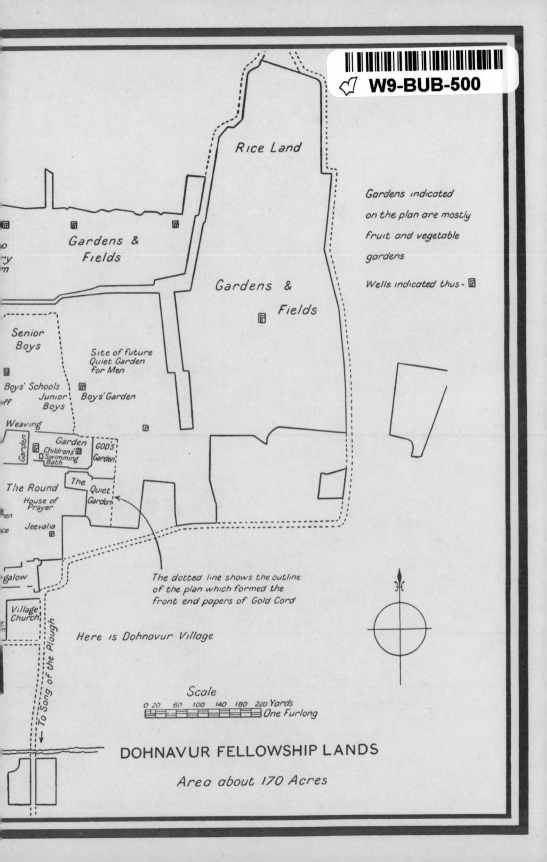

Rice Land

Gardens indicated
on the plan are mostly
fruit and vegetable
gardens

Wells indicated thus -

Gardens &
Fields

Gardens &
Fields

Senior
Boys

Site of future
Quiet Garden
for Men

Boys' Schools
Junior
Boys

Boys' Garden

Weaving

Garden

Garden

Childrens'
Swimming
Bath

GOD'S
Garden

The Round

House of
Prayer

The
Quiet
Garden

Jeevalia

galow

The dotted line shows the outline
of the plan which formed the
front end papers of Gold Cord

Village
Church

Here is Dohnavur Village

To Song of the Plough

Scale

0 20   60   100 140 180 220 Yards

One Furlong

DOHNAVUR FELLOWSHIP LANDS

Area about 170 Acres

A Chance To Die

The Life and Legacy of
Amy Carmichael

Other Books by the Same Author

Through Gates of Splendor

Shadow of the Almighty

Love Has a Price Tag

Discipline: The Glad Surrender

Passion and Purity

A Lamp for My Feet

The Savage My Kinsman

These Strange Ashes

The Mark of a Man

Let Me Be a Woman

A Chance To Die

The Life and Legacy of Amy Carmichael

Elisabeth Elliot

Fleming H. Revell Company
Old Tappan, New Jersey

Library of Congress Cataloging-in-Publication Data

Elliot, Elisabeth.
    A chance to die.

    Includes bibliographical references.
    1. Carmichael, Amy, 1867–1951. 2. Missionaries—
India—Biography. 3. Missionaries—United States—
Biography. 4. Dohnavur Fellowship. I. Title.
BV3269.C32E44 1987   266'.0092'4 [B]   87-4386
ISBN 0-8007-1535-7

To all who loved Amma

Contents

Contents

Illustrations

Acknowledgments

Members of the large Dohnavur Family in India, England, Ireland, Australia, New Zealand, and Canada have made it possible for me to write this book. They "don't go in much for credit lines," they told me, so I do not give their names. I have tried in personal letters to tell them how grateful I am. I say it again here—thank you, from my heart, for:

Your prayers, first of all. I have been upheld.

Your hospitality;

Your generous sharing of all extant data, including your own private correspondence from Amy Carmichael.

Your time—for patient answering of sometimes rude questions, both in interviews and by letter; for your willingness to read the manuscript, make corrections, offer suggestions. Some of your suggestions I have not followed. You bear no responsibility for the final result.

A special thank you to Dr. Eric Frykenberg of the University of Wisconsin for information on the early history of Christianity in South India for chapters 14 and 20.

11

Be earnest, earnest, earnest—
Mad if thou wilt;
Do what thou dost as if the
stake were Heaven,
And that thy last deed before
the Judgment Day.
Charles Kingsley

"Hereby perceive we the love of God, because He laid
down His life for us, and we ought to lay down our lives for
the brethren." How often I think of that *ought*. No sugary
sentiment there. Just the stern, glorious trumpet call,
OUGHT. But can words tell the joy buried deep within?
Mine cannot. It laughs at words.
Amy Carmichael, letter written in the
Old Forest House, 1922

Every day we experience something of the death of Jesus,
so that we may also know the power of the life of Jesus in
these bodies of ours.
2 Corinthians 4:10 (PHILLIPS)

Preface

To Amy Carmichael I owe what C. S. Lewis said he owed to George MacDonald: as great a debt as one can owe another. I cannot pay it. But it is my hope that this biography will introduce its subject to a generation which has not had the privilege that was mine. I "met" her when I was fourteen. Mrs. P. W. Du-Bose, headmistress of a small boarding school in Florida, used to quote often in school vespers from Carmichael books. I was captivated, and told her so. She lent me the books.

Dohnavur became a familiar place. I knew its bungalows, its paths, its people; I breathed its air. Amy Carmichael became for me what some now call a role model. She was far more than that. She was my first spiritual mother. She showed me the shape of godliness. For a time, I suppose, I thought she must have been perfect, and that was good enough for me. As I grew up I knew she could not have been perfect, and that was better, for it meant that I might possibly walk in her footprints. If we demand perfect models we will have, except for the Son of man Himself, none at all.

The first of her books that I read was, I think, *If*, which became her best-seller. It was not written for teenagers, but for seasoned Christians with the solemn charge of caring for the souls of others. It was from the pages of this thin blue book that I, a teenager, began to understand the great message of the Cross, of what the author called "Calvary love." I saw that the chance to die, to be crucified with Christ, was not a morbid thing, but the very gateway to Life. I was drawn—slowly, fitfully (my response was fitful), but inexorably.

In a far more secular and self-preoccupied time Amy Carmichael's vision of the unseen and her ardent effort to dwell in its light, making any sacrifice for its sake, seems hardly believable, let alone worth trying to imitate. Will we be put off by her awesome discipline, her steadfastness, or perhaps by the cultural shift or the difference in vocabulary (saturated as it was by the English of the King James Bible and the mystics of centuries ago)? She spoke often of the "country whose forces move unseen among us." That country is our country. We are its citizens as she was, if we call ourselves Christians. If its forces moved in Dohnavur, they move unabated here, too, where we live. If we are unaware, perhaps we have not listened, have not taken time to observe. Have we been deafened by noise, some of the worst of which passes for music? Has our vision, spiritual as well as physical, perhaps been impaired by the glittering images of the ubiquitous screen?

In spite of much that militates against quietness there are people who still read books. They are the people who keep me going. I write especially for those who bring to their reading a mind not hidebound by the sensibilities of our own time, but prepared to contemplate the Eternally Relevant; to seek in this book specifically the truth and the hidden meaning of a single life.

We read biographies to get out of ourselves and into another's skin, to understand the convulsive drama that shapes, motivates, and issues from that other life. Our current vocabulary includes such terms as identity, role models, self-image, self-actualization, liberation, upward mobility, and fulfillment, worries that never crossed Amy Carmichael's mind. How shall we, accustomed to popular seminars on rights and how to feel comfortable, receive and transmit a faith that prized what the world despises (the Cross) and despised what the world prizes (all that dims the Cross)?

The Christian life comes down to two simple things: trust and obedience. What does that mean, exactly? We could hold a seminar and talk about it. Visual aids are better. Look at a life. Amy Carmichael set her face toward that other Country. Her education, experience, and environment were incidentals, a mere framework within which she lived for eighty-three years, loved, feared, trusted, suffered, celebrated, failed, triumphed, and died. Through all the lights, poses, moods, and disguises we discern the common human elements that make up all of our lives.

I offer the testament of one whose loyal answering of her Lord's *Come follow* has made an incalculable difference to me. May it make a difference to my readers.

ELISABETH ELLIOT
Magnolia, Massachusetts

A Chance To Die

The Life and Legacy of Amy Carmichael

Chapter 1
Tide Pools, Pink Powder, and Prayers

She managed to stuff her two little brothers up through the skylight and then squeezed herself onto the slate roof. Glorious freedom. They stood up triumphant in the fresh wind that swept across the Irish Sea. The water was blue today, which to the girl (perhaps seven or eight years old) meant that it was happy. On some days it was green and angry, on others gray and anxious. Over the rooftops of the village they could see the stony beach and, far off across the water, the great rock called Ailsa Craig, and two rounded hills, the Paps of Jura. Now for the rest of the adventure. Gleefully the three children slid down the slates and paraded triumphantly around the lead gutters—until they saw, gazing up at them, the astonished faces of their parents.

The girl was Amy Beatrice Carmichael, great-great-granddaughter of one Jane Dalziel. It was said that King Kenneth II of Scotland (A.D. 971-995) had offered a reward to any of his subjects who would dare to remove from the gallows the body of the king's friend and kinsman who had been hanged. One stepped forth and said in Gaelic, "Dal ziel," *I dare.* So Dalziel became his name. That spirit was not much diluted in the child on the roof.

The parents on the ground were David Carmichael, descendant of Scottish Covenanters, and Catherine Jane Filson, descendant of Dalziel. Years later Amy found spiritual significance in this union, as she found spiritual significance in almost everything. Because her mother's ancestors were friendly with certain persecutors of the Covenanters, it was as though persecutor and persecuted were at last united. "So you see," she wrote, "after all, cruelty and wrong

The Carmichael house in Millisle.

are not the greatest forces in the world. There is nothing eternal in them. Only love is eternal."

Amy Carmichael was born December 16, 1867 in the gray stone house, one of three large houses in the village of Millisle on the north coast of Ireland. Below the Carmichael house, close by the seashore to this day, stands a row of old stone cottages with low doors, thick walls, and small-paned windows. In the street that runs along by those cottages are the water pumps and the iron rings set into the stones to which horses were tied. It is not hard for a visitor in the late twentieth century to imagine a little girl, wrapped in a woolen shawl, trying to hurry along that street with her little brother while carrying a pot of soup sent by their mother for one of the poor cottagers.

The rocky beach was her favorite playground, where she would lie prone beside its tide pools and gaze and gaze. There were live things in those pools, things which held endless fascination for the child. Her powers of observation were exquisite, her sympathy boundless—even, as we shall see later, for creatures the rest of the world thinks worthy of nothing but death.

20

The house was surrounded by a garden where there were roses, ivy, apple trees, yellow whins, and heartsease. There was a high wall with a large gate opening onto the principal street of the village. Not far away stand today the ruins of an old flour mill, its windows bricked up, the roof disintegrating. On the seashore can be seen what is left of the quay where grain was unloaded. Amy's great-grandfather had leased the mill a hundred years before she was born, and her father and uncle William, whose house was just down the road, managed it together. Coming from the lowlands of Scotland, the family joined the Presbyterian church built by the Anti-Burgher Seceders, a group who, because of doctrinal disagreements, had separated themselves from the Church of Scotland. Convinced of their obligation to live for the good of others, the two brothers supported the church with their generous tithes, bought a pony carriage for the minister, and were benefactors of the Millisle National School which was used not only for the three R's but for Sunday school and evangelistic services.

The love which formed the climate of the Carmichael home was a sinewy one, without the least trace of sentimentality, holding not only the conviction of her father's side of the family, and the courage of her mother's, but the toughness of Irish Presbyterians, the ruggedness bred by winters on that cold sea, and no-nonsense principles of child rearing.

There was no question in the minds of the Carmichael children as to what was expected of them. Black was black. White was white. Their parents' word could be trusted absolutely, and when it was not obeyed there were consequences. Five kinds of punishment were used: being stood in a corner with face to the wall, forbidden to go out to play, slapped, "pandied," and (worst of all) given Gregory powder. A pandy was a stroke with a thin flat ebony ruler. The child was required to stand still, to hold out his hand at once and not pull it away, to make no fuss, and finally to say politely, "Thank you, Mother." He knew that the worst was coming when he found a tray set up in the dining room with a pitcher of hot water, a small pitcher of cold milk, a teacup, a teaspoon, and a bottle of pink powder. It was too late for apologies. The mother mixed the potion, the child received it, thanked her for it, and drank it down.

One day Amy and two of her brothers were swinging on the garden gate when an idea struck her. They had been told that the seeds of the nearby laburnum tree were poisonous. "Let's count how many we can eat before we die!" said Amy. It was not long before they began to feel uncomfortable, and wondered what would happen next. Gregory, of course, was what happened next, and they were sent to bed to meditate on their sins. Some notion of the mother's strong determination can be gathered from Amy's report of one occasion when she cried, "Oh, Mother, I've such a pain!" The calm reply, "Have you, dear? I hope it will do you good." "But Mother, I can't bear it! It's a *dreadful* pain." "Is it, dear? I'm afraid you will have to bear it."

A nursemaid attempted to frighten the children out of their habit of swallowing plum stones by telling them that a plum tree would grow out of their heads for each stone they swallowed. Amy was charmed by the idea of having an orchard of her very own, within such easy access. Deciding that twelve trees would provide her with plenty of plums to eat and to give away, she gulped down twelve stones.

When told how exceedingly naughty she was, Amy used to think, "If only you knew how much naughtier I could be, you wouldn't think I'm naughty at all."

The seven children—Amy, Norman, Ernest, Eva, Ethel, Walter, and Alfred—were called daily to family prayers by the sound of a bell. Probably the servants also were required to attend. Amy remembered the sound of her father's voice reading the Scripture, a "solemn sound, like the rise and fall of the waves on the shore." Her ear was trained in this way, from those earliest years when a child's powers of memorization by hearing are nearly miraculous. For the rest of her life the majestic cadences of the Authorized (King James) Version of the Bible shaped her thinking and every phrase she wrote. A child, even when apparently distracted, learns far more than adults dream he can learn. Amy did not by any means always attend perfectly to the reading. Once she found a mouse drowning in a pail of water just at the moment when the prayer bell rang. She fished it out, hid it in her pinafore, took her place at prayers, and hoped it would not squeak. It did.

Amy, about five, with mother, Eva, Norman, and Ernest.

Whenever there was a meeting at the little whitewashed church in Balleycopeland, the Carmichael family was there. Amy envied the farmers' children, whose station in life was clearly very different from hers. The farmers' wives, on their part, may have pitied the mill owner's children, and sometimes offered them peppermints as they went into church. They were instructed to refuse politely—to smile and say, "Thank you very much, but my mother would rather I didn't." It was one thing to go to church with village folk. It was something else to do all the things village folk did. Their children snuggled down during the long service (never less than two hours) and sucked on pink and white lozenges. The smell reached the Carmichael pew—"but such solace was denied us."

Only psalms were permitted to be sung on Sundays, but hymns might be used in the Wednesday evening prayer meetings. Once when the theme of the prayer meeting was "Our Departure from this World," Amy amused herself by counting up all the various things hymn writers said you were supposed to do at the precise moment of departure. How a dying person could manage them all she was at a loss to know, but was pleased with the prospect of shouting, "while passing through the air, 'Farewell, farewell, sweet hour of prayer!' " What else could it mean but that very prayer meeting?

Amy had an extreme sensitivity to others' pain. When her mother told her the story of Calvary for the first time, she rushed out into the garden to try to forget "thoughts too dreadful to be borne, for how could anybody hurt another so, specially One who was so good? And there on the lawn stood a boy cousin, and he had fastened a frog to a monkey-puzzle tree. It looked like a crucified thing . . . I was frantic. In a passion of pity I tried to get it off the horrid spikes, but I could not reach up to it. So I tore into the house to call someone, and as I ran, suddenly the thought came, 'Now all the frogs will go to heaven.' "

A lesson in the mysteries of prayer—a tough one for any adult—came when Amy was three years old. Taught by her mother that God was a hearer and an answerer of prayer, One who could change water into wine, she determined to test His powers. Kneeling by her bed that night she asked for the one thing she most passionately longed for: blue eyes. Surely there would be no difficulty for the Lord in this. The little girl went to bed with perfect confidence. She jumped out of bed at dawn, pushed a chair to the chest of drawers, climbed up and looked in the mirror—into the same brown eyes. She never forgot the bewilderment she felt until, somehow, an explanation was given (did the Lord Himself speak to her, or did someone else?): *Isn't NO an answer?* So prayer was not magic. Like her earthly father who loved her, her heavenly Father might also say no.

Given a dollhouse complete with lovely furniture and properly dressed dolls, Amy displeased her old nurse, Bessie, by emptying the house and filling it instead with moss, stones, beetles, and earwigs—things she found far more interesting than the toys nice children were supposed to like.

Their father took them for walks even on Sundays (Sunday walks were frowned on by Presbyterians in those days), through fields of pink clover or blue flax, to the ponds to see swans and, on weekdays, to watch the great black dripping wheel of the scutch mill where the woody fiber was beaten from the flax to make linen.

They had books—all the children's books that could be had then—and toys, which included a toy telephone soon after the telephone was invented. There were always pets—Daisy, the yellow and white cat, Gildo, the collie, Fanny and Charlie, the ponies. David and Catherine Carmichael loved beauty and tried to surround their children with beautiful things, keeping far from them, when possible, all that was not beautiful. They gave them a microscope and lenses to encourage them to study and observe, taught them capillary action by pointing out how water climbed from grain to grain in a lump of sugar, demonstrated electricity by rubbing a piece of amber on a coat sleeve till tiny scraps of paper flew up to it.

Amy's grandmother lived in a small house close to Strangford Lough (Gaelic for lake or sea), in a place called Portaferry. The tide there was said to be the second strongest in the world. The children were allowed to go rowing within certain limits. One evening Amy and her brothers passed the limits, were caught in a swift current, and swept toward the bar. "I was steering, my brothers were rowing hard, but they were powerless against the current. 'Sing!' they

shouted to me, and I sang at the top of my voice the first thing that
came into my head:

'He leadeth me, O blessed thought,
O words with heavenly comfort fraught;
Whate'er I do, where'er I be,
Still 'tis God's hand that leadeth me.' "

J.H. GILMORE

The children did not attend school in the early years, but were
taught by a succession of governesses. One of them, "an unfortu-
nate Englishwoman," did not stick it out for long, and when she
departed they all trooped down to see her off—"We wanted to be
sure she went!" Her replacement, Eleanor Milne, was much beloved, like an older sister to the children. She taught them poetry,
told them stories of the great martyrs of Scotland and England. The
last words of Ridley to Latimer stuck in Amy's mind: "Be of good
cheer, brother, for God will either assuage the fury of the flame, or
else strengthen us to abide it." When he and Latimer were chained
and the fire kindled, Latimer said, "Be of good comfort, brother
Ridley, and play the man. We shall this day light such a candle by
God's grace in England as I trust shall never be put out."
As the sternness of an Irish winter, with its gloom and wetness
and icy winds, puts apple cheeks on both old and young, so the
sternness of Christian discipline put red blood—spiritual health—
into the girl who could not have imagined then the buffetings she
would be called on to endure. But it was a peaceful childhood nevertheless, its discipline balanced by buttered toast and raspberry jam
in front of the nursery fire, the soft soughing of the wind in the
chimney as the children listened to stories, the sweet, sweet sound
of a mother's singing, pony rides, tree climbing, swimming in the
frigid sea. It was a peaceful home in a peaceful village. Amy's testimony long afterwards was: "I don't think there could have been a
happier child than I was."

Chapter 2
The Hope of Holiness

When Amy was twelve she was sent away to Marlborough House, a Wesleyan Methodist boarding school in Harrogate, Yorkshire. Naturally she was homesick. Is there, for anyone who has grown up in a secure and loving home, anything to compare with the first experience of complete separation from that home? It is pure misery from which there seems to be no possibility of escape, for it is the parents themselves who have decided that this is "best." The child feels that nothing could be worse; yet he trusts his parents. It seems that the "earth is removed and the mountains are carried into the midst of the sea." Amy's upbringing forbade her to make much of anything appointed, nevertheless she needed solace of some sort. She found it—in a white lily that stood in a pot in the bow window, in a box of chrysanthemums sent by her mother from the little greenhouse at home, and in a saucer of moss on the dinner table which reminded her of one of her father's stories: Mungo Park, an explorer, was comforted by seeing moss and feeling that the One who made it would care for him.

The taboos and restrictions of Methodism would seem intolerable in the twentieth century, even to the dedicated. To Amy they were perhaps not more stringent than the Presbyterianism she was used to. She did not find schoolwork nearly so pleasant as it had been at home, and only one teacher, the botany master, knew how to make lessons "shine." Certainly there were no complaint boxes at Marlborough House, nor were students in those days required to evaluate the performance of each of their teachers. Looking back years later, Amy judged that the faults lay mostly with herself—

"many things happened which should not have happened, because I had not learned to set to, and work at things which seemed to me dull and not useful. This was a great pity. I have often been very sorry about it." Unfortunately for us she saw to it that no record of the story was left which she did not believe would edify the children in India, except for a single incident. The wild Irish girl was "quite naughty" that time, but felt that the end surely would justify the means. It was the year of the comet, 1882. Amy went, on behalf of the girls in her dormitory, to request permission of the principal to stay up to see the comet. "Certainly not," was the verdict.

Missing the celestial show was simply not to be borne, so Amy tied threads to the toes of each of the girls, promising to keep awake and give them a yank as soon as the rest of the house was asleep. At the signal, they all crept to the attic, holding their breath when a step creaked, and found themselves face-to-face with the principal and teachers. "We had time to see it beautifully before anyone had recovered sufficiently from the shock of our arrival to order us back to bed. That was a woeful night for me, I was sure I would be expelled and that would break my parents' hearts. Happily that did not come to pass. There was a rather solemn hour next morning, for the matter of threads tied round toes showed such purposeful audacity that it could not be passed over. It was taken for granted that I was the ringleader, but in the end I was forgiven."

It was near the end of her three years at Marlborough House that Amy experienced "the one watered moment in an arid three years." The Children's Special Service Mission held meetings in Harrogate at which one Edwin Arrowsmith spoke. She had no recollection of his talk, but remembered singing the lovely children's hymn by Anna B. Warner, "Jesus loves me, this I know, for the Bible tells me so." In those quiet minutes she understood what she had not understood before—there was something else to be done. All her life she had known of Jesus' love. Her mother had often told her of it, sung to her about it, and Amy had, as it were, nestled in Jesus' arms as she had nestled in her mother's. She realized now, at the age of fifteen or so, that she had not "opened the door" to Him. "In His great mercy the Good Shepherd answered the prayers of my mother and father and many other loving ones, and drew me, even me, into His fold."

It seems that competition with American flour necessitated a move to Belfast where the Carmichael brothers built a new mill. Amy's family found a house in College Gardens, and soon afterwards because of financial difficulties she and her brothers were withdrawn from the boarding schools. Amy's lessons were in subjects deemed suitable for young ladies—music, singing, and painting. She was thoroughly discouraged with the last, in which she had especially wanted to do well. She held up alongside a real sunset an oil sketch of a sunset. "The contrast was so tremendous I resolved to spend no more time on that." Her father took her to London, where she was filled with wonder at the great sights of the Tower, Westminster Abbey, Windsor Castle, St. Paul's, the British and Kensington Museums. They went to hear the famous singers, and one day, seated in the gallery of the House of Commons and peering down through the lattice, they saw the great William Gladstone.

When Amy was nearly eighteen she saw her father talking gravely to her mother by the dining room window. The matter was money, something not discussed in front of the children, so it was not until later that Amy learned the truth. David Carmichael had lent some thousands of pounds to a friend who needed to make a new start in life. When the time came for repayment, the money was not forthcoming. Not long after this blow, Carmichael contracted double pneumonia. He died on April 12, 1885, fifty-four years old. Amy recalled that the last thing she had read to him was from Milton's *Samson Agonistes:*

> All is best, though oft we doubt
> What the unsearchable dispose
> Of Highest Wisdom brings about,
> And ever best found in the close.

If going to boarding school did not seem to Amy a major crisis—lots of girls went to boarding school—surely the death of her father must have. Yet in her story, written for the children, there is only the laconic statement, "on an April Sunday morning while the church bells were ringing, our dear father died," followed by the lines of poetry which she said had been with her ever since. Not a word about what this sorrow meant to anyone in the family, least of all to herself. Not a hint that she was devastated, nor even tempted for a moment to doubt that all was best. It is, in fact, difficult to find anywhere in the writings of Amy Carmichael anything akin to the poet's admission, "oft we doubt." If any doubts rose in her mind—at the moment, perhaps, of watching her father's coffin lowered into the ground—she would not in any case have put them on paper. Did she speak to her mother of what it had meant to her, or seek reassurance that her mother had no doubts? We are not told. Mrs. Carmichael needed a stronghold. That much we know. It was faith, not doubt, that moved her out of herself, out of self-pity and despair. She found what she needed in the words of Nahum 1:7, "The Lord is good, a strong hold in the day of trouble; and he knoweth them that trust in him." Years later, Amy discovered in the margin of her mother's Bible, next to that promise, a tiny notation: "Found true all along the line ever since." The strength of her example was not lost on Amy.

Being of an acutely sensitive nature, Amy must have felt deeply the loss of her father. The happy, peaceful, predictable routine of her home life was profoundly shaken. If she had been born a hundred years later, she would very likely have been encouraged to be angry, told she had a right to express her anger and her sorrow and her bewilderment and her rage, and generally to disintegrate. These were not the expectations of her friends and family. Nothing could have been further from her expectations of herself. Instead, she threw herself into serving others. She became like a second mother to her brothers and sisters.

"The time when she impinged on my life was during about five years after our father died," wrote her sister Ethel. "She lived an amazingly full life in those years, taking classes in painting and other subjects, teaching Eva and me during a period when we were not well enough to go to school, and starting various 'good works.' . . . If anybody asked me what were the strongest impressions Amy made on me in her youth, I think I would say—her enthusiasms."

The preoccupations of seventeen-year-old girls—their looks, their clothes, their social life—do not change very much from generation to generation. But in every generation there seem to be a few who make other choices. Amy was one of the few.

The decisive moment which determined the direction of her life came on a dull Sunday morning in Belfast as the family was returning from church. They saw what they had never seen before in Presbyterian Belfast—an old woman lugging a heavy bundle. Amy and her brothers turned around, took the bundle, and helped her along by the arms. "This meant facing all the respectable people who were, like ourselves, on their way home. It was a horrid moment. We were only two boys and a girl, and not at all exalted Christians. We hated doing it. Crimson all over (at least we felt crimson, soul and body of us) we plodded on, a wet wind blowing us about, and blowing, too, the rags of that poor old woman, till she seemed like a bundle of feathers and we unhappily mixed up with them."

There was an ornate Victorian fountain in the street, and just as they passed it, "this mighty phrase was suddenly flashed as it were through the grey drizzle: 'Gold, silver, precious stones, wood, hay, stubble—every man's work shall be made manifest; for the day shall declare it, because it shall be declared by fire; and the fire shall try every man's work of what sort it is. If any man's work abide—' "[1]

Amy turned to see who had spoken. There was nothing but the fountain, the muddy street, the people with their politely surprised faces. The children plodded on with the bundle of feathers, but something had happened to the girl which changed forever life's values. That afternoon she shut herself in her room. It was time to settle some immensely important things, and things of that sort Amy Carmichael settled alone with God.

She began about this time to gather the children of the neighborhood to her home for meetings. Henry Montgomery of the Belfast City Mission used to take her through the city streets on

---

1. 1 Corinthians 3:12–14.

Saturday nights. She saw something of "the other half," and began teaching a group of boys in a night school, always ending with what she called a "good-night service," probably her chance to give them something from the Bible, perhaps a gospel song, and prayer. She started a program called the Morning Watch to encourage boys and girls to spend a regular time each day in Bible reading and prayer. She gave them pledge cards, blue with a gilt edge, which they could sign. When they met on Saturday mornings, each would tell what had helped him during the week, or confess failure to get up in time. It can't have been too dull an hour, because two of her brothers joined. Another member recalled that it was always a happy time and everybody loved Amy.

She initiated a weekly prayer meeting for schoolgirls in their own homes, then moved it to Victoria College when some of the staff and students joined them. She worked at the YWCA, and had a class at Rosemary Street Presbyterian Church for "shawlies," mill girls who, too poor to buy hats, covered their heads with shawls. This was something of a shocker to the proper church members. Not only were they unaccustomed to the presence of such "common" folk, but the idea of Mrs. Carmichael's permitting her daughter to venture into the slums to fetch them was deplorable.

Not one to refuse even unnecessary risks, Amy was more than ready to take risks for the sake of others. She had certainly been sheltered, and she knew it. The shawlies were not sheltered. *What sort of life did they lead?* she wondered. Her brother Ernest, working for the railways, knew things she didn't know. She pressed him for information as to the sort of conversation the shawlies must hear. He wasn't sure she ought to know, but Amy would not be put off. He told her a few things. She intensified her prayers that the girls would grow up pure and good.

This zealous work with young people went on for more than a year. Amy poured herself into it, but felt that she was not really building as she had determined to build, in gold, silver, and precious stones. Something told her all this activity might amount to nothing more than a heap of wood, hay, and stubble unless she began living a holy life, a life that would *help others.* She was full of misgivings. The list of her activities must surely have seemed an impressive one to those who looked on, but to the girl herself they were nothing. They were empty. Nobody was truly being helped as she believed they should be. What had she missed? How could she live the life she longed for? How to be holy? Was there any hope of it for her?

Chapter 3
Mutton Chops Don't Matter

In September 1886 Amy was invited to visit friends in Scotland, and it was there that a second spiritual crisis took place. They went to Glasgow where a convention was being held "on Keswick lines," that is, teaching that was given each year for one week in a large tent in Keswick, in England's Lake District. The tent meetings had their origin in 1874 in a six-day conference at "Broadlands," the country estate of the Right Honorable W. Cowper-Temple. The chairman was Robert Pearsall Smith. The purpose, articulated by Smith's wife, Hannah Whitall, was "the promotion of holiness or the Higher Christian Life." Canon Wilberforce and George MacDonald were among those attending, along with "nonconformist bankers, ritualistic curates, peers with parsons, novelists with temperance reformers."[1]

There was a spirit of such unity, a sense of being lifted to such heavenly heights, a springing up of such hope of an unbroken walk with God, that it was decided to repeat the meetings on a larger scale. Five weeks later, a second conference was held in Oxford, attended by the Vicar of Saint John's, Keswick, Canon Dundas Harford-Battersby, a former Anglo-Catholic. Both of the Smiths were speakers, as well as a mining engineer named Evan Hopkins. Through their messages Harford-Battersby received "a vision of faith, a sight of the glory of the Lord . . . I shall never forget what I saw then, to my dying day."[2] He also met Robert Wilson, owner of

---

1. J. C. Pollock, *The Keswick Story* (London: Hodder and Stoughton, 1964), p. 20.
2. Ibid, p. 28.

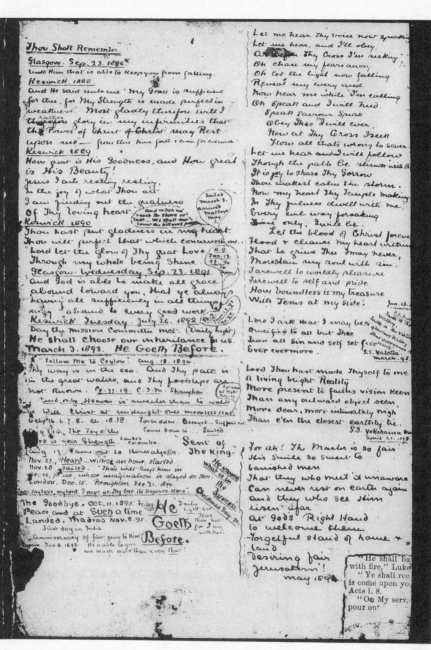

Flyleaf of Amy's Bible.

coal mines in Cumberland, and the two became close friends. The following year the vicar wrote to Wilson to propose "a numerous assemblage to look for and wait for a blessing at God's hands." The largest hall in Keswick accommodated only four hundred, so a tent was hired, and the famous Keswick Meetings began. It was a "spiritual clinic," a place where Christians might come "to have the great Physician, the Lord Himself, diagnose and heal their spiritual ailments."[3]

Keswick teaching spread to other places, and so it was that Amy Carmichael attended the meeting in Glasgow.

The hall was full of a sort of grey mist, very dull and chilly. I came to that meeting half hoping, half fearing. Would there be anything for me? *Could* there be anything? I don't remember feeling there was anything (my fault) in either of the two addresses. The fog in the Hall seemed to soak into me. My soul was in a fog. Then the chairman rose for the last prayer . . . "O Lord, we know Thou art able to keep us from falling." Those words found me. It was as if they were alight. And they shone for me.

The restaurant where her friend took her for lunch was not a five-star. The mutton chops they ordered were badly cooked. *Mutton chops?* thought Amy. *What does it matter about mutton chops? The Lord is able to keep us from falling! To keep us from falling!* This, this at last, was what she had prayed and agonized for. She wrote down the date, September 23, 1886, in her Bible.

If mutton chops didn't matter anymore, neither did clothes. When Amy got back to Belfast, the long mourning period for her father was over and it was time, her mother said, to purchase a few pretty dresses—among them, of course, an evening dress for parties. They went to the shop. The shopman displayed his loveliest things. Suddenly Amy decided she could not have them. She was now, in the language of the apostle Paul as interpreted by the Keswick people, "dead to the world." To Amy, the world meant fashion, finery, luxury of any sort. She would follow Him who had no

---

3. Steven Barabas, *So Great Salvation* (London: Marshall, Morgan, and Scott, 1952), p. 39.

home, no earthly possessions beyond the bare minimum. She would be "dead to the world and its applause, to all its customs, fashions, laws." For a girl with her eye for beauty, it is the measure of her commitment that she did not hesitate to relinquish all that seemed to her inimical to the true life of discipleship.

Entertaining her brothers and sisters was certainly not inimical in Amy's mind to that life. Bursting with vitality, she went skating with them on the ponds of the Royal Botanical Gardens. She taught them to identify the orchids in the conservatories, and conceived the idea of helping them to establish a shop in which they learned about money through the sale of small items to other members of the family: pencils (halfpenny each), india rubbers (one penny), blotters, pens, paper ("cream laid, superfine"). Another project was a family magazine, *Scraps*. Volume 1, number 1, page 1, reads:

As it is usual in publishing the first issue of any journal to give the reasons for beginning it, together with its politics etc. we will try to relate the circumstances which led up to the existence of *Scraps*. By having a family paper it was thought that a great deal of pleasure as well as profit might be the result, and that by spending an evening now and then in reading and discussing the items which might appear in such a paper a great deal of amusement and perhaps a little instruction might be gained. It was therefore proposed by Amy and seconded by Norman that such a paper should be at once begun.

The handwriting is Norman's, elegant and sweeping. A list of rules follows, including the requirement that each member must pay an annual subscription rate of six pence, and must choose a *nom de plume*. Norman became "Namron," Ernest "Oddfellow," Eva "Lulu," Ethel "Atom," Walter "Blanco," Alfred "S.S.I." (for Silly Silly Idiot), and Amy, not surprisingly, "Nobody." Mother was elected president, Amy editor.

The pages of *Scraps* were decorated with cartoons, illuminated headings, and delicate pen-and-ink drawings. None is signed, but Amy's later drawings on her missionary letters lead me to assume that the finer work in *Scraps* is hers—exquisitely detailed ferns, cattails, grasses, flowers. There are several watercolors (one shows a shoreline with cottage and trees, masts and sailboats on the water) and a beautiful oil of autumn leaves. Alfred contributed ink drawings—one shows the cook, "Queen of the Kitchen," a dour woman with warts and hairy moles, standing on a stool, a band around her tight curls, an apron pinned to her dress, sleeves rolled up, laced boots; another a "Mill Girl" swathed in a voluminous black shawl; a third a drawing of the cover of a book, *Mill Girls and All About Them,* by Amy Carmichael.

The editor saw to it that there was, in addition to whimsy and humor, plenty to edify. She reported her conversation with a Bible scholar about soul and spirit. She quotes Shakespeare, Dryden, Kingsley, and Coleridge, includes a vocabulary study with the etymology of *tantalize, burglar,* and *pecuniary.* Some of her early efforts in poetry appear, ranging from doggerel:

> Oh we are a jolly family
> We are, we is, we be—
> And very wise and careful
> And exemplary are we!

to:

> Think truly, and thy thoughts shall be
> Spotless with God's own purity.
> On every thought-bud let us bear
> The stamp of truth, and love and prayer.

From *Scraps* we learn that the usual rising time was 4:50 A.M. and that for breakfast the Carmichaels ate brown bread, white bread, bacon, toast, oatcake, marmalade, and tea, with finnan haddie and soda bread added for Sundays. All were expected to dress for tea, to respond when the tea bell rang, and to remain afterwards for prayers. "Tea," the evening meal, usually meant potatoes, bread, perhaps a bit of sausage or fish, and, of course, pots and pots of tea. No wonder the Christmas hamper from Grandmother in Portaferry was welcomed—she sent turkey, geese, and vegetables. Mice and cockroaches also lived in the house, we find, in spite of various cats and a dog named Scamp.

It was a pious Presbyterian home, and the children's language was strictly watched. "Queen Motherie" remonstrated upon Eva's "most inelegant exclamation, 'Cricky!' " "But there's nothing nice left to say, so I can't help saying it!" was Eva's defense. The others, sympathetic to the urge to swear, offered alternatives. Why not "Beetles!" or "Earwigs!"? Ernest wrote when April Fool's fell on a Sunday, "Of course we were all very pious, doubly so as we would not have a chance of being ever so pious on a Sunday for another seven years."

The Christmas number of 1887 carries a set of character sketches of the family, by "Nobody." Namron is a sweet child, kindly, loving, unselfish, "in short, very dear in every way. As for faults—a difficulty in believing himself to be mistaken is about all I can say, and this fault is so overruled by good-temperedness that it is almost indeed dormant. When his beloved sister Nobody was ill he nearly carried her upstairs." Oddfellow was "one of those youths to whom absence makes the heart grow fonder. When you are away from him you realize that you are worth something to him. . . . I think I won't name his faults, for since beginning to write, I have become conscious that my own are so numerous and so far out-weigh other people's, that the less I say about them the better." Eva: dear, frisky, amusing, loving, innocent, "has a large stock of love ready to draw upon for Birthdays, Christmas, etc. and when one is really ill, there is nobody kinder, she would buy tons of chocolate if thereby she could ease the sufferer—if she had the cash." Atom: "a gigglety creature, packed full of condensed electricity, very fond of lessons, sweets, rowdyism, wrestling, with a large amount of natural affection." As for S.S.I., "a dear little jolly old fellow. He is our sunshine." Blanco was, "of all good-tempered willing fags [flunkies, "go-fers"] he is the goodtemperedest and willingest." Mother: "There never was such a mother—so good, so loving, so unselfish, so perfect in every way, we can only thank God for her and try to make her shadowed life bright with our love." Of Amy herself one of them wrote:

> Our eldest sister is the light of our life,
> She says she will never be a wife.

40

Such a promise from a twenty-two-year-old girl might have been taken as a challenge meant only to be refuted. It is to be doubted that Norman and Ernest, at least, took her seriously, and perhaps she did not expect them to. At any rate she kept her word.

That promise may have been partly the fruit of a visit to Belfast during 1887 of Hudson Taylor of the China Inland Mission. In meetings sponsored by Keswick he said that every hour four thousand "pass through the gates of death into the darkness beyond— Saviorless, hopeless."

"Does it not stir up our hearts," Amy wrote in *Scraps*, "to go forth and help them, does it not make us long to leave our luxury, our exceeding abundant light, and go to them that sit in darkness?" She quoted these lines:

> Listen! Listen, English sisters
> Hear an Indian sister's plea—
> Grievous wails, dark ills revealing
> Depths of human woe unsealing,
> Borne across the deep blue sea.
> We are dying, day by day,
> With no light, no cheering ray.

It was a strange providence that brought into Amy's life during those very meetings one whom she was to learn to love to such a degree as to make her obedience to the call to heathendom excruciatingly more painful than it would otherwise have been. He was the chairman of the Belfast conference, and the man who with Canon Harford-Battersby had arranged the first Keswick tent meeting, Mr. Robert Wilson. He was a man "of massive frame and of great strength, bearded and burly," his son recalled. "His movements were slow, his humor deep under a solemn exterior, he was sparing in speech and if pressed to a course he thought wrong took refuge in Quaker silence."[4]

At the close of the Glasgow meeting Mr. Wilson asked if there were questions, and Amy's aunts, who were staying with the Carmichaels, had several of a doctrinal nature which Amy wrote out on

---

4. Pollock, op. cit., p. 30.

a pink card with a gold edge. Mr. Wilson asked if he might call at their home.

"He was not quite seventy years old then,[5] but he had wavy silver hair. His eyes were as blue and as candid as a child's, and his face was like a child's too in its fresh colouring; his big frame almost filled our biggest arm chair. He made a beautiful picture as he sat in the firelight."

Amy did not know it then, but she had "turned a corner of the road of life."

---

5. In fact, he was not quite sixty.

Chapter 4
The Tin Tabernacle

Early in 1888 Mrs. Carmichael called the children into the dining room one evening to tell them that nearly all of their money had been lost. They knelt together around the table as she committed the matter to God. What seemed overwhelming did not overwhelm her, for she believed that there was nothing she could not expect His wondrous kindness to do. "He has been so kind about other things that we cannot doubt but that He will care for this too."

There is nothing in *Scraps* to indicate that their life was interrupted. Amy's work with the shawlies grew until it began to cause a certain disturbance among some of the church people. To have this crowd of crude and unorthodox characters filling and overflowing the large hall, the prayers of two or three of them sometimes rising simultaneously, was unsettling, to say the least. One official stood in the doorway watching them with folded arms and knitted brows. There must have been some sighs of relief when the crowd grew so phenomenally that they needed a hall that would seat five hundred. The church had no such facility. Amy spotted an advertisement in a magazine for a building made of iron that could be erected for five hundred pounds. It was an awesome sum for her but she knew how to pray and taught the mill girls to pray. An experience when she was ten years old had planted a seed in her mind about the matter of finances for God's work. Sent out by her grandmother in Portaferry to collect funds for some charity, she approached a man who had just finished building himself a new house. He refused to give anything. Stunned, the little girl pondered the wisdom of asking money from people who don't really love God. *Why not,* she thought, *ask God to make people who love Him want to give?* Amy and the shawlies did exactly that.

Not long afterwards, Amy was fulfilling one of the more odious duties of a girl in her time, "returning calls" with her mother. This meant sitting in drawing rooms with a cup of tea and a piece of cake balanced precariously on the saucer, trying to be polite when one couldn't help thinking of better ways to spend the time. But the God who teaches us to pray has many ways of answering, and that afternoon's boredom resulted in the hostess's mentioning Amy's work to a friend. The friend asked Amy to lunch.

An old house, a charming garden, a butler at the door. A table set in a sunny room. White cloth, shining silver. An old lady "like a white violet." A few days later, a letter saying she wished to give the hall. Amy did not doubt that this was God's answer.

One thing, however, was lacking. Where would they put it? They asked God. Not one to fold her hands if God might be expecting her to do something besides pray, Amy went straight to the office of the owner of the biggest mill in that part of the city and asked what he would charge for a slice of land. He mentioned a ridiculously small sum. The hall was put up on Cambria Street. Amy named it The Welcome and sent out printed invitations to its dedication, to take place on January 2, 1889.

> Come one, Come all,
> To the Welcome Hall,
> And come in your working clothes.

The invitation described the organization as "The Mill and Factory Girls' Branch of the YWCA." She invited her minister to dedicate it. "The windows were in and the curtains were up in time," she wrote, "in spite of the croakings of the Tin Tabernacle's raven friends." Above the platform she hung a long strip with the words, *That in all things He may have the pre-eminence.* She meant it. She herself ("Nobody") sat that evening, not on the platform as would have been expected of the prime mover of the enterprise, but in the middle of the audience. Two students of American evangelist D. L.

Moody opened the work of The Welcome with a mission in which, for the first time in the British Isles, was sung the gospel song, "I know whom I have believed." "Souls were won every night," Amy recorded, but then for a time there was nothing, no power, only deadness. It was her fault, she believed—she had grieved the Holy Spirit by levity following a meeting. "There was nothing wrong in the fun, but it was not the time for it."

Her brothers and sisters were interested in their big sister's work at the "Tin Tabernacle," and no doubt helped her there occasionally. In one issue of *Scraps* Norman refers to "the most charitable of all charitable objects, The Amy's Mill Girls' Society."

It must have been a lively place, judging from the weekly schedule:

Sunday 4:30	Bible Class
" 5:30	Sunbeam Band Meeting
Monday 7:30	Singing Practice
Tuesday 7:30	Night School
Wednesday 7:30	Girls' Meeting
Thursday 7:30	Sewing Club
Monday and Friday 1:20	Dinner Hour Meeting
Wednesday 1:20	Dinner Prayer Meeting
Thursday 4:00	Mothers' Meeting

First Wednesday in the month—Gospel Meeting—All Welcome.

It was too much for Amy to do by herself. She needed help. What kind? She looked as usual in the Bible for guidelines, and found them in the book of Ezra. When the exiles returned to Jerusalem, they set about rebuilding the temple of the Lord. The enemies of Judah and Benjamin asked to join in the work, claiming that they worshipped the same God. The leaders refused their offer, saying that this house was no concern of theirs but a task which Cyrus, King of Persia, had assigned to the Jews alone. This caused offense and slowed the work, but the Jews stood fast on the principle. Amy would not think of building in any but substances that would survive fire—gold, silver, precious stones. The Lord led her into this truth at the very beginning, she told her "children" later, "and He has kept it as a settled thing in my heart ever since." She prayed for the right kind of helpers. They came—a band of loyal friends and cousins whose gifts she herself had the gift of recognizing and encouraging.

Methods for raising money which were generally taken for granted by churches and other religious organizations were to Amy thoroughly secular, wholly out of keeping with a life of faith, and unthinkable for The Welcome. She wrote a long piece on the subject for *Scraps*.

We must have money. We can't build spires ninety feet high without it, we can't decorate our churches with elegant windows without it, we can't issue costly programmes for our social meetings without it, we can't furnish our sanctuaries with real polished mahogany without it. . . . How are we to get it? You may touchingly plead for the 865,000,000 heathen abroad. You may paint a picture terrible and true of the state of the home heathen at our doors. You may work yourself into hysterics over these and other intensely real realities but you won't get the money. So another plan must be devised. We shall get up a fancy fair.

A clipping from the newspaper advertising a **Grand Bazaar to Liquidate a Debt on Argyle Place Presbyterian Church** is pasted in, describing everything from a "fairy palace of a thousand lights," a Punch and Judy show, ventriloquism, and a shooting gallery, to THE FULL BAND OF THE GORDON HIGHLANDERS. Amy, giving free rein to her imagination, offers other possibilities:

Idle young ladies who like to do good will work sofa blankets, smoking caps, babies' petticoats, and tea cosies. . . . They will entrap old men and young into buying just one ticket for the exquisite chimpanzee which some kind friend presented to aid us in the liquidation of our church debt (he was sick of the creature however, and glad to get rid of it). . . . Nobody will escape without being regularly besieged by gypsy women, Queen Elizabeths, Mary Queen of Scots, Robinson Crusoes, Robin Hoods, knights, pages, fools, apes and asses, just to buy this very cheap pincushion at 5/11, and this beautiful pair of slippers at £1.19.10, and this sweet baby doll with real petticoats at 19/6—and nobody will escape our clutches without being pretty well fleeced—that I can honestly assure you. Oh yes! we shall get the money for our poor dear little church, and everybody will have the pleasing consciousness of having devoted themselves to the noble cause of screwing, wheedling and extorting money out of a selfish, thoughtless public—for the Cause of God! Ah, there is where a little incongruity seems to come in. Let us fancy for a moment we are a band of Israelites who want to build a magnificent abode for the Mighty Presence to dwell in. We convene a committee . . . Moses says, stroking his beard meditatively, "Ah, the people's tastes must be considered, in the present state of society we cannot do otherwise, though of course it is not a desirable course to pursue."

"But brother," remarks Aaron, "the Tabernacle must really have decent curtains, and if they are to be of goat's hair they will cost quite a large sum of money, and then they must be embroidered. . . ." Then Bezaleel speaks: "You speak, my brethren, as if nothing but the curtains should be considered, but there is a great amount of carving in wood and cutting in stones to be thought of and various curious things to be devised out of gold and silver and brass. These too will cost money." There is a silence. Moses looks puzzled when in a very hesitating voice Aholiab says, "Have not we, Bezaleel, got both time and talent to devote to this work? Could we not spend and be spent in the service of the sanctuary?" But he is quite squashed by the head-shakings of the committee. Such a thing would never do. "What would become of our families if we worked for nothing? Really Aholiab should be ashamed of himself—such an idea!" etc. etc. Suddenly Moses' face brightens. "Just what I remarked at first," he says pleasantly, "In the present state of society we must conform a little to the world. We'll have a Bazaar!"

Isn't it a pretty picture—far superior to: "And they came both men and women as many as were willing-hearted, and brought bracelets and earrings and tablets and jewels of gold, and every man that offered, offered an offering of gold unto the Lord."[1] Three things we may notice:

1st as many as were willing-hearted

2nd brought their own possessions

3rd unto the Lord.

Now we give unto Mrs. So and So who wrote us a begging letter, or Miss So and So who called the other day with a collecting card and unfortunately we were in and could not get off without giving her something. . . . May there not be some clue to the money mystery in these thoughts, taking as our keynote three sentences, not very much believed in nowadays:

"The silver and the gold is Mine."

---

1. Exodus 35:22.

"Ask, and ye shall receive."

"My God shall supply all your need."

1. Is the work for which we want the money God's chosen work for us, or our chosen work for Him? If the former, will not He see after the money necessary? If the latter, then how can we expect anything better than we have?

2. Can we expect a blessing to follow money given grudgingly?

3. Should we not see that our Root is right, before expecting flowers and fruit?

These principles, discovered when Amy was alone with her Bible and her God, written down only for the small circle of readers of *Scraps,* were never laid aside. Years later their influence was felt by thousands.

Chapter 5
The Inescapable Calling

Exactly the sort of place I should have chosen if I had been asked to choose!" That was how Amy described the place where she was living later in the year 1889. An old friend of the family, Jacob Wakefield MacGill, had asked her to come to Manchester, England, to begin a work similar to that of The Welcome. Her mother was invited to be superintendent for the women of a rescue home there, so the move was made. Amy lived in a slum, teeming with people—tough, hardworking, hard-drinking people. At night she heard the yells and screams of fights. In the morning it was factory sirens and the clatter of wooden clogs as people went to work in the dark and cold. "But what I remember most vividly is that the most loathly sort of 'puchie' used to crawl through the thin walls."

It was good missionary training. If one is preparing to storm the bastions of heathendom, it won't do to blench at creepie-crawlies. Another lesson Amy learned was to do at a moment's notice whatever was required—Uncle Jacob had no patience with those who wouldn't. She learned to do without things most precious—privacy and quiet. The neighborhood was not what her family would have thought "safe," and once, walking to the railway station, she was mobbed by hooligans. She walked on unafraid, cheered by the story of a brave ancestor who had marched through a hostile crowd. In Amy Carmichael the faith of her fathers was living still.

Amy was happy in the work with factory girls, but sickness brought it to a halt. "What asses bodies are!" she said.

Eighteen-eighty-eight was the year of the fourteenth Keswick convention, and Amy's friend Mr. Wilson, cofounder of Keswick, whom she had met in Belfast, invited her to attend. Having heard Keswick teaching in Belfast and Glasgow, she was eager to go to the tent in Keswick. Since its beginning the movement had suffered from various "winds of doctrine," but by 1888 had been corrected and steadied, largely under the leadership of Bishop Handley Moule, who wrote in 1890 or thereabouts:

> Keswick stands for the great and eternal truths, some of which, so to speak, it takes for granted but never forgets: the glory of our Lord Jesus Christ. . . . His death for us upon the Cross: Keswick is firm as a rock upon the sacrifice of the death of Christ, and the benefit of pardon, utterly unmerited by us, which we have because Jesus died.

Sanctity was the great emphasis of Keswick, which Moule defined thus:

> To be like Christ. To displace self from the inner throne, and to enthrone Him; to make not the slightest compromise with the smallest sin. We aim at nothing less than to walk with God all day long, to abide every hour in Christ and He and His words in us, to love God with all the heart and our neighbor as ourselves. . . . It is possible to cast every care on Him daily, and to be at peace amidst pressure, to see the will of God in everything, to put away *all* bitterness and clamor and evil speaking, daily and hourly. It is possible by unreserved resort to divine power under divine conditions to become strongest through and through at our weakest point.[1]

What Keswick stood for Amy Carmichael stood for. The great principles enunciated in the tent described precisely what she most longed for and were echoed in her writings for the rest of her life. Before the convention she had been pondering the agonizing question of the fate of those who had never heard of Jesus Christ. It was as though she heard "the cry of the heathen," and could not rest because she could not gladly stay at home and do nothing about them. During that week she prayed specifically for rest from that

---

1. Bishop Handley Moule, *Thoughts on Christian Sanctity.*

"cry," though the thought that God might actually call her to go to them did not cross her mind. The convention was "an unforgettable time," and resulted in "a new committal of one's whole life."

Mr. Wilson, a widower whose only daughter had died when she was just Amy's age, had by this time become a close friend of the Carmichael family. The children, who called him "the D.O.M.," for Dear Old Man, visited him often in his home, Broughton Grange. He was a lonely man in a bleak household with two bachelor sons in their late thirties. Amy's visits became more and more indispensable to him, until he asked her mother if Amy might become his "daughter." She consented, and so it was that the "corner" she had turned at the Belfast convention in 1887—her meeting Mr. Wilson when he called at their home—led to a new and important phase of her missionary training.

In 1890 she moved to Broughton Grange, God's "appointed school," in a beautiful setting in England's Lake District, above the river Derwent, with a glorious view of the Cumbrian Range from Skiddaw to Scafell.

Wilson was a Friend (Quaker), but for years superintended the Baptist Sunday school and later attended the Anglican church on Sunday evenings. Amy, the Irish Presbyterian, learned to value the silence of the Quaker meetings and the beauty of the Anglican service. The varied ways in which Christian worship found expression illuminated for her the Keswick motto, chosen by Wilson, "All one in Christ Jesus."

One day as the two were driving a gig along a country road they came upon a stone breaker. Pulling up the old horse, Charlie, the D.O.M. turned to Amy. "Which blow breaks the stone?" he asked. Then, pointing with his whip he said, "Thee must never say, thee must never even let thyself think, 'I won that soul for Christ.' It is the first blow and the last, and every one in between."

It was he who told her of the three inscriptions over the doors of the Milan Cathedral. One, with a carving of roses, says, "All that pleases is but for a moment"; another, with a carving of a cross, says, "All that grieves is but for a moment"; and over the great central door are only the words, "Nothing is important but that which is eternal."

It is not surprising that the Wilson sons found Amy's presence in the house disturbing. Her relationship with their father was at least unusual, probably an interference with whatever communication they had had with him, and certainly an interruption to the routines they were used to. They did not welcome her, and she knew it, but years later, when missionary work thrust her into close quarters with others whose styles differed from hers and whose approval she did not win, she saw that this aspect of Broughton Grange had also been a part of her necessary training.

Amy helped in meetings of the Scripture Union on Tuesday evenings, where the Wilson sons participated. The fact that she was the one who usually gave the address and was immensely popular with the children who attended may not have enhanced the fellowship she had with the two men, any more than did her inviting a number of girls to the Grange on Saturdays. They would take over the library, play games, have a Bible class, tour the garden, and devour milk and gingerbread.

The year 1890 marks the first publication (unless we count *Scraps*) of a piece by Amy B. Carmichael. She made a tour of the villages of the Clyde with Miss Hannah Govan of the Faith Mission. *Bright Words,* the organ of the mission, carried Amy's story about a shawlie, "Fightin' Sall," converted at The Welcome.

Amy always took note of spiritual milestones, keeping records of the dates on which God had met her in some special way. None marks a greater crisis than January 13, 1892. It was on that snowy Wednesday evening that the categorical imperative came, not just once but again and again: *Go ye.* The "rest from the cry of the heathen" for which she had prayed at Keswick four years before had been "only half answered," and now it was clear that she was to go. But how could she? The D.O.M. needed her. She had taken it for granted that she would stay with him until he went to heaven, but "crashing through that thought came a word I could not escape and dare not resist." How did the word come? Was it audible? Visible, like the handwriting on Belshazzar's wall? Was it a deep impression on her impressionable mind? She had had a talk with her "Fatherie" that afternoon. She went back to her own room, and, as clearly as a

Amy at Broughton Grange, about twenty-four.

human voice, she heard God say, GO YE. It was inescapable, irresistible.

The next day she sat down at the writing table in the beautiful old house. The house she could relinquish. The gorgeous view of the river and the gentle mountains she could do without. But the Dear Old Man? Yes, she could get along, by the grace of God, without his fatherly love. But could she break his heart? Simply walk out on the old man to whom she was light and comfort and joy? What of her mother?

"My Precious Mother," she wrote, "Have you given your child unreservedly to the Lord for whatever He wills? . . . O may He strengthen you to say YES to Him if He asks something which costs."

She wrote of "those dying in the dark, 50,000 of them every day," of her own longing to tell them of Jesus, and her misgivings because of the claims of home, and of how, only a few days before, she had written down for herself the reasons for not going: her mother's need of her, her "second father's" need, the possibility that by staying she might facilitate others' going, her poor health. Examining those reasons she wondered how God saw them. Were they good enough?

She could not finish the letter. It was too excruciating. Next day she tried again.

"I feel as though I had been stabbing someone I loved. . . . Through all the keen sharp pain which has come since Wednesday, the certainty that it was His voice I heard has never wavered, though all my heart has shrunk from what it means, though I seem torn in two."

She quoted the words of Jesus, which cut deeply: "If any man will come after me, let him deny himself and take up his cross and follow me. For whosoever will save his life shall lose it, and whosoever will lose his life for my sake shall find it."[1] "He that loveth father or mother more than me is unworthy of me."[2] "To obey is better than sacrifice."[3]

---

1. Matthew 16:24, 25.
2. Matthew 10:37.
3. 1 Samuel 15:22.

Faith does not eliminate questions. But faith knows where to take them. Amy must have spent many hours kneeling in that room, poring over her Bible, looking up to God with the questions: Who of her friends would understand? What if she should make a mistake and thus dishonor Him? Was the call mere fancy? What about leaving the D.O.M.? Might he die? But if she stayed would she not rob him of the greatest blessing? Her brothers and sisters—had she still some responsibility to help her mother with them? Health—was it foolhardy of her to imagine she could "take it" on the mission field? And money. Lord, what about money? And her widowed "Motherie." What about her, Lord?

On January 16, in firm, clear handwriting, Mrs. Carmichael wrote, "My own Precious Child,

> He who *hath* led *will* lead
>   All through the wilderness,
> He who hath fed will surely feed. . . .
> He who hath heard thy cry
>   Will never close His ear,
> He who hath marked thy faintest sigh
>   Will not forget thy tear.
> He loveth always, faileth never,
> So rest on Him today—forever.

"Yes, dearest Amy, He has lent you to me all these years. He only knows what a strength, comfort and joy you have been to me. In sorrow He made you my staff and solace, in loneliness my more than child companion, and in gladness my bright and merry-hearted sympathizer. So, darling, when He asks you now to go away from within my reach, can I say nay? No, no, Amy, He is yours—you are His—to take you where He pleases and to use you as He pleases. I can trust you to Him and I do. . . . All day He has helped me, and my heart unfailingly says, *'Go ye.'* "

She wrote more—of the sufficient grace she could count on, of the everlasting love, of the smallness of life, of her willingness to give her child into the loving arms of God. As for Mr. Wilson, "God has his happiness in *His* keeping."

Mr. Wilson wrote to comfort Mrs. Carmichael in the giving up of her "dear Child for the Lord's work amongst the heathen. I know something of what it must cost you. . . . It hardly seems a case for anything but bowing the head in thankful acquiescence when the Lord speaks thus to one so dear. . . . The future seems changed to me. . . . She has been and is more than I can tell you to me, but not too sweet or too loving to present to Him who gave Himself for us."

Sometimes Wilson comforted himself with the words about the colt Jesus had asked His disciples to fetch: "If any man say unto you, Why do ye this? say ye that the Lord hath need of him."[4] He needed Amy far more desperately, surely, than the man needed the colt. But it was the same Lord who asked for her. Who could say no?

---

4. Mark 11:3.

Chapter 6
Small Shall Seem All Sacrifice

The two Wilson sons were shocked to learn of Amy's decision. By this time they had come to terms with her lively presence in Broughton Grange. What had once been upsetting had become a part of their lives, and, though probably neither had allowed himself to admit it, they had, like Henry Higgins, "grown accustomed to her face." Suddenly she was about to abandon them all and go off to some godforsaken place forever. Their protests were ostensibly on their father's behalf. It was for his sake that they had tolerated her moving in with them, and certainly the old man needed her. How heartless of her to leave. It was, in effect, a breach of contract.

The Wilsons were not the only ones who were unsympathetic. Some whose names were well-known as Keswick leaders spoke "words that cut like knives." Someone suggested that the D.O.M. would be dead before Amy was through the Mediterranean. Even Mrs. Carmichael's sisters wondered if the girl was not enchanted by the notion of a foreign land. "If they only knew how torn in two I feel today," Amy wrote to her mother. She was beginning to understand a little of what it might mean to "bear shame" for the sake of Christ. She was ashamed to think that as a follower of a Savior who was "despised and rejected," she herself shrank from being merely misunderstood and misjudged. So this was what those stark Scripture passages meant: dead to self, alive to God—"dead to all one's natural earthly plans and hopes, dead to all voices, however dear, which would deafen our ear to His."

The old man himself, though his heart was breaking, did his best to be cheerful and comfort Amy. He had made it clear at the beginning that hers was not a binding arrangement with him, and was prepared to say so to those who accused her of a breach of faith.

One old friend, Mrs. Bell, a Quaker, actually clapped when she heard of Amy's call.

The "Go ye" part of the call had been crystal clear. Autumn of 1892 seemed to be the right time. She would sail then. But where? That was the vague part. Africa? China? She had often thought of both. Perhaps it was the solidity of her confidence in the Great Shepherd that prevented her worrying much over the geography. He would get her where she belonged, wouldn't He? Perhaps, too, a certain charming insouciance was a part of her nature. But now the island of Ceylon (Sri Lanka) came constantly to her attention. Why not go to Ceylon? She knew next to nothing about it—it wasn't "all flat," there were a lot of rats and insects there which at times "feed upon live missionaries." It was not long, however, before Ceylon dropped out of sight and Amy began thinking of China again and of Hudson Taylor's reminder of a million a month dying without God. She met a Mrs. Stewart, missionary from Fukien, China, and this seems to have been all that was necessary to convince her that she should go to Fukien with the Stewarts in the fall, probably under the Church of England Zenana (i.e. women's) Missionary Society. Plans were made, but on July 16 word came that Mrs. Stewart could not return that autumn. Amy accepted it as part of the Master Plan, not dreaming that if she had gone she would most likely have been murdered three years later as were the Stewarts and several single women missionaries.

At the end of July Amy and Mr. Wilson went as usual to the Keswick Convention. By this time missionary meetings had become a regular part of it. In 1887 thirty young people had volunteered for missionary service, and the next year someone sent a ten-pound note to the chairman "as the nucleus of a fund for sending out a Keswick missionary." It was in 1892 that the first one was chosen to be sent and supported by that fund: Amy Beatrice Carmichael. In her *Daily Light,* a book of daily Scripture readings arranged for morning and evening, she recorded in the margin of July 26, "Definitely given up for service abroad." The opening verse for that day was, "By faith Abraham . . . called to go out . . . obeyed"[1] Looking back after fifty years Amy declared that she was "no more fit to be a Keswick missionary than a Skye terrier puppy." That estimate never caused her to question the validity of the call—or, we may assume, the judgment of the One who issued it.

Sometime in August Amy decided that she would offer herself to Hudson Taylor's China Inland Mission. The wheels of mission boards in those days did not grind nearly so slowly as they do now. There was no psychological screening, no language schools, no jungle camps to survive. On August 10 she and Mr. Wilson left Broughton Grange for London. One evening as the two sat by the fire in the home of Miss Soltau, who was in charge of women candidates, "Fatherie" said to Amy, "Thee must sign thy name Carmichael Wilson in the C.I.M. papers. I would not have the world think that thou art not my child any more." Later he changed his mind. "Thee had better write, 'Wilson Carmichael.' " So it was that for many years she was Amy Wilson Carmichael.

Wilson returned home. That night Amy was overcome with sorrow for the Dear Old Man. She stood by the window of her little bedroom, tortured with thoughts of his desolation. Miss Soltau came and stood beside her:

The window had been open, and the little white dressing-table cover was powdered with smuts. As a tortured heart does always notice trifles, so I noticed those smuts. The words broke from me, "They say that if I leave him he will die. Even so am I right to go?" "Yes," was Miss Soltau's answer, "I think even so, you are right to go."

It was a tremendous answer. She must have added something about trusting our Father to deal tenderly with His servant who had truly given me to Him, though his heart still clung to me. But all I remember of the next few minutes is that with her arms around me I entered into peace. Often, through the many years that have passed since that night, I have been helped by the memory of her courage in the ways of God to strengthen a younger soul who was being torn as I was then.[2]

---

1. Hebrews 11:8.
2. Mildred Cable and Francesca French, *A Woman Who Laughed: Biography of Henrietta Soltau*, pp. 154ff.

Geraldine Guinness, who later married Hudson Taylor's son Howard, was staying at the mission at the same time. One day she handed Amy a little folded slip of paper. On the outside she had written, "Love and deepest sympathy, my dear Amy, and *many* thanks for your precious, helpful words yesterday. Geraldine. A little question, Darling—see over." On the inside:

> *CAN YE? Mark 10:38.*
>
> *Can ye drink of the cup that I drink of? And be baptized with the baptism that I am baptized with?*
>
> *CAN GOD? Psalm 78:19.* Ye shall *indeed . . . for with God all things are possible.*
>
> *Now is my soul troubled—and what shall I say? Father, save me . . . Father, glorify Thy name. For this cause came I unto this hour. John 12:24–28.*

On the back of this note sometime later Amy wrote:

> *Give and it shall be given unto you, good measure, pressed down, shaken together and running over. Luke 6:38. God's Good Measure.*
>
> *An exceeding and eternal weight of glory. 11 Cor. 4:17,18. Lord, I believe. Help Thou mine unbelief.*
>
> *Who for the joy that was set before Him—endured.*
>
> *As seeing Him who is invisible*
> *O small shall seem all sacrifice*
> *And pain and loss,*
> *When God shall wipe the weeping eyes,*
> *For suffering give the Victor's Prize,*
> *The Crown for Cross.*
> *"I will trust and NOT be afraid.*
> *Jan. 1892[3] Jan. 1893[5]*
> *Sept. 1892[4] March 3, 1893[6]* from today till He come."

---

3. The date of her hearing the GO YE.
4. To the China Inland Mission Home in London.
5. "Go to Japan" (see chapter 7).
6. Sailed for Japan.

The paper is dog-eared, insect-eaten, stained. She must have carried it in her Bible for the rest of her life.

Miss Soltau took her shopping for the things she would need in China. Together they packed them in two airtight tin trunks. Everything was ready.

No, it wasn't. The mission doctor refused to give approval for Amy to go to China, so back she went to Broughton Grange. The D.O.M. was ecstatic. "The Lord has given me back my Isaac!" he said. So it was the old peaceful grange life again. Amy played with her dog, Scamp, rode the pony Wilson gave her, helped with his writing, spoke in women's meetings. But one thought never left her: "This is not your rest." Doctors' verdicts notwithstanding, she knew she had to go.

Chapter 7
The Rending

On January 13, 1893 "the thought came" to Amy that Japan was the place for her to go. She had been praying and waiting for months, sure that she was not to "nestle down," that God in His time would make things plain. The battle with her feelings for the Dear Old Man was not finished. The words of Matthew 10:37 were always with her: "He that loveth father or mother more than me is not worthy of me."

If it was in fact God's leading, it was not by any miracle such as a pillar of fire, an audible voice, an angelic visit, a star, or handwriting on the wall. It was not by the ordinary methods by which, in combination, God seems to nudge us in the path of righteousness: circumstances, common sense, godly counsel, biblical principles. It was a thought. We may believe that God can impress such a thought on a mind surrendered to Him, and leave it at that. The pitfalls are many, however, and the story of Amy's next year or two may illustrate this.

She knew no one in Japan, but the D.O.M. did. Barclay Buxton, a missionary with the Church Missionary Society, was the leader of the Japan Evangelistic Band, a group of young people not necessarily associated with the CMS. Wilson wrote to tell him of Amy's "strange feeling" (her words) that she was to go to Japan, and asked if he had a place for her. Instead of expecting that Buxton's reply, negative or affirmative, might be an indication of the will of God, they were so confident of the validity of their first feeling that they followed another one. Both "felt" she should head for Japan at the earliest possible moment. A party of CIM women was to sail on

March 3 for Shanghai. Why not go with them? Buxton could send his reply there. Amy confidently booked a passage.

The few weeks that remained before she was to part with her beloved "Fatherie" were filled with anguish. Mr. Wilson believed God had given her to him as if she were his own lost daughter brought back from the dead, and his "flesh and his heart failed" at the prospect of Broughton Grange without Amy. No doubt she kept her sunny disposition with him, and they comforted each other with the promises of Scripture—anyone who relinquishes anything for the Lord's sake will not go unrewarded. But there were times alone in her room when all the waves and billows washed over her.

"Never, I think, not even in Heaven shall I forget that parting," Amy wrote fifty-two years later. "It was such a rending thing that I never wanted to repeat it. . . . Even now my heart winces at the thought of it." At about the same time she told a friend what she had never told anyone: "The night I sailed for China, March 3, 1893, my life, on the human side, was broken, and it never was mended again. But *He has been enough.*"

The steamship *Valetta* of the Peninsula and Orient Lines left the dock in Tilbury where many friends of the four women had gathered to say good-bye. Farewells to those leaving nowadays by jet plane are nothing compared to the protracted agonies of dockside partings. Now the traveler simply disappears into the jetway. It is a mere walking into another room. Then it was gangplanks, hours of visiting on board, the "All ashore!" the deep-throated whistles, the throwing off of moorings, the slow glide away from the dock, the almost imperceptible widening of the great gulf between voyager and loved ones, the straining to discern till the last possible moment the diminishing face. When Amy sailed, friends stood on the wharf and sang, "Crown Him with Many Crowns, the Lamb upon His Throne," and "Like a River Glorious is God's Perfect Peace," one of the Keswick hymns. The ship was within a stone's throw for an hour, so the singing went on and on, the same hymns sung again and again, the words taking on an ever more poignant significance:

Crown Him the Son of Man
Who every grief hath known

64

The Rending

That wrings the human breast,
And takes and bears them for His own
That all in Him may rest.

MATTHEW BRIDGES

Amy stood by the rail, watching intently the dear wrinkled face of the old man. Each, "on the human side," was broken. When, many years later, she held up before prospective missionary recruits the standard of the Cross of Jesus, no one could say she knew not whereof she spoke. If there was peace in her heart at that moment, it was nothing less than Jesus' last gift to His own—"*My own peace,* such as the world cannot give. Set your troubled hearts at rest, and banish your fears."[1] It was the peace her friends were singing about, "like a river glorious." But it did not utterly cancel the pain. As the ship rounded the last corner there stood the Dear Old Man again, having hiked a half-mile down the docks for a last glimpse. They were close enough to call out Bible verses to each other and a phrase Amy remembered from the farewell meeting, "Jesus has two nail-pierced hands. He lays one upon each and parts us so—*He* does the parting."

When the speck that was the dearest face finally disappeared, did she rush to her cabin and throw herself on the bunk sobbing? Not likely. Perhaps she waited by the rail until England dropped from sight, reviewing all the way the Lord had led her. Like Abraham, she did not know where she was going, and found comfort in the words of Genesis 12:1, "unto a land that I will show thee." Like Abraham, she had by faith obeyed what she believed to be the voice of God.

How would she spend the weeks between England and Colombo where she would transship? She considered the options. There were games. She loved games. But she was a missionary now, and a missionary hasn't time for games. She prayed for opportunities to speak of Christ to the sailors and fellow passengers. The captain himself asked her to put up Bible verses in his cabin "as a witness to all" that he had come to know the Lord Jesus Christ.

---

1. John 14:27 (NEB).

She wrote to the Keswick friends that she was "peacefully miser-able," that is, seasick. She paraphrased a hymn:

Peace, perfect peace, though seasick we can sing,
For even so we are beneath His wing.

On the first Sunday a service was held in the salon. Rough weather took the starch out of most of the passengers—"we sang hymns somewhat faintly"—and the congregation dwindled until a gentleman from first class suggested that the "Salvation Army ladies" (he had heard them singing hymns when they embarked—they *must* be Salvation Army) should address what Amy called the "survivors." She and a German missionary gladly complied. She also held a Bible study down below the main hatchway each morn-ing, "a little 'All-One-in-Christ' picture, a native Indian gentleman who is searching the records of the world's religions to find the true one; a poor simple Lascar who once met a missionary who told him about Jesus and who clings to Him very wistfully as his '*own* One,' a Chinaman, comical and eager who loves Him 'muchly,' and a nice old Ayah . . . met with us to read His book together."

In the Bay of Biscay they sang another Keswick hymn, one stanza of which reads, "O how great Thy lovingkindness, vaster, broader than the sea."[2]

Behind us lay the calm, dark waters stretching away and away, before us they shimmered in a glory of color and gold, above was the glow of even-tide, underneath were the everlasting arms of a Love limitless as the en-compassing ocean. . . . As we entered the Mediterranean He commanded His stormy wind to lash the quiet waters into a glorious fury. . . . Through the mighty rush and roar the old psalm sung itself chorus-fashion over and over, "The floods have lifted up, O Lord, the floods have lifted up their voice. . . . The Lord on High is mightier than the noise of many waters."[3]

As they steamed past the coast of "Darkest Africa" Amy saw one tiny light which typified for her how few spiritual light-bearers

---

2. J. Mountain, "Jesus, I am Resting, Resting."
3. Psalms 93:3, 4.

there were, and begged her correspondents not to go on leaving "the voiceless silence of despair" unanswered.

While traversing the Suez Canal they passed caravans of camels, pacing through the sand, followed by blue-robed, white-turbaned Arabs. As they passed camps, small boys rushed out and called for "baksheesh," a handout of money. Seeing the "solemn Sinai ridge" with its bare red peaks and rolling desert, Amy thought of the people of Israel standing far off while Moses went up the mountain and into the thick darkness where God was. At Aden she saw for the first time "the great Need, face to face"—swarms of curio vendors and diving boys, clad in chocolate brown and little else, "without Christ, without hope, without God in the world." Ceylon, a wonderland of rest to their sea-weary eyes, seemed like "a great peopled hothouse minus the glass." In Colombo the missionaries were "taken possession of by brothers and sisters in Jesus," driven over red sand roads to a bungalow where breakfast waited. Amy sat down to the little organ—glad of one that remained steady after the stormy passage—and played Samuel Rutherford's hymn, "The Sands of Time are Sinking," a Keswick favorite, as well as Frances Ridley Havergal's "Like a River Glorious." In Colombo as in Penang, Singapore, and Hong Kong, Amy asked to see the mission work, and seemed to have Old Home Week with many who had been to Keswick, knew the Keswick songs, read the Keswick magazine, *The Life of Faith.*

When they boarded the SS *Sutlej,* they found their cabin already occupied by rats and cockroaches. This was a matter for prayer first ("We went and told Jesus"), followed by action ("then we spoke to the steward"). Amy printed a card with the words *In everything give thanks,* decorated the corners with the initials of their chief woes, and hung it in the cabin.

On the back of her last shipboard letter, dated April 13, there is a note, "Friday, April 14th—Arrived safely at Shanghai. 'So He bringeth them into their desired haven.' Found letters welcoming me to Japan. 'He goeth before.' "

After a brief stay she was put on board the SS *Yokohama Maru* bound for Shimonoseki where she was to be met, and "off I went without a fear." The ship was caught in the tail end of a typhoon, making landing impossible, so the captain put her into a madly tossing steam tug full of very seasick Japanese. The tiny tug was buffeted and flung about till everybody was finally "tumbled together out onto the shore."

Amy was surrounded by a crowd of shouting, gesticulating people, not a white face anywhere. She did her best to explain her predicament. The crowd was friendly, it was certainly interested—it was, in fact, transfixed at the sight—but it was helpless. As she told the story later, she said she laughed till she was positively aching at the absurdity of the whole affair. A foreign port. Nobody to meet her. Not a word of any language she could understand. The girl from the Irish village on the North Sea, standing in the pouring rain beside her pile of luggage on the shore of Japan, laughing. "All this was part of the going forth unto a land I knew not, and everything was just right, and if things went wrong it was so much the more fun. I knew they would come right in the end. And they always did." So with the charming lightheartedness of faith she only wondered, *What next?*

There was a sudden rush of Japanese from all quarters. "They carried my boxes and me off to a hotel (made of paper as it seemed to me) and I sat down tranquilly on the mats and waited to see what the angels would do." They were on the job. Somebody beckoned and she followed. A rickshaw was waiting, in she got, and off she went into the unknown again. "It seems unbelievable but it felt quite natural to me." The rickshaw bounced through many streets and stopped at a house where a white man appeared. He turned out to be an American trader, thoroughly stunned to find this cheerful diminutive foreigner at his door. He was able to direct her to the home of missionaries, an American girl and an old lady, who had been expecting not Amy but the missionary who was to have met her, who had been delayed because of the storm. "Perfect saints they were, and that evening I was safe with them."

During the few days' wait for the lady who was to meet her Amy walked one day along the seashore, talking with one of the Shimonoseki missionaries. A casual remark was dropped which elicited an astonished question from Amy. "You don't mean to say," the missionary replied, "you think all missionaries love one another?" Precisely what she had thought. How could it be otherwise? "No faintest foreshadowing of the purposes of God was mine that morning," she wrote, "but I remember the thoughts that rushed through me then. What of 'See that ye love one another with a pure heart fervently'?[4] Was such a life of love lived *nowhere?*" It was a gray day, with a gray sea, a gray drizzle, and gray thoughts. But it spurred her to prayer, to an earnest beseeching that the Lord would enable her to love as He commanded us to love.

---

4. 1 Peter 1:22.

Chapter 8
The Romance of Missions

S uch a Hallelujah welcome was waiting for me here," wrote Amy of her arrival in Matsuye on May 1, 1893. "Praise Him who went before to search out a Resting-place. May it be a place of victory too, for His own glory's sake."

Amy, always assuming that her correspondents, and later the readers of her books, were as saturated as she was with the language and imagery of Scripture, rarely bothered to cite references. Here she was thinking of the Ark of the Covenant of the Lord that preceded by three days the people of Israel as they journeyed, to "search out a Resting-place." Whenever the Ark began to move, Moses prayed for victory over their enemies. Amy moved day by day in the spiritual company of those Israelites, guided as surely as they were, by the Lord, and sheltered by the Ark of His presence, which came to rest in Matsuye.

This was an old feudal town with a pagoda-shaped castle on a hill. The town lay between two inland lakes, one of which opened into the sea. Amy sketched a corner of the castle on one of her letters, but sketches could not catch the beauty of it all—"blue and green, brown and purple, opal lights, and changeful shadows, sunset glories on the waters." The houses were built so that one could look straight through to the garden at the back, where there were dwarf pines, rock work, tiny pools and bridges and lanterns. It seemed to Amy that everything in the houses was made of paper—walls, windows, trays, dustpans, baskets, brooms, strings, handkerchiefs. The walls had a convenient way of sliding back into themselves when not needed. If anyone wished to see out, he had only to touch the paper

71

with his tongue and the translucent became transparent. "An eye-hole being thus expeditiously manufactured, what need of glass?"

The Reverend Barclay Buxton was a young man then, one whose name, for Amy and many others, always wore "a little crown of light." She refers to a "shadow that was with him always," but does not explain. It was something that might have darkened his whole life and witness, but because it did not she learned that it is possible for those who love the Lord to choose to rejoice. He was a man of great charm and gifts of leadership. They were people of means and had brought with them many English manners and conveniences, including a governess for their three small sons. They lived in a large house and employed servants as the English of their station in life always did, whether in England or abroad. Here Amy was to spend the first months of her stay in Japan in a lovely room which, to her great delight, commanded a view of the mountains.

Buxton was not the stereotypical British colonial, nor the missionary depicted by Hollywood, who spurned the society of "the natives." There was "not a suspicion of the foreignizing element" in the church in Matsuye, which was a converted Shinto temple— "rather a thorn in the flesh to the Devil, I should fancy," wrote Amy. The Christians held a welcome meeting for her on the first Saturday evening after her arrival. She went to church, probably for the first time in her life, without hat or shoes. What this meant for a Victorian girl from her cultured home, with her great personal reserve, no twentieth century American or European can imagine. She sat, as everyone did, on the floor, Buxton beside her, interpreting in a running undertone the speech of greeting.

In a letter which began, "This is to be a home-letter in the strictest sense of the word, and isn't to be trotted round," Amy answered some of the questions folks at home were asking. Why "trot round" the answers to such trivial questions? What did she wear? In the summertime, cotton dresses, as few layers as possible, for the temperature often stayed in the nineties. In winter, "my blue serge dress and cap (that last dear little bit of home). For coats, my myrtle one with the cape—so warm and light—and for knock-about my good old pilot." When it was bitterly cold she almost lived in her "big tweed."

It did not take Amy long to see that European dress was a distraction. Why add an altogether avoidable distraction to the many unavoidable ones of being foreign? If Hudson Taylor could wear the queue and gown of a Chinese, why couldn't she wear a kimono? She departed from standard missionary practice and asked her colleagues' indulgence if she wore Japanese dress at least on Sundays. A sensible idea, they realized, and soon all adopted the practice. She had a dark-blue kimono with pale-green finishings, cool and graceful, with the words "God is Love" embroidered on it. "One soon forgets its presence in proving its power to draw one to the people. . . . I am keeping to my own shoes and stockings, however—the native ones being beyond me as yet." The text furnished an opportunity to explain to the curious her reason for being in Japan. Her hair was a matter of astonishment to the people—"No oil at all!" said one old lady who bowed most devoutly, sidled gently over, gazed at the foreign hair, and patted it. "Is it always fuzzy like that?"

One day she was telling the Good News to an old lady by interpretation. Just when she seemed ready to turn to Christ in faith, she noticed Amy's hands. It was very cold that day, and Amy was wearing fur gloves. "I cannot remember whether we were able to recall her to what mattered so much more than gloves, but this I do remember, I went home, took off my English clothes, put on my Japanese kimono, and never again, I trust, risked so much for the sake of so very little."

What did she eat? the folks at home wanted to know. When in the Buxtons' home she ate more or less what she had always eaten, including a proper English afternoon tea. This was the "hour of hours" to her, for "be it known, though fairly Jappy in other times and places we are thoroughly English then, and revel in the most un-do-without-able of English luxuries." These included condensed milk, potted meat, bread, and "real" tea, which was three times stronger than Japanese tea. When traveling, however, it was a different story. "Native fish paste, pale mud color and nasty; semi-boiled animal, nature unknown; eggs young and old; perfectly raw fish, brown seaweed, black beans in a liquid like senna tea; chicken (usually a fowl of much experience) in sugary juice; leathery scraps floating about in some terribly fishy liquid; sliced bamboo, lily roots, odoriferous radish, sea-weed, sea-ears, sea-slugs, plus pickle, plus rice."

Before she left England, Amy had imposed on herself the discipline of drinking tea without cream and eating toast without butter, in preparation for hardships to be endured. It did not work. It was dull and boring, and it made everyone else nervous, so she gave it up. The Lord knew where her heart was—where He led she'd follow, what He fed she'd swallow. She found when the time came that she didn't really mind anything nearly as much as she had feared she might. The promised grace was always supplied. The great thing was to learn to be thankful, for "in Japan we don't know what hardships are." She was thinking of the rigors of missionary life in inland China or Africa. Admittedly, however, there were occasions during her missionary journeys when, because of seasickness or sheer exhaustion, she could not bring herself to swallow the black liquids or the sea-slugs. Then she would, as unobtrusively as possible (which sometimes meant under the quilts) pull out of her bag bread and tea of the familiar variety.

Amy tackled the study of the language at once. It was a great gulf fixed between her and the people with "dark eyes, dark windows of darker souls," and she felt the helplessness of the alien. She was surprised and delighted to find that it was possible to start giving out the Gospel by means of an interpreter. A Christian Japanese girl, Misaki San, became her "mouth," her travel companion, her teacher.

"The honorifics are peculiar," Amy wrote. "For our 'go slowly' they have quite a touching appeal, 'augustly leisurely going, deign to be;' if you are hungry, you explain with polite frankness that your 'honorable inside is empty,' and if you want to say somebody has died, you say he has 'honorably deigned to cease to become.' " Upon arrival at one of the small country hotels she was greeted with the announcement that a chicken had "deigned to cease to become," and that a bath was "on the boil."

When she had been in Japan for one month she felt it was high time she took a missionary journey. She wrote long, long letters at every stage, filling twenty or more of the thinnest pages imaginable

Saturday. Have just come in from visiting with Miss Porter. We went to one of the few upper-class houses wh. is open to the Gospel in this part of the Country. Its head, ~~was out~~ was out, & we had a nice time with his wife & daughter, a dear ~~little~~ girl of about seventeen, the only Christian there. Think how hard it must be for her. Her learned father laughs at the N. T. she says, but she believes, and is "kept by the Power of God," true to Him in the midst of all the hindrances & inducements to forsake Him. After the usual lengthy preludes. bowing, tea, &c. Mrs. Porter read from John &c. to her Mother who is inquiring into the Jesus doctrine, & listening so brightly, putting in a word here & there to make it meaning clearer, I expect she will win both parents yet.

Part of the entertainment was without beginning & end, middle upon her strings the picture was such a movement & dainty coloring wished I cd. send you it, just had during ... I was ... Mrs. P. explained one more, & I am back painting on silk. the So here she is, only somewhat more attired! Their music is written in character instead of notes & looks as Bach's unmusical as the it sounds!

a "musical" performance all being a monotonous of two notes only. But pretty to. The graceful ... up for much! I as I saw it, & as if she slipped away, & returned were quite what So she departed with a lovely very thing! she was simply Gekkin-Playing

Portion of a letter from Japan written on rice paper.

with her round, clear handwriting and delicate drawings (storks, centipedes, people, fish, swordplay, incense burners, pagodas). There was an audience, of course. People hung over her shoulder, studying the writing. "Oh!" said an old lady when Amy explained that she was describing to her family the silkworm business in that village, "Our honorable worms and we ourselves are going to England in a letter!"

On the first leg of this first journey she and Misaki San traveled by *kuruma,* the Japanese rickshaw. "Sometimes after a plunge of unusual severity, my kuruma-man would turn with a cheerful 'Oh!' and a glance to make sure I was still safely inside." The roads were nothing but ruts, the ride so jolting that it could not be borne for many hours at a time, so the two women would get down and walk. They traveled in melting heat in crowded trains; in sampans and other boats of various descriptions where they and everyone else were seasick, and in a *kango,* a sort of sedan chair. The batterings and buffetings of such travel, the discomforts of the tiny hotels, the horrors of the menus could not but have been severe lessons in discipleship for the girl who had lived in the peaceful seaside village, the pleasant house in College Gardens, and the beautiful estate of Broughton Grange. But the girl was a disciple. That had been a clear and final decision, and all subsequent lessons she saw not as "culture shock"—the term had not then been invented so she did not have to bother about that sort of thing—but as the expected terms of her chosen discipleship, the first condition of which is, according to the Master's words, "He must give up all right to himself."[1]

Amy described in smallest detail everything she encountered, "comical topsy-turvy ideas and odd customs," seldom losing her spiritual perspective or, what is equally important for a stranger in a strange land, her humor. She was a realist, but never a pessimist or a sentimentalist. "Last night as we splashed into pools and knocked up against posts (wind and rain made carrying paper lanterns impossible) I laughed and thought of the Romance of Missions.

---

1. Matthew 16:24 (PHILLIPS).

Throw a love-halo round us, as shining as ever you like, but don't, if you wish to be true, adorn us with one more romantic."

The "private" lives of the people were, in the foreigner's eyes, rather shockingly public. People sat in their open front windows, discoursing, smoking, nursing babies. Then there was the custom of The Tub. The wooden family bathtub was often set in front of the house. "The blaze below, the steam above, with a parboiled head in the midst thereof, reminded one rather painfully of the early Christian martyrs, but nobody seemed to mind." Amy minded, "But I refrain—!" was all she said about that.

Amy's notions of privacy had no meaning at all for the Japanese. At night in the little hotels, when she lay down on the floor on quilts, she was surrounded by solemn eyes. One man gazed, she "regretted to say, at my nightdress, which I could only thankfully remember would look like full dress to him. Oh dear, it was dreadful, but too funny to mind very much." On a later journey, when she was traveling third class (there was no other option) with the Buxtons and other members of the Japan Evangelistic Band, the captain, a European, insisted on Mrs. Buxton's taking his own cabin and the others making the salon their bedroom. This meant that Amy and two single women shared the salon with Mr. Buxton and a bachelor named Consterdine. Amy told herself that this was really no more inappropriate than overnight railway travel, the resemblance being nearly strong enough to invite an attack of "H.S."— homesickness. But suddenly the captain reappeared with a carpenter, three youths whose duty seemed to consist in running around, a curtain, a flag, a hammer, and some nails. A partition was rigged up, and Amy fell asleep under the full blaze of the Rising Sun on the Japanese flag. When she woke and saw the great red ball, she realized how far she was from home. "Don't be a baby, Amy," she said to herself, "Sing a chorus and look ahead":

> The Lord of the Harvest will soon appear
> His smile, His voice we shall see and hear.

The taken-for-granted delays in Japan were hard on Europeans. Amy and the Buxtons had packed for a long voyage but the ship sailed six days later than scheduled. Why should it matter? What difference did three or four or six days make, after all? One could simply look upon the 144 hours as "a welcome little hemming-up time," but one of the band (Amy does not say which one) regarded them as so much "hanging on." Surely they were going to be late for everything they were making the journey for if they went on in this happy-go-lucky style. Mr. Buxton, never ruffled, pointed out the obvious: "God knows all about the boats." The lesson, applicable to anything that troubled her, stuck with Amy, along with another of his sayings, "Good for the flesh!" (spoken when someone objected to their singing as they walked along the road).

Perhaps no part of the cost of being a foreign missionary is greater than the loneliness. The alien experiences a sense of utter isolation, and is tempted to cling with greater tenacity to others of his own language and culture. Amy had a co-worker in the mission named Florence, whom she referred to in her letters as "Twin." At a missions conference they found that in the posted dinner lists, Twin and a friend named Mina had been seated side by side.

Well, I was very glad that dear Mina should have Twin, and I don't think I grudged her to her one little bit, and yet at the bottom of my heart there was just a touch of disappointment, for I had almost fancied I had somebody of my very own again, and there was a little ache somewhere. I could not *rejoice* in it. . . . I longed, yes *longed,* to be glad, to be filled with such a wealth of unselfish love that I should be far gladder to see those two together than I should have been to have had Twin to myself. And while I was asking for it, it came. For the very first time I felt a rush of real joy in it, His joy, a thing one cannot pump up or imitate or force in any way. . . . Half-unconsciously, perhaps, I had been saying, "Thou and Twin are enough for me"—one so soon clings to the gift instead of only to the Giver . . . :

Take my love, my Lord, I pour
At Thy feet its treasure-store.
Take myself and I will be
Ever, only, all for Thee.

FRANCES RIDLEY HAVERGAL

After writing this, Amy felt inclined to tear it out of the letter. It was too personal, too humiliating, but she decided the Lord wanted her to let it stand, to tell its tale of weakness and of God's strength. She was finding at firsthand that missionaries are not set apart from the rest of the human race, not purer, nobler, higher. "Wings are an illusive fallacy," she wrote. "Some may possess them, but they are not very visible, and as for me, there isn't the least sign of a feather. Don't imagine that by crossing the sea and landing on a foreign shore and learning a foreign lingo you 'burst the bonds of outer sin and hatch yourself a cherubim.' "

Forty years later Amy described for one of her "children" a transaction that had taken place when she was alone in a cave in Arima. Having gone there to spend a day in solitude she faced with God feelings of fear about the future. Loneliness hovered like a spectre on the horizon. Things were all right at the moment, but could she endure years of being alone? The devil painted pictures of loneliness which were vivid to her many years later, and she turned to the Lord in desperation. "What can I do, Lord? How can I go on to the end?" His answer: "None of them that trust in Me shall be desolate."[2]

Her mother ventured to ask in a letter whether Amy "loved anybody very much." Her answer was evasive. Had she met someone who made the possibility of marriage seem attractive, in spite of her early decision to remain single? Mr. Consterdine's name had occurred once or twice in her letters—apparently a single missionary, kind, protective, thoughtful in small ways. A young woman of Amy's beauty, gifts, and exuberance of spirit could not possibly have escaped the notice of any European bachelor who might have been around. If Mr. Consterdine or anybody else had proposed to her, she covered it with complete silence. She was a Victorian, with a Victorian's scrupulous modesty, and she had given over all matters of the heart to Him to whom alone hers was open.

---

2. Psalms 34:22.

Chapter 9
The Unrepealed Commission

Breakfast at the Buxtons' was at seven-thirty, followed by the reading of *Daily Light*. Then came Japanese and English prayers, and from nine till half past twelve language lessons. The midday meal was dinner. Everyone else in the house had time after dinner for rest and play. Not Amy. Rest and play? Perhaps for some it was necessary, but certainly not for her. Such an expenditure of time for a new missionary! She used the hour to teach English to a little boy who was eager to teach her Japanese—"a comical interchange of information!" Tea was next, then visiting, when Amy and Misaki San went to the village of Yokobama to try to find hearers for the Gospel. They usually had another tea there, then an hour's Bible reading with a young man.

The schedule was unrealistic. Amy's associates told her it couldn't be done, so she tackled it with a smile. She couldn't do it. After a few months she was forced to quit the English lessons and have a bit of quiet after dinner—not to rest, of course, and not to play, but to write letters. She told the folks at home that her poor head was tired and stupid, she had not studied for some weeks, and the enjoyment she had had at first in her lessons had taken wings. "Quiet," however, was a relative term. She could get away by herself to write, but "downstairs squeaks a concertina (to be borne for the sake of the cause), outside screams a baby (I wish I had some soothing syrup), from one quarter wails a street cryer, to whom nobody seems inclined to attend, from another hammers a cooper. But the worst of the worst is the nerve-distracting shriek of a terrible tin horn performed upon by a youth who has yet to learn compassion."

Nights were often broken by noise—a gang of boys, for example, thundering with all their might and main on the front door. "Now we have a highly respectable cook-san, who is the happy possessor of a kind heart and a thick head, foreign clothes (always too tight and minus a button or two). He is strangely obtuse as to puddings, but in matters of this sort he shines. The thundering ceased and he held a parley. It ended in tumultuous defeat on the part of the insurgents, and a victory, flat but satisfactory, on his: they retired from the field, he subsided into his quilts, and we went to dreamland."

After nearly a year in Matsuye, Amy wrote in the letter she called her "Scrapperie," read by many people at home, "I shall never, never, never learn Japanese. You may put it on my tombstone: expired in despair. I am in the middle of my lessons, and have stopped short to tell you so. I answer all Misaki San's expostulations by assuring her that it is much more important for me to warn you to send out no more missionaries to a land with such a language, than to go on longer trying to learn it." The length of the words alone *(tokiakashiteoagemoshimashoka* for example) was daunting.

Here is the last straw which has broken the final back of my resolution . . . I wanted to say, "I like fine weather better than wet"—not a complicated expression, one would imagine. It is the twist of construction that staggers me: "Rain of coming down bad honorable weather than even good honorable weather of days of side good is."

You may learn pages of this, poll-parrot-fashion, but how to form other sentences in such a world? . . . Poor Misaki San is taking it quite seriously and I am scribbling under a perfect hailstorm of "Ah, Weesong [her pronunciation of Amy's middle name, Wilson] San, dozo stop and learn more. Please say not so! Ah, Weesong San!"

But all was not by any means lost. On the anniversary of her arrival in Matsuye she wrote that she had actually been the speaker at a little meeting, meant to be for children only, but men and women, "who would not otherwise waken up enough to trouble to come" were attracted by the singing and crowded into the room. The children, "little wild rabbits a few weeks ago, as tame as pet ones now, clustered close about me." When the room was jammed past toleration they moved into the courtyard and Amy spoke simply, helped by some men who translated into child language, "crumbling the bread, as it were."

"We had just finished when an old woman who had been listening with great delight to her small grandchild's performances in the sing-song line, came up to me and pulled my sleeve, saying, 'All alone you have come, and *well* we have understood.' Wasn't it good of Him? I was half afraid they hadn't quite. I thought of the last first of May and thanked God and took courage."

Her letters describe dozens of meetings, always beginning with singing, always with distractions multiplied—the smokers smoked and tapped their tiny metal pipes loudly on the charcoal braziers, mothers nursed babies, undressed older children and rubbed them down, gongs sounded for prayer in nearby temples, terrible-looking idols gazed down from shelves in the houses where the meetings were held. Sometimes, in the middle of a hymn, "a splash in the near distance tells us that somebody is in the middle of something else—but I refrain. Oh, the strangeness of it!"

It was one thing to speak in a public meeting, but the thought of approaching a family as they sat in front of their own house filled her with fear. "Go and tell them about Me," she heard her Master say. She had gone a few yards beyond them and it seemed silly to turn, "the usual 'buts' rose—I don't know enough, may make mistakes and do more harm than good. Still that solemn Voice I am learning so slowly to recognize, spoke on—'Go and tell them about Me.' It *must* be His, so I went. . . . In the simplest colloquial I repeated 'God so loved the world,' told them the very little I could, and left them sadly enough. It was so *little*. . . . My words are so few and so broken as yet, but pray that somehow He may use it to bring glory to His dear name."

As in Belfast and Manchester, Amy sought out the factory girls. She cut an even stranger figure in their part of town than she had in the city slums at home. She was showered with stones and followed by jeering boys, but never mind. When she invited girls to a meeting nearly eighty came, making Amy cry as she remembered her girls at the two Welcomes and how they had sung "God be with you till we meet again."

Her great longing was to have a "single eye" for the glory of God. Whatever might blur the vision God had given her of His work, whatever could distract or deceive or tempt others to seek anything but the Lord Jesus Himself she tried to eliminate. Why waste precious time, painful effort, on lesser things? Someone suggested that more girls would be drawn to the meetings if she offered lessons in sewing or embroidery and administered only a mild dose of the Gospel. But these girls worked from five in the morning till half past six in the evening. They had one day off in ten. They hadn't time for foolishness. Furthermore, so far as Amy could see, there was no scriptural warrant for "consecrated fancywork and chatter," for "fleshly things rather than spiritual." "I would rather have two who came in earnest than a hundred who came to play," she said. "We have no time to toy with souls like this. It is not by ceremonial teamaking and flower arranging, not by wool chrysanthemum-making and foreign sewing-learning, but *'by My Spirit, saith the Lord.'*"[1]

The young men of Japan were beginning to learn English, which she regarded as the "open Sesame of the world's great treasure caves and poison caves too." She must do something about that, give them an antidote for the Western books full of falsehood and skepticism that were making their way into Japanese. Somehow she fitted afternoon Bible classes for them into her schedule, beginning with the book of Daniel.

Meetings in tiny dark rooms, meetings in courtyards, meetings on the street, meetings for women, for children, for men, for young men, factory girls, farm workers; meetings in the afternoons, meetings in the evening, often beginning at ten o'clock when the people came in from the fields, and lasting till midnight—no wonder Amy was exhausted. Once while waiting for a late-night meeting to begin she lay down behind some kind Christian women on a dirty mat on the floor, chilled by draughts, assailed by odors, and fell asleep. She woke to hear her name announced as the next speaker, "and before anybody had time to wonder anything, I was wide awake in my

---

1. Zechariah 4:6.

place, text found and all. A curious preparation for speaking, you will think, but I think He gave it to me, so it was all right."

Amy felt that her ability to sleep in such conditions ought to prove to her fellow missionaries that she was robust enough to "live native." Why on earth did they make such a fuss about her wanting to do this? Their attempts to teach her the wisdom learned through longer experience than hers made little impression, and she continued to try to persuade them to allow her to discard all Western ways. "If there were less of what seems like ease in our lives they would tell more for Christ and souls. . . . We profess to be strangers and pilgrims, seeking after a country of our own, yet we settle down in the most un-stranger-like fashion, exactly as if we were quite at home and meant to stay as long as we could. I don't wonder apostolic miracles have died. Apostolic living certainly has." She did promise her concerned friends that she would not go against the combined wisdom of them all and rush into a life of extreme austerity, but she was deeply troubled by their objections. "Satan is so much more in earnest than we are—he buys up the opportunity while we are wondering how much it will cost."

She felt keenly her own helplessness, awkwardness, and ignorance, and begged her friends at home to pray. All other powers but prayer seemed infinitesimal and useless by comparison. As she thought of the giants of faith like Elijah or Hudson Taylor, she knew that she was nothing but a baby, "shamefully, yes, shamefully small. 'That which I know not teach Thou me. Lord, teach us to pray.' " She deplored the tendency she found in herself to do more talking and writing about praying than actual praying. She lacked practice, she wrote, so it was small wonder she was an infant in prayer speech. Would her friends at home help? Would they, when they wakened in the night or were busy at work and her name flashed into mind, would they recognize it as God's telegram to remind them to pray? Would they telegraph back? "Don't let a moment slip. More may hang upon your instant yielding than you know or shall know till the great Then comes."

Amy's attempts to give her readers the verisimilitude of an actual experience by painting verbal pictures were never more ardent than when she tried to arouse spiritual concern for those who had never heard of Christ. She described a chilly little hotel where she sat trying to dry her clothes over a hibachi while she wrote. Behind her was the "honorable place," a slab of wood on which were arranged golden persimmons, a spray of blossom, burning candles, and a bowl of incense, offerings to a relative whose anniversary of "deigning to cease to become" they were celebrating. Above the offerings hung a picture of a Buddhist dignitary. In the next room was a shrine with ancestral tablets and a many-armed idol of the goddess of mercy. Lamps swung before it, prayers were chanted. It cut deep into her heart to think of the emptiness of it all, the sadness, the cry of the silence of death.

You who can resist the half-articulate pleading of many and many a heart today, can you resist this? From millions of voiceless souls, it is rising now—does it not touch you at all? The missionary magazines try to echo the silent sob. You read them? Yes; and you skim them for good stories, nice pictures, bits of excitement—the more the better. Then they drop into the wastepaper basket, or swell some dusty pile in the corner. For perhaps "there isn't much in them." Very likely not; "there isn't much" in the silence any more than in darkness, at least not very much reducible to print; *but to God there is something in it for all that.* Oh! you—you, I mean, who are weary of hearing the reiteration of the great unrepealed commission, you who think you care, but who certainly don't, past costing point, is there *nothing* will touch you?

Chapter 10
The School of Prayer

The new missionary who is sure of his call can hardly help expecting to see miracles when he reaches the place of service. Amy Carmichael had had a glimpse, through her work with the shawlies, of how the "other half" lived, had experienced what it is to be a quaint figure presenting a hardly credible message, and knew that not by any means all who hear it find it even interesting, let alone compelling. She had seen some fruit, however. God had honored her faith and her labor of love, and there were many "trophies" of grace to show for it. Surely in Japan where the need was far more acute she could expect even greater miracles and trophies. She prayed for them. She worked as hard as she could for them. She believed God's promises. But again and again her letters express her consciousness of the weakness of her own faith and the overpowering might of the obstacles to be removed. Heathendom was a felt presence, never more overwhelming than in an Eastern carnival or *matsuri*. She wished she could describe such a scene with a fire-dipped pen—even with a pen dipped in her own heart's blood if that was what it took to rouse the people at home from their lethargy.

We are riding together in a kuruma, a Japanese girl and I, spinning along through deserted streets, dark and still. We hear the beat of drum, the clang of cymbal, the hum of a thousand voices. Suddenly it breaks into a roar and we are in the midst of it all, caught in the whirl, swept along through streets all shining with crimson light, over bridges reflected in crimson-lit waters, under arches dropping with crimson fire. It is as if the stars had fallen upon earth, changing color as they fall. A burst of "Nebuchadnezzar's orchestra" in full swing drowns our voices, should we try to speak. . . . Onward rushes the mighty rabble—men and women in exchanged attire and gaudy colors flit past and mingling with uncanny monster forms they dance the wild matsuri dance, with abandonment inconceivable, every step a parody, every gesture a caricature. Dragons, griffins, reptiles, fishes, birds there are, all dancing, waving fans, shouting, howling, singing, *noising* in one form or another, in chorus perfectly bewildering. Old crones with wrinkles showing through the paint, babies wrapped in rainbow hues, gazing with astonished eyes, children gay as butterflies and as bewitching, men of good position in grotesque masks, women of the gentler order forgetting all refinement in the strange glamor of the hour—endlessly on and on they swarm. . . . A huge car is coming, drawn by scores of revellers, festooned with flowers and tinsel, wreathed with chains of light. Standing within it and walking before and after are girls robed in silks and crepes, palest shades of pink and blue, glittering with embroideries of gold and silver. Pale, expressionless faces are theirs, dead, vacant, joyless, their heavy half-shut eyes hardly glance at the revelry around them. The weary feet drag slowly on. We turn away heart-sick, for this is heathendom indeed. Our kuruma man speaks: have we seen enough? Ah yes, and far more. He takes us home, and we leave behind us the chaos of sound and color and mirth all hollow and sin all dark and in the silence of a pain we cannot conquer we find ourselves just spirit-crushed, and with no language but a cry.

The passion of her pleas for prayer and for understanding, the vividness with which she tried to depict what she was up against, were inspired by a genuine conviction that the work she was called to was without question God's work, and could not possibly be done without the help of God's people—"prayer warriors" who would share the bitterness of the battle with her. There was another bitterness which probably added to the urgency. Rumors reached her from England of continued criticism of her having gone off to Japan. This would vitiate the prayers she needed so badly, so she reminded her friends of her call in 1892, "Go ye," and in 1893, "Go to Japan." She confessed that she had made some mistakes during the year that intervened between those calls, mistakes due partly to the fear that if she did not find out immediately where she was to go, the strength to obey would fail and the light of the Lord's smile would be gone. "So I tried and we tried—and failed.

He had to teach us to Be Still and Know. Then when His time came His will was clear." She asked her supporters to believe that it was God's constraining hand which had beckoned her away, God's voice which would not let her stay. "Please, please, what you can't approve of, won't you forgive and don't let the prayer help He means you to give us be lost, for we need it so."

One experience in particular showed how greatly she needed it. Early one morning she was told that a man nearby was possessed by a "fox spirit." This spirit was worshipped in Japan, shrines were dedicated to him, and stone foxes were often set side by side with Buddhas. What this demon was doing to the poor man sounded very like New Testament stories—"Wherever he is, it gets hold of him, throws him down on the ground and there he foams at the mouth and grinds his teeth."[1] Amy went straight to her room and asked the Lord why she couldn't cast him out. "Because of your unbelief," was His answer. She spent hours on her knees before she asked Misaki San if she believed the Lord Jesus was willing to cast the devil out of the man. Misaki San was startled, but after some thought and prayer, declared that she believed. Amy's impulse was to go at once, but she remembered that the disciples were told that such a demon required fasting as well as prayer. So she and her friend did both, having sent a message in the meantime to ask if they would be permitted to see the man. Yes, came the answer, but he was very wild. He had six foxes, and was tied up.

After some hours of which Amy said only that they were solemn, the two went to the house. Stretched on the floor, fastened crosswise on two beams, bound and strapped hand and foot, his body covered with burns and wounds, lay the man. Little cones of powdered medicine had been set on his skin and lighted. They burned slowly, with a red glow. Nothing had so far daunted the fox spirits, but Amy called to mind that the power of God had conquered a demon whose name was Legion. She told the crowd in the room that her mighty Lord Jesus could cast out the six spirits. At the name of Christ a fearful paroxysm took hold of the man, hellish power was loosed, and blasphemies which even she could recognize

---

1. Mark 9:18 (PHILLIPS).

as blasphemies poured from the man's mouth. He struggled, was forcibly held down, the women knelt and prayed, the struggle increased. Satan seemed to be mocking them. "Can you think how I felt then?" Amy wrote. "The Lord's name dishonored among the heathen, and *I had done it!* Far, far better never to have come!" But she heard the Shepherd answer: *My sheep hear My voice and I know them and they follow Me. All power is given unto Me. These signs shall follow them that believe: in My name shall they cast out devils. Fear thou not for I am with thee.*[2]

Amy assured the wife that God would answer, and the two went home. An hour later a message came—the foxes had gone, the cords were off, the man was himself again. Next morning he asked to see Amy and Misaki San. Unrecognizable except for the burns, he offered them a spray of scarlet pomegranate blossom and sugared ice water. He and his wife gladly knelt with the women as they prayed, joining in with "Hai! Hai!" (yes, yes).

Amy's letters to the Keswick magazine, *The Life of Faith,* are full of stories of prayer answered. One tells of a man and a boy who often discussed the Christians' claim that God answers prayer. No, it could not be. But one day the boy was in charge of delivering the cakes to a wedding. He carried them very carefully, but as he stepped from a sampan a fear crossed his mind—something would happen to the delicate little cakes. A few minutes later he stumbled and dropped them. There was no time to go back for more, no time even to open the fragile boxes. What should he do? He thought of the Christians' God, and there on the road prayed his first prayer, "Please let none of the cakes be broken." It was not until the marriage ceremony was over that the guests were given their boxes of pink and white fan-shaped cakes. Not one was so much as cracked. Back went the boy to his friend. "Now I know that God hears prayer, for God heard *me.*"

One day Amy gave a New Testament to a student who took it and said, "It will be a seed." Seeds need to be watered. Prayer was that water, and Amy prayed. On the other side of the world another student, reading a letter from Amy asking for prayer for the Japa-

---

2. John 10:27; Matthew 28:18; Mark 16:17; Isaiah 41:10.

nese student, "put in five solid minutes' prayer." He was Paget Wilkes, an Oxford undergraduate then, who went to Japan, worked in Matsue, and led to Christ that student for whom he had prayed.

An insight into Amy Carmichael's understanding of the nature of prayer is given us in her story of what happened at Hirosi. This was a large Buddhist village where only eight or nine Christians shone "like stars in the night." Amy planned to visit the village, but wanted to prepare herself by praying along the lines of whatever God intended to do there. If she could be sure of that, she could pray with faith. Years later she discovered that Julian of Norwich had held a similar view of prayer: "I am the Ground of thy beseeching: first it is My will that thou have it; and after, I make thee to will it; and after, I make thee to beseech it and thou beseechest it. How should it then be that thou shouldst not have thy beseeching?"

As she prayed, Amy felt "pressed in spirit" to ask for a soul, one soul. Next day she went to Hirosi with Misaki San, and a young silk weaver "crossed the line"—became a Christian—that evening. A month later they went again. It was two souls she prayed for this time. The silk weaver brought a friend who "found peace," and an old woman also turned to the Lord. Two weeks passed. Again they went, again they asked God what He wanted to do, and the answer was that four souls were to cross the line. By this time other missionaries in Matsue had joined in prayer. One of the men felt it was a bit much to ask for four souls, but agreed to ask for two. Things looked anything but encouraging when the women arrived. The Hirosi Christians balked at asking for four. Nobody in town seemed in the least interested. The devil fired his usual darts of doubt: "You can't expect conversions every time. It's quite presumptuous. Fancy going back to Matsue empty-handed! etc."

Matters were enormously complicated by Amy's having dropped what she thought an unarguable suggestion, that new converts should burn their idols. *Burn* their *idols?* Impossible to let it be known that Christians must do this—it would turn back all inquirers. Amy was adamant, facing what she termed "the Calvary side of the work, a thing to be lived through alone with Calvary's Christ." They "prayer-meetinged" her, asking the Lord to open her eyes, show her the foolishness of transgressing Japanese custom. Then they besought her not to mention idols again. But truth was dearer than success. "I could not buy a soul at the cost of sacrificing truth. The fact that many might and probably would be turned back could not be a proof that this course was wrong, because in John 6:66 we read 'From that time [speaking of the "hard saying"] many of his disciples went back, and walked no more with him.' The servant is not greater than his Lord." In the meeting that afternoon the people gazed and smiled and felt nothing. It seemed a prison of mocking spirits. Amy was about to close when a woman said, "I want to believe." Then her son came and knelt. On the way back from the meeting Amy stopped at the home of Christians who had a friend waiting to ask her the way of salvation. That friend was number three. Where was number four? "Why," said a man, "It must be my wife. She wants to be a Jesus-person, but she is away at her own village." She came back early the next morning and confessed before her relatives her desire to be a Christian.

For weeks afterwards Amy felt an irresistible divine pressure to ask and receive according to 1 John 5:14, 15: "This is the confidence that we have in him, that, if we ask anything according to his will, he heareth us: And if we know that he hear us, whatsoever we ask, we know that we have the petitions that we desired of him." The petition this time? Eight souls from Hirosi. Again there was resistance from the Christians there. To ask for something they did not receive would be "a very bad happening." Amy had no doubt God wanted to give the eight, and offered to stay longer to give Him time. No, they could not possibly arrange more meetings. So Amy, not about to capitulate, read prayer promises. The dear old undershepherd, a man of "perfectly Gladstonian ambiguity and circumlocution," had locked horns with Amy over every issue that arose, his whole soul protesting against her categorical imperatives. This time he saw that protest would be futile. Slowly he rose, slowly spoke, "You are a Jesus-walking one; if His voice speaks to you, though it speaks not to us, we will believe." Their trust, greater perhaps in Amy than in God, was rewarded. In His mercy (He knows the measure of faith He has given to each), eight more "stars" now shone in Hirosi. Later in India, bearing very great responsibilities for decision making, Amy remembered the undershepherd's words and was strengthened in her resolve when Indian fellow-workers questioned her judgment.

And what about the next visit? Sixteen? No. No number at all was "laid on" Amy's heart. They went to Hirosi, they had the usual meetings, they prayed together with all the Christians there, some came to Jesus, but Amy did not know how many. "We parted in a sort of singing silence."

When she wrote the Hirosi story for her "children" she acknowledged, in a veiled way, that she had suffered pain because of those Christians. She did not elaborate. "I do not think that is a thing to talk about."

Fourteen years later Barclay Buxton's nephew joined him in Matsuye. He often visited Hirosi, and found that the converts from Amy's time were still firmly rooted in faith.

Utter holiness, crystal pure, was Amy Carmichael's desire. She did not see how any true Christian could have a lesser. "If we are not clean when we bear the vessels of the Lord," she wrote in May of 1894, "we may profane His holy name in the things which we hallow. Our very service a defiling thing! . . . The need of Japan: prophets of her own who can and will dare, Elijah-like, to stand alone for God, speaking His word faithfully, be that Word like as a fire, like a hammer, marking out, for lifelong loneliness, the man who is 'the Voice.' "

She herself set the example and paid the price, sometimes in conflict with fellow-believers both European and Japanese. The matter of using pictures of Christ, a common practice among missionaries, was unthinkable to Amy. No one, she felt, had a right to presume to imagine God the Son. Who could possibly separate manhood from Godhead? She shrank in dread from such holy ground, and reminded those who disagreed that the apostles had avoided all appeal to the senses, trusting in the power of the Word alone. The Church, she said, resorted to pictures only when her power had gone.

The merest suggestion of anyone's choosing missionary work because it was noble and grand, or a mission field because it was pleasant, horrified her. How could people at home write of a "delightful" missionary meeting? Had they absorbed nothing of needs unmet, cries unheeded, griefs uncomforted? Did they attend for nothing but the tea and cake, the conversation, the chance to examine exotic curios, and then tell themselves that they were doing all that could be expected of them? "Missionary work is a grain of sand, the work untouched is a pyramid. . . . Face it. Look and listen, alone with God. Then go, let go, help go. But never, never, never think that anything short of this is being 'interested in missions.' Never, until this point is reached and passed, delude yourself into believing that you care at all." Her own experience at Keswick was anything but "delightful." The tent, thronged and still. Wave after wave of silent prayer, rising solemnly to God. Brief, burning "soldier-words" from soldier-souls. Silent battles raging within. A long hush. A cry as of pain, unavoidable, demanding an answer. She had given her answer, and on countless occasions in the field had had to reexamine her motives. A young missionary once said to her, "I would go home tomorrow if I could. It is all a miserable disappointment, and I thought it would be so nice." She besought her friends, girl friends, and cousins at home to consider the cry and the call, to welcome all tests of whatever sort before they crossed the seas, and to learn to die to self in any shape or form. Experience had quickly taught her that she could not survive the storms without the anchor of the constraining love of Christ and what she called the "Rock-consciousness" of the promise given her, "He goeth before."

Chapter 11
Japanese Head

T he first missionary, a tough man named Paul, found that his apostolic duties entailed some stormy buffetings. He was hard pressed, bewildered, hunted, struck down; he was starved, imprisoned, beaten, shipwrecked; he was afflicted with something that needled his flesh. During Amy Carmichael's first fourteen months as a missionary she was "buffeted" in other ways. She was hard pressed, sometimes bewildered, and finally struck down. Her experiences caused her to meditate on the great vulnerability of the physical body, the same body in which the Life of Christ is mysteriously revealed.

Writing from Imaichi, a town to which she had gone because the only missionary had had to take sick leave and Amy could not think of leaving it alone, she quoted the hard-pressed apostle, "We glory in our *weakness* that the power of Christ may rest upon us."[1] The text was followed by an ellipsis, then:

Back again, and now on reading over the last few lines they seem perfectly prophetical! On Sunday I collapsed. . . . A touch of fever, then a fainting fit. . . . a terrible comedown, for I always declared nothing could make *me* faint. All such weakminded nonsense I quite scorned. The only time I ever lost consciousness for a moment was through the agony of sympathy experienced for Alfred [her brother] when he gashed himself and had to get sewn up. . . . But this time, over I went and before I came back all the humiliating attentions attendant upon such departures had been showered upon me and they left me very wet.

---

1. *See* 2 Corinthians 12:9.

She had an explanation, albeit a feeble one. She had lost her umbrella overboard. While sun helmets were not worn by missionaries in Japan, it was taken for granted that European heads could not tolerate sunshine. Umbrellas were a must.

It was a hot day. When she got to the hotel a hot bath, as always, was waiting. It was the last straw. There had been mention in letters to her mother of divers afflictions. In January when the eight converts were given in Hirosi she wrote that she could hardly think because of acute neuralgia. In May she told her mother she might be going to China for a "change of thought," as the climate of Japan was "dreadful upon brains and eyes." A Keswick letter written early in June assured everyone that she was feeling fit again, having allowed herself the luxuries of butter on her bread and milk in her tea. These dainties were supposed to do what the unidentified black liquids and sea-slugs did not seem to be doing—put muscle on her. So her troubles were due to more than the loss of an umbrella.

When she came to after the fainting fit she found herself "environed by wet towels, doleful faces, and a general sense of blurs." Then she remembered she was expected at a meeting. No "weak-minded nonsense" must interfere with that. The power of Christ, while it did not exempt her from a momentary lapse, would enable her to carry on. She banked everything on the promise of Isaiah 40:31, "They that wait upon the Lord shall renew their strength . . . they shall walk, and not faint," took herself by the scruff of the neck, marched herself to the meeting, and spoke. It was a late meeting, followed by a long talk with a woman who came to Christ. There was no doubt in Amy's mind it was worth it. Later she acknowledged that she had given Isaiah's word the meaning she wanted it to have, not a good thing to do.

"Japanese head" was the doctor's diagnosis. No one seemed to be very clear as to exactly what sort of head this was, but it was extremely painful, foreigners were susceptible to it, Amy had succumbed, and was ordered to take a long rest. This was a terrible interruption of her plans, but the threat of telltale letters to her loved ones persuaded her to submit. "I am getting meek in my old age, you see."

Before she left she had the thrill of attending the baptism of the

Misaki San and Amy.

first believers in Hirosi. Afterwards the church group was photographed, along with Amy and her co-workers. "I wish it were possible to keep from this mode of embalmment," she wrote, "but one can't without hurting kind feelings and making a fuss." For the rest of her life she resisted being photographed, giving in only rarely under pressure from people she loved. She could not understand why anyone should wish to be preserved as he is when Christians have the sublime hope of being some day like Christ.

Saying good-bye was agony. The Japanese were kindness personified, and of course expected her to return within six weeks or so, but how would it look to them? Would they know she couldn't help having to leave, or might they take her for another of the many quitters? "You are going to China for your weakness," one of them wrote. "Please come back." Something told her that she might not be back as soon as they expected.

On board ship for Shanghai she found a note from her beloved Misaki San: "I know you will miss me, but Christ is sitting by you now, so please talk with Him to forget me." Sleep was hard to come by in the crowded and smoke-filled hold, so she lay on her plaid on deck amid the noise and funnel dust. For the second leg of the journey she succumbed to what, on principle, she had set herself firmly against—she took first class. "I don't believe the Lord Jesus or His disciples would go in for it. It does not seem to me honoring to our Master, this missionary habit of going by the easier rather than the harder way, when *He* chose the harder. It is as if we put ourselves a little above Him." First class on such a steamer might be compared to third class on a British ship, though a bit less comfortable, and she couldn't help being thankful for cleanliness, privacy, quiet, and, in place of the cabin boys on the coastal steamer, a woman "who wore *clothes!!*" Amy suffered the usual woes of storms and seasickness, heat and headaches. Nevertheless she found some sailors she could speak to of Christ. "Well, miss," one of them said, "we thought the sea'd beat you this time." She had asked for strength, and it came, amid the howling and clashing, roar and rush, but it gave out at the end of her talk and she had to be helped back to her cabin. She learned next day that several had trusted Him who is "mighty to save" and had signed a pledge to abstain from alcohol.

By July 10 she was comfortably ensconced in a room of the China Inland Mission in Shanghai. She made it her own by hanging family photos and the mottoes she cherished: FAITH IS THE VICTORY, CHRIST IS CONQUEROR, NOT I BUT CHRIST, JUST FOR TODAY, and a single embroidered word, RABBONI, Mary's word when she saw the risen Christ: *My Master!* On the table lay a calendar with the words, "The Lord thinketh upon me." She reminded her correspondents of the million a month dying without Christ in China, and the eighty thousand dead of plague in Hong Kong in the previous few weeks.

"To any whom the Hand Divine is beckoning: count the cost, for He tells us to, *but take your slate to the foot of the Cross and add up the figures there.*"

The temperature was in the nineties, but the mission house was cool with punkahs (huge fans suspended from the ceiling and operated by a coolie with a rope) waving continuously and cups of hot tea, the Englishman's cooler, always available. Amy's "brain oppression" lessened, and as she saw others who were far more in need of a change than she, she felt ashamed that she had given in to "tiredness." But, she hastened to explain, her giving in was only because of the fear that she might give trouble to others. She assured her friends that she was not thin—she was, in fact, the "opposite of a shadow"—and that "promotion" (to heaven) was not imminent.

Amy had been in Shanghai only a week when, feeling refreshed and without excuse for indulging herself any longer in such comfort, she asked God what was next. The answer came as it had when she went to Japan.

"On the eighteenth of July the word of the Lord came unto me saying, 'Go to Ceylon.'" The CIM people were horrified. Was she well enough to go? Did she know what she was doing? Why Ceylon? How could she go alone? Only the last question was settled. Another missionary was making the voyage and would look after her. Forthwith Amy booked a passage for Colombo. Off she sailed on July 28, sure of one thing: *He goeth before.* "Only whoso has felt the Spirit of the Highest in this most solemn way will understand at all," she wrote—pages and pages of explanations to the homefolk who would worry about their "Keswick Child." It never once crossed her mind that she needed counsel, let alone permission, from those who had sent her. She felt one in spirit with Abraham, "not knowing whither," and with Luther, "Here I stand—I can do no other."

"I am prepared for much blame, or at best misunderstanding, but I cannot help it. One *dare* not do anything but obey when that Voice speaks." How did it speak? In three ways: through the Word, with unanswerable force, through the inward leading of the Spirit, and (often but not always) through circumstances. She felt confirmed by all of these, although her friends found no confirmation for the last, nor was Amy herself sure there was any infallible warrant for that one in the Bible. The old saints appeared to have gone often in what seemed direct opposition to existing facts. She could see, however, that circumstances, which are all of God's ordering, might be confirmatory witnesses.

She reviewed the circumstances of this move: She had not wasted much strength in learning Japanese, had had no house or settled station, and few responsibilities in Matsuye, hence would not be missed. Fellow-workers had helped by prayer and by mending and packing her things. The passage to Ceylon cost only ten pounds. When she stopped in Colombo en route to Japan, friends there had remarked that the Lord might send her back to them. God had brought helpful people all along the way. Could there be any doubt that He was in charge? She pleaded all these proofs to her worried loved ones.

"All life's training is just exactly what is needed for the true Life-work, still out of view but far away from none of us. *Don't grudge me the learning of a new lesson.*"

In Hong Kong she caught a chill. On August 2 she wrote in the margin of her *Daily Light,* "Very ill—fever—alone—kept—comforted." She was brought (she admitted it) to the very end of herself, of self-strength, self-energy, everything. "What if I never reach Ceylon at all?" she wondered during a turbulent, fevered night. "What if God's work for me is to give all up and go home by the next boat?" It would certainly look as though her call was false, her faith misplaced, her Master's voice misunderstood.

When she recounted the journey years later, selective memory had obliterated all but the faithfulness of God. Every one of the imagined (and, as she found, real) objections people had raised was gone. She told her "children" that it had never occurred to her that anyone might misunderstand. The need for explanations had faded from memory, along with the battles fought all the way to Ceylon. She had not reread the shipboard letters describing the wrestlings of mind and soul—"Oh, just awfully the Devil came with doubts and fears!"

Chapter 12
Not Much of a Halo in Ceylon

At dawn of the day the ship was to dock in Colombo a small, tired woman stood on deck, tortured with fear, weak, "utterly unfit for the great dim unknown, coming now so close to me." A moth, Amy said, could have crushed her then. She picked up her *Daily Light* and read, "The joy of the Lord is your strength."[1] A flood of sunshine fell across the mists and she decided she would trust and not be afraid. Welcomed and invited to stay at a mission cottage in Colombo she was immediately made one of the circle, but felt helpless, trustless, wondered why she had come, and longed for solitude and quiet.

The D.O.M. had word of her whereabouts. What on earth could his darling girl be up to now? Off to Ceylon! Was she about to pull up all stakes in Japan and join another mission? He cabled her at once, advising her against joining any mission in Ceylon. Then he wrote, expressing his serious concern about the move she had made without so much as informing the Keswick Mission Committee in advance. She was devastated. She had left it all in God's hands, believing He would make things as clear to her constituency as He had made them to her. "But it has not been so, and I see my wrongness and cannot be sorry enough."

She found that "a tiny band of girl-witnesses unto Him" (three single missionaries whose leaders had both died of fever) had been praying for a new leader to be sent to the village of Heneratgoda. To them it was perfectly obvious that Amy was the answer. To her

---

1. Nehemiah 8:10.

it was not. *She,* their leader? The thought filled her with new fears, but as they met and prayed together she believed that while she was not meant to lead them she could be "the string to the beads."

Making it clear that she must not be regarded as a member of the Village Mission of Heneratgoda she moved into their thatch-roofed hut. Its floor was composed of what Amy's Victorian sensibilities allowed her to describe only as "mud and *horror."* During every minute of every hour they were under the meticulous scrutiny of many eyes ("these good folk seem fond of character-study"), a thing unsettling, of course, but "an easy way of entertaining one's friends—*live and let look!"* She found beauty in the surroundings, always particularly observant of birds.

Yesterday I had five delightful minutes watching a honeysucker. There, in the bright sunshine like a bit of blue flame among white flowers, the tiny chirping thing flitted to and fro. Now poising itself on a spray of shining blossom, diving its curved beak deep into each fragrant flower, never marring a petal, now fluttering in and out of the bush on which they grow, its clear electric tinting showing well against the green, and now for a moment motionless, half hidden in the whiteness, a little living jewel in a snowdrift of sweet flowers.

With her usual determination and earnestness—never mind that she was supposed to be convalescing—she plunged at once into meetings. "Bright lamp shining in the midst of bright flowers, bright dark eyes shining upon us, bright praise songs rising from lips closed till now, soft moonlight shining upon all." Here she was in a new field of service, a new language to learn, the old, old story to tell. Children were most open to hear that story, and she began to gather them, "dear little brownies with necklaces and bangles, such a contrast to the quaint tots of Japan, the queer little imps of China." When one three-year-old refused to join the singing, she forfeited the privilege of sitting on Amy's lap. A thumb went into her mouth, she sulked, was put on a chair in the corner, and told she was a sinful child. Three times in an hour the child fell off the chair. When she was told she could not go home till she was good, "a smile of much delight lit up the sweet contentment of her face and she remarked triumphantly that she did not want to go home. The opposite tack was tried at once and within five minutes the fight was won and with more mischief than penitence, I'm afraid, the monkey declared herself 'good.' "

Heathenism in all its forms Amy found appalling. She described a celebration which took place just across the lane from their little house:

Through the moonless dark we can see the flare of torches, the glimmer of lamps, the flicker of tapers. The woman there was ill, they had a devil-dance over her, now she was recovered and they were paying the vow to the demon who had withdrawn as requested. One man is playing a sort of long-shaped tomtom, hung round his neck, two more are dancing up and down and round and round on a marked circle, sacred to the presiding spirit. Two or three boys are arranged in corners to yell at given periods. On the ground lies the woman. Behind the performers three altars stand, decked with creamy water lilies, lit with tapers floating in split coconuts, and on each there is rice in little piles, a few coins, and sprays of the exquisite areca flower. All around there are people, men and women and boys. They will go on all night. In the early morning the dance will vary, they will sing something different too. At present it is a continuous drum thump, bangle-jingle, weird cry, and monotonous chant. They are propitiating the demon and at the same time trying to frighten him away. . . . "Doctrines of demons" are no myth here. . . . I turned to my Bible: "Be strong and courageous, be not afraid or dismayed, for the King of Assyria nor for all the multitude that is with him, *FOR* there be more with us than with him: with him is an arm of flesh, but with us is the Lord our God to help us and to fight our battles. And the people rested themselves upon the word of Hezekiah, King of Judah."[2] And so, I think, may we.

When this woman from the windswept seacoast of Ireland found herself "away in the heart of heathendom with my sister-girls in this dark, dark jungle" she was telling the straight truth as she saw it. She turned with an instinctive deadly nausea from any coloring of the facts, any slightest bending of the truth in order to create a more interesting picture. She was far ahead of her time as a missionary reporter. The constituency was accustomed to a certain triumphalism in missionary stories. Not that there were none like Amy who told it straight, but there were many who popularized

2. 2 Chronicles 32:7, 8.

mission work by dramatizing the successes and skipping lightly over what was far more commonplace than success. "There isn't much of a halo in real life," she wrote, "we save it all up for the missionary meetings."

The original letters (reprints of which Amy had expressly forbidden) show evidence of another's attempt, if not to color the facts, at least to sweeten them a bit. Someone had crossed out parts not thought suitable for reprint, such as mention of fleas, lice, or "slimy, crawly things," filthy slime through which she had to wade, and, in a reference to the inability of the Singhalese to focus their minds, the editor has deleted Amy's aside, "if minds they have."

The hard work of visiting—"Do you throw a halo around it?" she wrote:

You go to a hut and find nobody in, you go to the next and find nobody wants you, you go to the next and find an old woman who says yes, you may talk if you like, and she listens in an aimless sort of way and perhaps one or two more drift in, and you go on, a prayer behind each sentence if you are speaking through interpretation (but I hope I won't have to do that always), an undercurrent flowing all the time, if you are sitting silently listening to somebody else speaking. Perhaps they are thoughtful enough to object—"We ourselves are Buddhists, why should we change? Do you kill animals? We don't want a religion like that."

If you ask them don't they eat eggs and fish, they say oh yes, but they wouldn't poach an egg (i.e. break the shell!), boiling it is different. They wouldn't kill a fish, they take it out of the water and it dies of its own accord. . . . It is so disappointing sometimes, just when you think you have got a little bit of the glorious Truth wedged in, when the heart seems touched perhaps by the wonderful story of Calvary, some little triviality comes up, and some question about pigs or eggs sends you back to the very beginning. But there are the bright bits, too, times when a flash of Heaven's own sunshine lights up the darkness of the darkest mud hut, and one such moment is worth a lifetime's plod.

Although Amy was told that it was a risky business in Ceylon for single women to visit Buddhist priests, she did it. Taking questions from a crowd also was dangerous. She did that too. A priest turned up in an open-air meeting one day and put these questions: You Christians believe God leads people who are in earnest to the Truth, do you? Yes. Do you deny that Gautama Buddha was in real earnest? No. How was it, then, that he did not find it? Amy's answer, recorded in a letter: "To our Father and his Father we may leave the gentle Buddha. To the Indian Prince Siddhartha (the teacher of whom Buddha was the deified incarnation), as to the Persian King Cyrus, He may have said, 'I have even called thee, I have surnamed thee, though thou hast not known Me.'—but what of those," she added to home friends, "who today are seeking and, so far as we are concerned, seeking as vainly as he? There are some such. In inland China Mr. Hudson Taylor found one. All old missionaries can tell of a few rare souls found blindly groping, if haply they might feel after Him and find Him. Oh that our skirts may be free from the stain of our brother's blood!"

Because of a doctor's verdict that it would never do for Amy to return to Japan—she had "brain exhaustion"—she had finally settled down, she wrote in November 1894, to study the Singhalese language. Her luggage was to be sent in a year or so from Japan, and the D.O.M. was shipping a box of clothing to Ceylon for her. She had reached a measure of peace. The Lord's field for her work would be Ceylon. "All is settled," she wrote on November 14.

On November 27 she learned that the D.O.M. had had a stroke. Within an hour she set out for Colombo, borrowed warm clothing from a missionary, and sailed for London the next day.

The journey was a nightmare from start to finish. She was so ill she could remember little except pain, fever, fear, heat, then, in Naples, icy wind. The Lord sent along His angels, one of them in Rome to rout her from sleep on one train and get her on the right train for Paris, another a Frenchman who piloted her across Paris to the train for Calais. A rough Channel crossing. Her mother meeting her in London on December 15. December 16—her twenty-seventh birthday. It is doubtful that there was any festivity. Then long days of blank. Finally the faces of beloved Keswick friends, a doctor's face. Through it all the urgent thought, "I must be well. I must get to Broughton Grange." She got there in time for Christmas.

Chapter 13
To the India of the Raj

"England was very good to me." Thus Amy summed up in her autobiography the ten months spent there.

She neglected to mention that she became a published author. Marshall Brothers of London brought out during that year (1895) her first book, *From Sunrise Land,* a collection of letters from Japan with illustrations by the author and William Wilson, the D.O.M.'s son.

It was not her idea. She had to be talked into allowing the material to go into print. Persuaded at last, she explained her primary reason in the introduction:

"These little letters were written just for 'home'; remembering this, your kindness will excuse mistakes and informalities. And the same plea applies to the little sketches scattered throughout. . . . Others could tell you far more, and far more worthily, of the showing forth of His hand in their part of the great Mission Trust. Will they believe that this thought presses, and that the more conscious of it we are, the more grateful we shall be for their prayer? *Please pray!* Please ask that the Master may stoop to use a thing so simple and so small, to lift even one into the Love wherewith He loves."

Rereading the book later she was, like most authors, not happy with it. Tolstoy is said to have lamented, when he read *War and Peace* years after it first appeared, "This must all be done over." In Amy's copy of *From Sunrise Land* she wrote, "Bad rhymes in parts, bad writing all through."

The D.O.M. was overjoyed to have her at home again, believing at first that she had been "given back" to him. He recovered from the stroke, but soon knew that he would have to relinquish her once more since she had no intention of staying. The doctors' verdict that the tropics were not to be considered again did not in the least deter her. If any mission anywhere would take her, she was going.

In the spring a letter came from a friend in Bangalore, India. The climate there, she wrote, was healthy and delightful. Good news for Amy's friends. Bad news for Amy—"it sounded much too easy." On second thought, her going there would "lighten things for those who found it hard to see that I should go anywhere," so she applied to the Church of England Zenana Missionary Society and went to London in May for an interview. She was not an Anglican, but was warmly recommended by Keswick leaders who were Anglican clergymen. In an informal meeting on July 26 at Keswick she was accepted. The next day she spoke at a missionary meeting in the tent. "Who can forget," wrote a clergyman, "Miss Amy Wilson-Carmichael's farewell address, ere she left for her life of sacrifice in India, as she unrolled a 'ribband of blue' with the golden words, 'Nothing too precious for Jesus?' "

Amy was with her dear "Fatherie" on his seventieth birthday, but both had to face the imminent, wrenching, second parting. "Of the blistering days before I sailed and of the goodbye I will say nothing. We shall all be together soon in the Father's Country."

She sailed on October 11, "with many a backward look at Japan," and a few wistful ones at China, the country to which she had felt drawn ever since hearing Hudson Taylor speak of its millions' spiritual need.

The country whose shores she reached in November of 1895 had been under British rule since 1600. London merchants had had their eye on the riches of India's spice trade, then under the control of Dutch privateers. Outraged when the price of a pound of pepper went up five shillings in 1599, a group of twenty-four merchants met to establish a small trading firm. The East India Company was chartered in December of that year by Queen Elizabeth I, giving them a monopoly of English trade with the "Indies," which comprised China, India, and Indonesia. It was not only pepper they were after. Wondrous tales were told of gems the size of pigeons' eggs, endless forests of pepper, indigo, cinnamon, and ginger, and potions guaranteeed to perpetuate youth and virility. In August of 1600 Captain William Hawkins anchored his galleon north of Bombay and set off inland to find the world's most powerful monarch, the Great Mogul. The emperor granted him not only trading rights, but offered a beautiful girl (an Armenian Christian, it was claimed) from his harem.

Profits began to pour in, merchants flocked to other Indian ports, and, with Britain's assurance that their object was *"Trade, not territory,"* they were welcomed. Predictably, conflicts arose with local authorities on whose territory the Company operated, and soon there were British forts in Bombay, Madras, Cuddalore, and Calcutta, to protect mercenary interests. England was "in over its head," almost unwittingly committed to a policy of intervention in every aspect of Indian life. In 1757 General Robert Clive, with an army of two hundred English and three hundred Indian soldiers, defeated ten thousand Indian troops at Plassey, losing only twenty-three men.

For a hundred years conquest followed conquest, even though orders came from London to avoid "schemes of conquest and territorial expansion," such schemes being "repugnant to the wish, honour, and policy of this nation." Not all governors saw things in the same light. Social diseases such as gang robbery, slavery, infanticide, thuggee (the practice of murder and robbery by thugs) and suttee (the immolation of widows on the funeral pyres of their husbands) were taken by some of them as typical of the country's life as a whole. Richard Wellesley, governor general from 1797 to 1805 and himself a campaigner against suttee, thought the natives "vulgar, ignorant, rude, familiar, and stupid," and therefore unworthy of any rights. "No greater blessing," he held, "may be conferred on the native inhabitants of India than the extension of British authority, influence and power." The modest trading company had become the sovereign.

While the Company regarded noninterference with Indian customs as most beneficial to its own interests, the Crown saw its responsibility to reform and civilize these "wily Asiatic intriguers," men of "degrading superstitions," as a divine assignment. Clash between Company and Crown was inevitable. If the British were going to "hew down the dense jungle of Hindooism" business might suffer, as the silver business suffered in Ephesus in New Testament times. Missionary work inhibited profiteering, so the Company forbade missionaries to evangelize. Yet the barbarous practices named above, together with the almost universal idolatry, offended the sensibilities of those Englishmen (among whom Radicals and Evangelicals were among the most influential) who had no immediate vested interests. These began to insist on reforms.

Certain benefits of British rule can hardly be denied—her legal, administrative, and educational institutions, her railways and, above all, her language, which became India's common one. But like most of the "blessings" of civilization, they were mixed. English became the vehicle of revolutionary aspirations which reached a climax in the savage Sepoy Mutiny of 1857. The fuse that fired it was small but significant. Cartridges for the new Enfield rifle had to be opened with the teeth. Religious scruples of the influential Brahman element in the army were deeply offended, since the cartridges, it was claimed, had been lubricated with cow's fat, sacred to vegetarian Hindus, and (for good measure) pig's fat, unclean to Muslims. They refused. Nevertheless the perspective of history would indicate that the matter was infinitely larger. It was East against West, white against black, an ancient people seeking to maintain an ancient culture against a highly confusing admixture of materialism, European culture, and something which called itself Christianity.

Britain succeeded in crushing this uprising, but the existence of the Honourable East India Company was terminated on August 12, 1858 by Queen Victoria, who then (providentially, it was believed) became Empress to 300 million Indians, her authority represented by a sort of king called a viceroy. Under him were two thousand members of the Indian civil service and ten thousand officers of the Indian army whose authority was sustained by sixty thousand British regular soldiers and two hundred thousand native troops.

Theirs was the India of gentleman officers wearing plumed shakos and riding at the head of their turbaned sepoys; of district magistrates lost in the torrid wastes of the Deccan; of sumptuous imperial balls in the Himalayan summer capital of Simla; of cricket matches on the manicured lawns of Calcutta's Bengal Club; of polo games on

the sunburnt plains of Rajputana; of tiger hunts in Assam; of young
men sitting down to dinner in black ties in a tent in the middle of the
jungle, solemnly proposing their toast in port to the King-Emperor
while jackals howled in the darkness around them; of officers in
scarlet tunics scaling the rock defiles of the Khyber Pass or pursuing
rebellious Pathan tribesmen in the sleet or the unbearable heat of
the Northwest Frontier; of a caste unassailably certain of its superiority, sipping whisky and soda on the veranda of its Europeans Only
clubs. Those men were generally the sons of families of impeccable
breeding, but less certain wealth; the offspring of good Anglican
country churchmen; talented second sons of the landed aristocracy
destined to be deprived of a heritage by primogeniture; the sons of
schoolmasters, classics professors and minor aristocrats who had
managed to squander the family fortune. They mastered on the
playing fields and in the classrooms of Eton, Harrow, Rugby, Win-
chester, Charterhouse, Haileybury, the disciplines that would fit
them to rule an empire: excellence at games, a delight in "manly
pursuits," the ability to absorb the whack of a headmaster's cane or
declaim the Odes of Horace and the verses of Homer. "India,"
noted James S. Mill, "was a vast system of outdoor relief for Britain's upper classes."[1]

Travelers to India by ship noticed a strange transformation in
fellow-passengers. Ordinary middle-class or lower middle-class
Englishmen began to assume an air of superiority and self-assertive-
ness. Ladies affected the airs of grande dames. The vocabulary
changed—instead of breakfast they now had "tiffin," the call for a
steward became, "Boy!" (derived from Hindi *bhoi*, Telugu *boi*, a
term which had come to be applied to a carrier or domestic servant). The bartender served up not whisky and soda but "chota
pegs." When the ship reached Port Said out came the "topees," the
preposterous sun helmets believed to be indispensable for Europeans. When the ship approached the port it was met by British officers aboard a launch which flew the Red Ensign, a flag with the
Union Jack in the corner. The arriving passengers became, with no
credentials other than the passage they had bought to India, the
lords of creation, acquiring at once the status of Sahib or Memsa-
hib. By virtue of being English and white they were given prefer-

---

1. Larry Collins and Dominique Lapierre, *Freedom at Midnight* (New York:
Simon & Schuster, 1975), p. 15.

ence on the railroads and in the shops. It did not take long to take such treatment for granted, so that if occasionally it was not accorded, they became first testy and then angrily insistent. Power corrupts. It corrupted soldiers, officials, planters, and their wives and children. It corrupted missionaries.

It was to this—in its later phase Rudyard Kipling's romantic and picturesque India—Britain's "rightful" empire for nearly three hundred years, that Amy Carmichael came. Perhaps it was not the climate only which made her feel it was "too easy." We have no reason to think that she harbored any doubts about the ethical basis of the "raj" (rule), but we can be certain that her soldier-soul shrank from the thought of its British comforts and its aristocratic British society.

The Church of England Zenana Mission Hospital, taking its name from the Hindi word denoting the part of a house where women were kept in seclusion, was in Bangalore, a city of South India with an altitude of three thousand feet. Amy arrived there, not in the buoyant good health her time in England was meant to have bestowed, but with dengue fever, a malady characterized with pain in limbs and head so extreme that its nickname is breakbone fever.

She was too ill to write or think, and found herself feeling "low and grovelly, not in the least a soldier." With excellent care from the English mission doctor and nurses, she recovered. The hospital was barrackslike, built high and dry in a sandy compound. "I am to be its 'prophet' "—meaning the hospital evangelist—"I can't help being as happy as happy can be." She loved the work, loved the climate, loved her fellow-workers, the doctor—"a splendid girl"—and Clare "who is, well, just Clare!" These three lived together in the staff quarters. Twenty minutes away were five single women missionaries, two of whom codirected the work. The scenery was flat, "nothing to touch Japan," the climate "fine—except in the long middle of the day, one almost forgets it is tropical. One can work *hard* in the morning, work fairly in the middle of the day, and work hard again (if allowed) in the evening, but this is not considered wise, for it is tropical after all, and this means a gradual substitution of water for blood in your veins."

With a beginner's aptitude for hasty generalizations she wrote that she found the Indian people "a series of contradictions. They are loving and lovable, cruel and needing-all-grace to love, bright and dull, eager and lazy to a degree perfectly incomprehensible at home. They are trustworthy and utterly the opposite, courteous and quite barbarous. They are everything you can imagine except, perhaps, straightforward. *That* the natural man in Eastern lands never, never is. In all sorts of trifles one is tried almost beyond endurance. Appointments are made to be broken, punctuality and speed are unknown—they don't understand our foolish fondness for getting on—'is there not a tomorrow?' " The comments are vivid and candid, meant for only a small circle who knew the character of the woman who wrote them. She acknowledged her own limitations when she added, "This is the average native character *on the surface*. Underneath there is much, much more, but one can't get at it until one can speak and I am far off that yet."

She praised God for Jeya, an Indian Christian woman whose name meant victory, "so dear and loving with me, calls me Sister, helps me with Tamil and interprets for me in the wards." As usual Amy did not waste a day in getting down to business, speaking to the patients in the dispensary. "I wish you could see the strange dark faces and beautiful seemingly eager eyes, and the rich, bright colors and graceful forms—it is all a pleasure in itself, but then there is the sadness of knowing that very little is really *going in.* These meetings are a 'sowing beside all waters,' but I long to be led to the truly seeking soul."

She had the luxury of a tiny room with its own "bath," which meant a place where she could dip water from a tub and pour it over herself. She managed to squeeze in also a wardrobe and chest of drawers. She thanked God for the privacy and accepted the lack of quiet, which "pulled one out of touch" with God—banging doors, crying babies, barking dogs, squawking crows, perpetual noises "of all sorts and conditions all day long and all night long, up to strong and awful attacks of the devil, the Prince of Heathendom."

Another luxury, taken for granted in the India of the raj, was servants. They worked, of course, according to caste—the houseboy dusted and swept, the cook cooked, the gardener brought the bath water, the dhobie came to collect the laundry, the "sweeper" emptied the latrines.

Amy's daily schedule went like this:

6:00 rise
6:45 tea, toast, and plantain (banana)
7:00 review language lessons
7:15 munshie (language teacher) comes
8:15 prayers in hospital ward
8:30 language lessons
10:30 breakfast
11:30 rest
1:00 study
3:45 tea
4:30 exercise, pony riding, letter-writing
7:30 dinner
8:30 housekeeping and accounts

Amy's Aunt Annie had little notion of the character of her missionary niece. She wrote to inquire if she read novels. "Do I ever read any novels?!!!! I have hardly time to read my Bible properly, much less anything unnecessary."

In keeping the household accounts she got tangled up in trying to sort out rupees, pies, and annas, but that was nothing compared to the battle of learning Tamil, "the Chinese of India," as Amy called it. In March she was "in the throes of grim despair," feeling she would never, never learn it. Somebody wrote from England, citing the story of Jericho, whose walls fell down after seven days' "compassing." "Fear went," wrote Amy. "I felt as if I could never be afraid again. Someone had prayed the prayer that rises straight up, and God had sent the answer straight down in the form of this story." By July the unfamiliar sound of the language was diminishing, but Amy chafed, wondering why she did not yet understand *everything*. She was thrilled to have succeeded in reading a Gospel in Tamil. The walls of Jericho were falling. In November, "it is bliss to be able to speak a little and to find that they understand. The next thing is to understand *them.*" She had finished the "most tiring half" of language study, but a month later she admitted that Tamil seemed an ocean in which she was not yet so much as ankle deep.

Chapter 14
Fashionable Christianity

F rancois Coillard, missionary of the Zambesi, wrote: "The evangelization of the world is a desperate struggle with the Prince of Darkness and with everything his rage can stir up in the shape of obstacles, vexations, oppositions, and hatred, whether by circumstances or by the hand of man. It is a serious task. Oh, it should mean a life of consecration."

These were words often quoted by Amy Carmichael. It would be impossible to exaggerate her sense of the seriousness of her calling, and, by contrast, of the apparent superficiality of much in India that called itself Christianity. "The saddest thing one meets is the nominal Christian. I had not seen it in Japan where missions are younger. . . . The church here is a 'field full of wheat and tares.' "

Since long before Amy's arrival in India conflict and competition had torn the Christian churches. Caste was a primary factor. The missions that since 1947 have together formed the Church of South India drew their church members largely from three barely compatible groups: the high caste Vellala landowners, the lower caste Paraiya field laborers (Gandhi called them "the people of God," the current term is "depressed classes") and, in the southern districts, the intermediate-caste Nadars or palmyra climbers. The work of certain foreign missions, the Salvation Army for one, was limited to lower castes. It is not to be wondered at, given the position of the Untouchables, that they were tempted by what Christianity seemed to offer: an identity hitherto denied them, a dignity and an equality not only with other Indians but even, in spiritual terms, with those Christians who represented power—the British of the raj. These were the "loaves and fishes" that drew the crowds. Who among them actually had "ears to hear" the words of the Master? This was the burning question.

Missionary social activities were not Amy's cup of tea. How to justify the time spent in this way? It was like making daisy chains while people were plunging blindly over a precipice. Once when the ladies were doing their fancy needlework and the men were reading missionary papers for discussion the question was asked whether anyone knew of an Indian who would work without pay.

There was a dead silence. The lady near me was busy matching her silks. All the others went on with what they were doing. Not one, so far as I could see, was astonished or shocked by such a question. At last one of the men said, "I must confess I don't."

But I felt as if a thunderbolt had fallen in the midst of that pleasant company. It wasn't that I thought the question referred to those who could not work unless their expenses were paid. To have one's expenses paid if one had not money of one's own is apostolic. No, it was not that; it was that no one in that room knew of any who (whether they had pay or not) were working purely for love of their Lord, who loved Him enough to work for love's sake only . . . I had half expected that in the moment's silence that followed we would be on our knees in shame and contrition before God. For if such things were true, whose fault was it? But no, the discussion passed on to something else and there was a buzz of conversation, that was all. I went to bed that night in much perplexity of spirit.

She longed to become one with the people. " 'He made Himself of no reputation and took upon Him the form of a servant.'[1] Pray that we may get down to the bottom of that verse," she wrote home. *"Then* we shall be in a position to ask our Indian brethren to come down and join us for Jesus' sake. Pray that we who are His sworn soldiers abroad may throw our kid gloves to the winds and FIGHT!"

Compared to the sari, the beautiful dress of an Indian woman, Amy's own wardrobe seemed ludicrously elaborate, impractical, and, worst of all, a dreadful distraction for the Indians, as it had been for the Japanese. It might even be dangerous for her. If she wore a sari she had a measure of protection by being less con-

---

1. Philippians 2:7.

spicuous in a crowd. She tried not to be prejudiced in favor of one dress over another; "it is only a surface matter after all." But she was not yet free to adopt Indian dress except on rare occasions. It simply "wasn't done."

Because Bangalore's climate, although one of the most healthful in India, was considered too hard for Europeans to bear year-round, it was customary for British residents to resort to the hills in April and May. Missionaries generally followed suit. To Amy this was an indefensible waste of time and money. She had no intention of going, but was forced to join the party of three women to the Nilgiris. If they rode in sedan chairs, as was expected, thirty-six coolies would be needed, eight for each chair, twelve to carry the baggage. Amy and the doctor chose to ride ponies. They went to Kotagiri ("hills of the Kota tribe"), where there were forests of fir, fresh mountain air, and pure mountain water.

As she had ridden her pony Scamp on the beach of Millisle, Amy rejoiced to gallop Laddie on the quiet roads of Kotagiri.

Oh, that you could see us as we tear along, our solar hats discarded, if it is evening, our hair, or mine at least, flowing free! We are called the mad riders of Kotagiri, and I don't think we much mind. This evening we came upon the elite of the little place, residents and visitors, congregated on the road. There was the good old Bishop and his sister, and the Bishop-to-be, his wife, and various old ladies and middles, and perambulators enclosing babies, and a dog or two. The small crowd parted with alacrity as we shot through, and we caught a fleeting glance of a gaze of astonishment and horror. There are two very mild old gentlemen who are fond of taking their walks abroad round the hill we consider our cantering-row. We delight to amble sedately past them, then, a yard or two ahead, break into our wildest gallop, and they remain behind in a state of apoplectic pie. . . . Once I ran over a man. I did not mean to—he wouldn't get out of the way and one can't stop short in mid-gallop. Lilian reported him not hurt, only somewhat surprised. All this will be over soon. When one is ready for work a bullock cart will be the order of the day. Just now I take it as an extra good gift which helps to keep me strong for the months of grind before me.

Amy, interested more in vocation than vacation, had taken along her helper, dear old Saral (her earlier helper having proved untrustworthy). This was a new departure. A British resort, remote from the sizzling plains three thousand feet below, was designed to provide refuge not only from the plains' flies and smells and heat, but from its hordes of the poor and the ignorant. It was, above all things, freedom from contact with any Indians of any station whatever that most Britishers prized. This, to Amy, was a freedom earnestly to be avoided. "My Missie is as my child to my heart," Saral said, and Amy refused to be separated from her. This caused consternation. Was this young Irish upstart going to have the old woman actually share her room? She was. And if Saral sleeps on the floor, why should I have a bed? was her argument. No, no, they could not hear of it. Amy gave in, for "our quarters are so very close together any vagaries would be speedily detected."

She carried on with her Tamil lessons, and took Saral out visiting the Kota tribespeople, aborigines who lived as simply as aborigines anywhere, in houses which seemed hovels to the new missionary, eating strange foods, following strange ways. "Not one has as yet, we hear, been brought to Christ, yet He loves them and He died for them." Saral spoke to them in her simplest Tamil. When a woman of the tribe died Amy and Saral went to the burning.

They had the Death Car there. . . . They piled the faggots round it. They lighted them, and a wild, wild wail rose up to the God who looked down and saw it all. Then the horn blew loud and long, and as the fire flamed, one part and then another caught, and as the terrible sound which they called the head-split cracked through the crackling of the wood, they seemed to put all the dread and horror of it into one intense yell.

Why do I tell it so? Why break through the pleasant scenes of home with this bit of the fiery barbaric? Why! Because it is true! *It is true!* It has gone on like that for thousands of years. It is going on today. Is there nothing in it which speaks? Has it not a voice for you? A voice, yes, and a Cry. The cry God heard when He said long ago, "The voice of thy brother's blood crieth unto Me from the ground." Some of you are not much giving, not much caring.

From Kotagiri she went to "Ooty," short for Ootacamund, another little paradise of English order and cleanliness in the hills, with shaded streets, comfortable bungalows staffed by sashed and turbaned servants, gardens redolent of jasmine, heliotrope, and roses. Here she stayed with Mrs. Hopwood, mother of the Miss

Hopwood described by Malcolm Muggeridge when he visited her some twenty years later:

> A zealous evangelical lady of some wealth who maintained a house named "Farley" to accommodate missionaries on furlough. . . . We knew little of her own family circumstances, but she spoke sometimes of traveling about Europe with her mother, and attending musical festivals. Music was her only "worldly" interest; otherwise she considered all forms of entertainment as belonging to the Devil's domain. Hymn-singing was a permissible indulgence of her taste for music, and whenever possible she threw herself into it with tremendous zest, often, in her own house, providing the accompaniment as well on a small harmonium she had. She must have been rather pretty when young, and even in late middle age, when I knew her, she had still a grace and charm and gaiety about her . . . I can see her now with her energetic step, going about the garden and in and out of the house; the chains and bracelets she was given to wearing jingling and tinkling with her movements. Always busy, always breathless, always smiling.[2]

The young Miss Hopwood, a missionary to Muslims herself, took Amy to visit the Todas, another aboriginal tribe who lived in "a collection of beehives." The two ladies climbed a tree overlooking the village and talked of the desperate need for workers.

Miss Hopwood, zealous and evangelical, was not more so than her new friend Miss Carmichael. Amy rang the bell one morning to gather the servants for prayers. The cook's small boy, pointing to the bell, said, "It's a god."

> I looked at the thing, it had a scratched face on the handle, and the face, he declared, was Ram's. I think the young scamp meant nothing more serious than a bit of mischief, but I knocked the bell handle off and pushed it into a fire which was burning near. He could never say *that* again! They all looked on, servants and coolies, and nobody said a word. Would a *god* let me do that? I asked them, and walked off, carrying the battered bell.

Walking on the hills with Saral she discovered three stones under a tree which Saral said were heathen idols. "To see those stupid

---

2. Malcolm Muggeridge, *The Green Stick,* Chronicles of Wasted Time, Vol. 1 (New York: William Morrow, 1973), p. 122.

stones standing there to the honor of the false gods, in the midst of the true God's beauty, was too much for us. We knocked them over and down they crashed and over they rolled forthwith. Oh the shame of it! It makes one burn to think of His glory being given to another."

Naturally there was an Anglican church in Ooty, "depressingly English," Amy said, with the usual Gothic arches and stiff pews. The governor of Madras, in gray frock coat and top hat, attended when on holiday there, and occupied the front pew which was reserved for him and his ladies. Indians who for one reason or another could not be refused admission were restricted to the pews at the back.

Far more to Amy's taste than riding to the English church in a proper carriage was trundling in a bullock cart to the convention held especially for missionaries. There she felt at home at once, away from the scenes of "fashionable Christianity" which were to her so strange and saddening. They sang the old Keswick hymns. "There was almost a Keswick feeling in the air. But the best of all was seeing the missionaries, specially the Tinnevellyites. Real Soldier-Missionaries." Among them was a man Amy had been hearing about: Thomas Walker. "Oh, he's a man by himself, very extreme, you know, a bit narrow-minded, but a scholar and a very fine man," was what she heard. She formed a mental picture: white-headed, rather cantankerous with wisdom and learning written all over him. She had taken along her Tamil grammar in case the addresses should be dull. When Walker spoke, her book remained closed. He was thirty-six years old, jet-black hair, dark, earnest eyes, a nervous gesture, wisdom and learning in evidence, but not a trace of the petty narrow-mindedness she had imagined. Following the meeting she was introduced to him in Government Gardens. They talked of how she might best learn Tamil.

"I would much rather live in a mud hut with the people around me than among English people in a bungalow," she told him.

"You could not stand it for long."

"I would rather burn out than rust out."

"That should be as God wills."

There was not a glimmer of a smile in his eyes. "I don't like you," Amy decided, and withdrew into the deeps of herself. "I haven't seen a Mr. Buxton yet," she wrote to her family, "and I don't expect to. There are not many on this side of the sea."

She could have no idea of how her life would be linked to the Walkers.

Chapter 15
Company, Church, Crown, and Hindu

Throughout her time in Japan, Ceylon, and India, Amy had written her *Scrap* letters monthly when possible, sometimes less often, her rule being that she would never write when she could do anything else. *Scrap* Number 7 was begun on September 23, 1896, the tenth anniversary of the Glasgow convention, where

a door was opened for me into a new life and I took the first step in. . . . Today as I thought of all that has passed since then, of the little *little* one has learnt or done or been, I felt as if one had not taken even a step into the land which opened out before one ten whole years ago. Tonight in my evening reading this verse came: "In His quiver hath He kept me close." I never noticed it before. It is the Revised Version of Isaiah 49:2. Is it not beautiful? And does it not fit into the verse linked always to me with September 23, 1886, "able to keep you from falling"? Dear friends, I don't often write of these inner heart-things in my Scrapperies, but to the glory of His name let me witness that in far away lands, in loneliness (deepest sometimes when it seems least so), in times of downheartedness and tiredness and sadness, always always He is near. He does comfort, if we let Him. Perhaps someone as weak and good-for-nothing as even I am may read this. Don't be afraid! Through all circumstances, outside, inside, He can keep me close.

Among the circumstances which called for trust in God's keeping power were the illness of her co-worker Clare, the constant presence of idolatrous customs—tom-toms keeping her awake at night, blood sacrifices being made within earshot, festivals, processions— the daily Tamil grind (she still wished heartily that her fellow-workers would consent to her living alone somewhere with Indians), opportunities to witness of Christ to individuals, some in hospital, some in other places.

There were encouragements—two Anglo-Indian girls who came for instruction and gave themselves to the Lord, a child who listened eagerly to the story of Jesus, a high-caste patient who returned to her village full of the Gospel story. When a single opportunity was missed, Amy chided herself. It had not crossed her mind to inquire whether a certain hospital servant could read. He worked for days before anyone thought to give him a Gospel. When someone did, it was Lilian, the doctor, not Amy. She confessed her dreadful failure to home friends, begging them to pray harder.

Saral came one day with an idea for drawing the women to hear the Gospel. She would teach them to knit with some pink wool she had been given, "and they will love me more and like to listen when I talk about Jesus."

Amy could not say yes to that. She explained that the Gospel needed no such frills. It is the power of God for salvation. Saral protested that there was nothing in the Bible which bore upon pink wool and knitting needles. Indeed there was—Zechariah 4:6, "Not by might, nor by power, but by my spirit, saith the Lord of hosts." There was no need for tricks which might open houses—houses were open. No need for methods of helping to humanize and fill bare and empty lives—"these women have a full day's work." To try to help God with pink fancywork was, she felt, plain unbelief.

At Ooty the Walkers had invited Amy to come to Tinnevelly to learn Tamil. Although she had not yet finished the examinations she was required to take in Bangalore, she made a visit in December of 1896, traveling by train from Madras to the hot plain. From the train window she saw temples in every village, idols under nearly every tree, people working in the fields with Siva's ashes on their foreheads. "It makes you feel as if you couldn't sit still. You must do something, try to do something, *anything!* . . . Oh to get into that stronger, calmer current, out of the feverishness of human haste. Do please, dear friends, ask that we may exchange the eagerness of the flesh for the earnestness of the Spirit and so move in the force of that Holy Wind that we shall be carried along by His great calm."

Tinnevelly is the mangled English pronunciation of the Tamil Tirunelveli, "Hedge of the Holy Paddy Field," a town and district at the southern tip of India, divided from the state of Travancore (modern Kerala) by a range of mountains called the Western Ghats or "steps." The plain, blistering hot in the dry season, was very beautiful after the monsoon, "a great garden, green with the wonderful green of young rice, and set with the shining silver of water." Other less-watered parts were barren with black soil, stunted trees, few palms. Its people formed an ancient and orthodox group of communities, with nearly three thousand Hindu temples, forty-two of them considered specially holy.

The Walkers of the Church Missionary Society arrived there in 1885. They were not by any means the first in that district to name the name of Christ. The Syrian Christians of the Malabar coast, whose records date from the fourth century, believed that the apostle Thomas brought Christianity to India. Roman Catholic missionaries landed in the fifteenth century, Saint Francis Xavier in the sixteenth. Far from wishing to transpose European culture to their converts, they went to great lengths to make themselves as Indian, that is, as Hindu, as possible. One Roberto de Nobili worked for forty-five years to convert "heathens," proclaiming himself a Brahman, adopting the sacred thread of the holy man, abstaining from meat, and keeping ritual purity.

By far the most colorful character, whose notions of identification with the people differed in marked degree from those of nineteenth century missionaries like the Walkers, was a renowned Catholic named C. J. Beschi. Calling himself Veeramamuni ("heroic and great sage"), he wore a purple robe, a white and purple turban, pearl and ruby earrings, gold rings, and bangles. He traveled in the grand style of a guru, riding in a palanquin (a conveyance borne on the shoulders of men by means of projecting poles), seated on a tiger skin with two servants to fan him, two to march in front bearing great bunches of peacock feathers, and yet another to hold a silk umbrella. A large retinue accompanied him—men with drums, fifes, tents, and caparisoned horses. Yet for all that, he not only preached the Gospel but produced a tremendous body of Tamil literature by which he meant both to convert the heathen and instruct new converts. He was so revered that he was made an official of the small realm in which he worked.

In the eighteenth century great waves of conversion to Christianity, Catholic and non-Catholic, swept Tinnevelly. In 1706 from northern Europe came bands of men who were renegades from the orthodox churches of their own countries, bringing with them a pietist brand of Christianity that demanded of its converts a radical change of life. They taught individual responsibility before God, which required a knowledge of the Word of God, and hence Bible translation and literacy. In short order they translated the New Testament into Tamil, set up printing presses, began turning out avalanches of Christian literature, and established "prayer-school houses," simple thatched buildings where people could congregate to learn to read and to pray and worship together. One wealthy converted Brahman widow had such a prayer-school in her home until it outgrew the space, whereupon she financed the building of a stone prayer-school.

This life-changing religion struck at the very heart of Tamil culture long before anyone dreamed of accusing missionaries of being colonialist or imperialist. The movement came from Germany and Denmark, while the East India Company was English and from the very beginning had kept a "low profile," accommodating itself in every way to Indian culture, realizing that its political power (a handful of Europeans ruling millions of Indians) as well as its material success depended on its being in actual fact a Hindu raj. This meant that its officials propitiated local deities, reinstated devil worship in places where it had long since died out, participated in and subsidized festivals and ceremonies, funded the building and repair of temples, and supported practices which the Company's constituency in England would have considered outrageous had they had any idea of them.

The growth of Christian congregations was startlingly rapid, doubling over and over for more than a century. The journals of Joseph Daniel Jaenicke, for example, in 1791 note "miraculous manifestations of divine grace" in conversions. Whole villages were often converted at once, and new villages founded, composed solely of new converts. Thus Christians became a power to reckon with, and, as the effects of their belief, particularly upon caste, became evident, intense opposition arose—intimidation, insult, violence, destruction of the prayer houses. This gave rise to the establishment of "Villages of Refuge," modeled after the cities of refuge set up by Joshua in the Promised Land.

For half a century there had been clashes and wars in South India between local authorities, and increasing struggles between the higher powers and the Company for imperial sway. This necessitated the building of forts and caused devastation, famine, and pestilence. Strong-arm men were brought in to persecute Christians, who were stripped, beaten, robbed, and sent into the jungles to starve. As often happens, persecution fanned the flames, and a new mass conversion swept Tinnevelly in 1802. In November and December over three thousand were added to the church. Complaints about the treatment of Christians began to reach Company authorities—did they not represent a Christian nation? Had not the "Hindu Christians," as they were called, a right to expect protection? The Company, while "officially" Christian as to its image in England, was, in India, unofficially Hindu in every meaning of the term—fully supporting a system of ideology, myth, ceremony, ritual, and institutions. Understandably, its opposition to the entrance of Christian missionaries was strenuous. It was not long before those authorities themselves were being accused of driving Christians from their homes, putting them in stocks, exposing them for as much as two weeks to broiling sun and chilling dews. To become a Christian, they declared, was an act of disloyalty to the Company's raj.

The Company's position was impossible. Since the India Act of 1784 it had become increasingly a public institution, more and more under the control of the British government. This meant, of course, that it could not escape the scrutiny of the "Lords Spiritual" of the Anglican establishment. The king himself was officially the head of the Church of England. Its bishops were members of the House of Lords. The Society for the Promotion of Christian Knowledge, a British organization, attempted to obtain religious toleration for

Christians equal to that enjoyed by Hindus and Muslims, but whatever the official response, the practical result was nil. Between 1806 and 1812 the Great Evangelical Awakening stirred up a vocal element of the Anglican church. Here was a whole country, by far the most important of the Empire, given over to what Anglicans could only call heathenism, with all its deplorable practices of child marriage, demon worship, widow burning (*suttee*, meaning "true wife"), and temple prostitution. Something had to be done about it. The Company was not without high officials who were Christians. These combined their influence with men like William Wilberforce, the abolitionist. Evangelical chaplains began going to India and new missionary societies demanded entrance and freedom to propagate the Gospel, not merely as a special privilege but as the right of any Englishman under the Crown.

In 1813 the Church of England refused to support in Parliament the renewal of the Company's charter unless the ecclesiastical establishment was admitted into British India. This was a powerful lever. It worked. In 1816 a Cambridge man obtained a military chaplaincy in the Company in Tinnevelly. He was James Hough, an ardent disciple of a leader of the Evangelical Revival in the Church of England named Charles Simeon. Under Hough a new phase of mission-minded Christianity began, resulting in the establishing of fifty-three congregations. Two years after his arrival came the Church of England with all its panoply, terrible as an army with banners. Groups outside the pale of the establishment became conscious of a sort of pecking order, with the Churches of England and Scotland at the top, and the earlier movements in descending order, according to the social classes from which they had come.

Hindus brought grievances to Company officials again and again as they saw their own way of life interrupted and obstructed by these meddlesome foreigners. In Calcutta, thousands signed "The Sacred Petition" of 1828 to His Majesty in London on the question of *suttee*. They felt that a widow's "voluntary and devout act" was a matter which was "altogether of too high and sacred a nature to admit of interference or question even from rulers of another Faith." The British were between Scylla and Charybdis. Only nine months later five hundred Christians from forty-seven villages in

Tinnevelly District addressed a petition to Parliament expressing first of all their gratitude for "the removal of the darkness of heathenism from these parts through the providence of our Lord, and the generous assistance of the people of Europe," then begging to put before the British public a list of deeds "being done in support of heathenism and in injustice to the poor by the Honorable Company." The list included the subsidizing of Hindu temples and exempting them from taxation. The Company had not only contributed "not the smallest sum" to help erect churches, but taxed them besides, giving rise to the reasonable conclusion that to the Company Hindu idols were the true gods. The petition mentioned also that since only those of highest caste could hold office or even enter the courts to make complaint or obtain assistance, Christians were nearly all excluded from entering. They had to stand afar off like any others who were "unclean" and call out, "as men invoke God, saying, 'Swami, Swami!' (Lord, Lord!)"

From Tinnevelly, one of the most important centers of old and wealthy Brahman power and pride, had come many of India's most orthodox and scholarly pundits. Hostilities smoldered and flames broke out. Hindu rights were being violated by some of the European officials who had appeared to be on the Hindu side, and by missionaries whom Hindus saw as their "declared and implacable enemies." Hindus were obsessed with fear since Tinnevelly had become "the emporium of missionaryism and proselytism." A society was formed dedicated to smearing sacred ashes, Siva's sign, on every forehead. Christians refused to be smeared. Mobs attacked villages, pulled down prayer houses, raped women, stripped and beat men. One missionary fortified his compound and posted guards. Government forces were sent in. In 1847 the use of the term "heathen" to refer to Hindus or Muslims was officially banned from all government documents.

Ten years later in North India the Great Rebellion took place, recognized by Queen Victoria and the rest of Great Britain as far more than a fanatical outburst against the greasing of cartridges with animal fat. Arguments over the meaning of the rebellion broke out and have continued ever since. Some saw it as a total rejection of British rule as represented by the East India Company. Whatever the case, the mutiny symbolized the end of Company raj and the formal taking over of rulership by the British Crown. The queen noted in her journal in November 1857 her feeling in the matter, which she believed was shared by her countrymen, "that India should belong to me."

The transition from Company to Crown rule, while enacted by Parliament, was formalized by the Queen's Proclamation of 1858. She rejected the first draft of this document as being too cold and unfeeling. Despite her distance from India and India's cultures, she had great sympathy for the Indian people.

> All the romance she had felt since childhood for brown skins, all the advice she had received from Indian travelers flooded her mind—the iniquity of a "fire and sword" system of government, the "immense field for improvement among the natives," the lies about mutilation of women and exaggeration of all kinds, the superior manners of the Indian "lower orders" compared with ours, the ill-treatment and insulting references to natives as "niggers"—out it all poured and was translated by royal alchemy into the moving words of a rewritten Proclamation:
>
> "Firmly relying ourselves on the truth of Christianity. . . . we disclaim alike the right and the desire to impose our convictions on any of our subjects . . . but all shall alike enjoy the equal and impartial protection of the law."
>
> As she wrote to Lord Derby, it was "a female sovereign" speaking from the heart to a hundred million Eastern peoples.[1]

In 1858 the existence of the Company which had operated in India for two and a half centuries, and had ruled for a century, was terminated by royal decree. The destiny of India now lay in the hands of the thirty-nine-year-old queen. She became Empress of India, her representative, the viceroy.

---

1. Elizabeth Longford, *Queen Victoria* (New York: Harper & Row, 1964), p. 281.

Chapter 16
Straight Against the Dead Wall

Amy spent her twenty-ninth birthday and Christmas with the Walkers in the town of Palamcottah (another English corruption of a Tamil name: Palaiyam-kottai), which had been the center of Christian work in Tinnevelly District for many years. The Anglican church in Palamcottah, like the one at Ooty, Amy thought "painfully English—built in the days when England did India's work, but life inside is native, and I do enjoy it. Today before the service began the singers of the place marched down in fine style, and stood before the porch making a joyful noise with voice and cymbal, violin and tambourine."

Walker, known as the Iyer (an Indian term of respect and affection), had been the chairman of the council of the Church Missionary Society, a position requiring much office work and, in 1895 and 1896, the painful task of purging the church rolls. It was a touchy matter, the weeding out of those whose names were on the registers but who were living as Hindus. Nominal Christianity was one of the most disturbing aspects of the missionary scene in Tinnevelly, and Walker was the object of calumny and scorn from those who could not see why the differences between Christian and Hindu needed to be so obvious. Other difficulties arose, and at last he felt he "could not go on turning the wheel in the direction it was turning," and dropped it. His resignation was accepted just at the time Amy arrived in Palamcottah.

The Iyer, a master of Tamil by this time, understood very well Amy's temptation to despair. During his own early struggles he had written to his sister, "It takes such a long time to get into the ins and outs of these Indian languages, and then, though you may know how to speak and what word to use, there is the enormous difficulty of proper pronunciation. However, on we go, trying and struggling. . . . I am only a stammerer in it yet." He read aloud to Amy from his own journals, which showed the plodding and the groaning, so that she might take comfort in seeing that she was not the first to be discouraged.

"But *you* were discouraged because you had set such a high standard for yourself!" she countered.

Walker quenched that nonsense by a crushing, "You know nothing whatever about it!"

An exigent coach, he insisted that Amy go through drill like any soldier before professing to fight. This included the study of Tamil classics, poetry, and proverbs, essential if one was ever to learn to "think Tamil." Remembering Misaki San's interpreting for her in Japan, she chafed at what seemed a wicked waste of time when she might be giving out the Gospel through interpretation, "but Walker says it's worthwhile and I am believing him straight in the face of my feelings." A few months later she wrote, "Never had a pupil such a teacher! But it is rather like a great Beethoven wasting his time over a stupid little scale-strummer." She wondered how she had ever had the courage to tackle the job. "It was the courage of ignorance—pure ignorance!"

Her second exam was to take place in early February. She dreaded it. She marked the year, 1897, next to the portion of *Daily Light* for January 23, in which she found strong encouragement: "Hope maketh not ashamed. I am the Lord . . . they shall not be ashamed that wait for me. Blessed is the man that trusteth in the Lord." Particularly comforting was the thought that God had once given words to a donkey.[1] Perhaps it was not too much to hope that the God who opened an ass's mouth would open hers and enable her to spout forth Tamil.

Walker, free now from administrative responsibilities, wanted to begin itinerant work in the villages. He saw in the new young missionary not only diverse and unusual gifts, but a deep and uncom-

---

1. *See* Numbers 22:28.

promising spirit of discipleship. He asked her to pray about the possibility of joining them in village work and perhaps beginning a work for women. The invitation came as God's seal on what she had longed to be doing. She prayed. The answer was yes, and in February they traveled by bullock bandy, a springless two-wheeled cart, the Walkers in one, Amy and Saral in another, to Pannaivilai, a day's journey from Palamcottah. Of this method of travel Amy wrote, "It is, except for the Chinese wheelbarrow, the most tiring way of going about I ever came across. The Japanese kuruma is bliss in comparison." Crash, bang, smash went the wheels on the rutted roads, jerking, pitching, lunging, and jolting the hapless passengers.

It was a clear moonlight night (we travel at night to escape the heat and to save time) and at first I couldn't think of going to sleep, and walked ahead of the bandies, disturbing various flocks of parrots who passed uncomplimentary remarks in consequence. When at last I settled down to slumber sweet, Saral rolled over on top of me, bumping me black and blue. The bandy threw her at me, she said. Then we stuck in the mud and Mr. Walker had to help to push us out. I wish you could have seen us.

She was delighted with the big airy bungalow at Pannaivilai.

No superfluous furniture, curtains, or antimacassars[2]—just three big rooms, like three big barns with a hayloft overhead! In the bedroom "barns," bed, chair, and table. In the center barn, table, chairs, plate press. A real barracks, truly! It is very cool to add to its charms, being so big and empty, and a wide shady verandah runs all round the house. We brought my baby organ, dear old Jappy texts, and what they irreverently call "*my remarks*" (Faith is the Victory, Christ is Conqueror) and we put them up and felt furnished. It is simply delicious being here, surrounded by brown faces only.

Amy gathered those brown faces around her whenever she could. A group of "heathen boys" who attended the mission school listened to the story of Solomon, illustrated by a picture roll. Amy

---

2. Crocheted doilies to protect upholstered chairbacks and arms from soil, specifically from "Macassar," a hair oil.

was alone, without Saral to interpret, and felt "like a bird in a cage too small for it. But oh, it was worth it all to be able to do, or to try to do, even so little as this. It's simply blissful to see that they understand." She told them how King Solomon had prayed not only in public (this did not seem strange to them—school always opened with prayer) but also alone. Did any of them do that? No. They could not possibly do it at home, one of them said. "So I told them they could in the jungle. They could easily go away there and be quite alone with God." One boy said promptly, "I will!"

One day three boys came asking for Bibles. Amy was astonished, for they were from "Christian" homes. Hadn't they got Bibles? No, they hadn't. Hadn't their parents? No. There wasn't one in the house. Had there ever been? They weren't sure. Amy, thinking she must have misunderstood their Tamil, went to Mrs. Walker who confirmed it all. Off they went to visit the Bible-less house. One scrap of an ancient bit of the Psalms was found. After prayer and talk the father agreed to buy a Bible.

"Do you see what this sort of thing means?" wrote Amy. "How can the Heathen know that He is the Lord when God is not sanctified in these people called by His name? For sanctified they cannot be when the Word is held in such small account. . . . Will you pray for these Christians of India? All round them there is the awful darkness of heathendom, and the darkness conquers the light unless that light is truly Divine." She learned of one congregation in which hardly a soul was converted, and whole villages of professing Christians with hardly one who understood what the name meant. There was a great palaver over what "giving up sin" might mean—surely not the breaking of caste or the burning of idols? Killing an insect or stealing a little rice while husking—such things might be sinful, of course. Toward these "heathen Christians" and those who made no pretense of being Christians Amy felt "pitiful, purposeful love."

No wonder that when the hottest weather came in April, requiring the customary trip to Ooty ("so one's brains won't liquefy"), Amy wished she could be allowed not to go. The Walkers believed it was best, so up to the hills they went. There were the usual pleasant sociabilities, some "of a most Christian character," such as "picnics finishing up with prayer," but it seemed "cruelty and wickedness to waste a moment when natives are waiting in the dark."

Amy gave readers of her *Scrap* letter a "deep look down" into that darkness in the form of the story of a girl named Pappamal. She was of high caste and wanted to become a Christian. "This is very rare, and means no end of difficulty to the Mission, as it is invariably followed by the closing of houses, emptying of schools, and endless law troubles, for the Hindus leave no stone unturned to wreck the work and injure the workers, and, if they can get at her, secretly poison the convert." Seen against the background of Tinnevelly's conflicts in the past, such violent reaction is not surprising. So long as Christians were limited to certain castes and posed no threat to the ancient and powerful cultural structure that is Hinduism, they could be tolerated. But for a girl to declare independence from caste and family in this fashion was an outrage. Pappamal was over sixteen, hence legally free to choose her own religion. She begged a missionary for help in escaping by night from her parents' house. Help was given. The parents found her, pleaded with her to return, but she stood fast. The Mission felt bound to protect her from "certain death" and decided to send her to Ooty. It was just at the time Amy was leaving for the hills, so she saw Pappamal safely into the hands of a Bible woman there.

Trouble erupted at once in Palamcottah. People who had been friendly glared at the missionaries. Doors of houses once open were slammed shut. In Ooty a man was seen prowling the mission compound, and soon the truth came out. The whole thing was a plot. He and Pappamal wanted to marry. As Hindus they were forbidden to because they were of different castes. She was to profess faith, escape from home, find asylum; he was to follow, profess faith also, then they would marry as Christians. That was not the end of the story. It came out bit by bit that the girl's parents were a part of the web, having connived to bring shame on the Mission, charging it with the crime of seducing a minor (she was not yet sixteen, they said). The Bible woman immediately wired Pappamal's father to come and take her. He refused, so the Bible woman personally escorted her to Palamcottah and publicly returned her to her family. She was shut up in solitary confinement. Word went round (and was confirmed by lawyers) that she would be killed, but in such a way as to evade proof. "Oh the dark dark deeds of this dark land!" wrote Amy. "It seemed like throwing the lamb to the wolves, only alas, the lamb herself was a wolf in disguise." Pappamal claimed that the missionaries had bribed her to leave home.

Only a few days later word came that the parents had, in fact, nothing to do with the plot; Pappamal had poisoned her mother so that she was unconscious when Pappamal escaped, and the father had been degraded by his caste, who refused him fire and wood. It was all the work of the suitor. The girl's horoscope had disappeared so no one could prove her age. Then the mission lawyer asked the mission to bribe the father's side of the case, as he feared it was going against them.

India was a land where "the veriest child can baffle the keenest. The Eastern mind and soul seems to me like a cabinet of secret drawers—you never know when you get to the last one."

Amy was staggered by the "terrible taking it for granted" that Pappamal would die. "I don't know about North India, but everywhere in South India there is only one answer when you ask why high caste converts have to be sheltered away from their homes, and why it is impossible for either a Mohammedan or Hindu woman to confess Christ in baptism while she lives at home. And that one answer is: It would mean death—or worse . . . As one of the lawyers said, 'She will be found down a well, and they will say she found her pain too much to bear and so put an end to it. Often it is so.' "

Two boys of the Vellala caste, one of the highest, told Amy that if they believed what she was telling them from the Bible they would be "beaten until they were dead." Her answer: "It would be the greatest honor in all the world to be beaten until you are dead for Christ!"

Happily Amy's brains did not liquefy in Ooty, but unhappily she came down with a fever that put her out of commission for two months. Always able to find something to thank God for, she learned during this time what true friends the Walkers were, she like a dear elder sister, he a wise strong elder brother. To them Amy was *tungachie*, little sister. In what Amy called "this happiest of missionary homes" she recovered, but language study suffered. She told her friends at home of the marvel of being able at last to understand Walker's sermon, adding a note in the margin, "but I expect it was only because it was an easy one."

Once in a while the thought that she would rather be in China came back, but she worked away faithfully where God had put her, teaching her Brahman boys whenever they turned up, spending a half hour in the evenings with Royal Jewel, "the jolliest little chap, very much in earnest (I hope)." The Indian headmaster of the mission school offered to give her two hours a day of Tamil if she would teach the schoolboys to sing hymns. Women came in the evening and learned from the Wordless Book, with its black, red, white, and gold pages, representing sin, the cleansing blood of Jesus, the purity He gives, and the glory to come. These women could argue. "God is everywhere, you say. Then He is in the stone, the tree. So we may worship the stone and the tree. Why not, if God is there?" Amy was heartened by reading the letters of Henry Martyn, earlier missionary to India, who wrote, "I have rightfully no other business each day but to do God's work as a servant, constantly regarding His pleasure. May I have grace to live above every human motive, simply with God and to God."

There were small excitements, such as the boys bringing her a freshly killed cobra and a scorpion that measured nine inches from nippers to tail tip. She was bitten by an unidentified "puchie." Since the pain was not great enough for an older scorpion and too great for a hornet, Amy took it to be a "young and innocent" scorpion. "All this is fine fun for me—I can't sober down into a proper missionary."

There were dialogues of an altogether sober nature with a new munshie of a high caste, with whom she felt she came "straight against the dead wall of Hinduism." He asked her to translate into Tamil an English tract he had brought. "Let us meditate on the All-Pervading Spirit, the Fountain of Bliss, the Incomparable One, Eternal, Immaculate, Incorporeal, Omniscient, Unalterable, Holy, Distant, and yet near, Light dwelling in tranquility, All-Comprehensive, Possessor of Perfect Felicity, pure intelligence, inexpressible, and inconceivable. . . ." Amy's progress in Tamil was obviously far greater than she dared to admit, for she translated this description of God and then asked how, if he believed all this, he could worship stones.

Then came a perfect torrent of exclamations and asseverations and repudiations, like a pent-up river flood suddenly let loose. "I shall bow down to a stone tonight! I shall! Yes! I read you this book now and tonight I shall worship a stone! No! It is not a stone I worship! It is the Divinity who has condescended to meet us mortals by means of this stone. He, the Great God is All-Pervading. He has entered that stone, how I know not, nor do I ask to know." Here he got beyond me and I could only listen and try to follow and catch the clue again. There he was, earnest, eager, far beyond me in mental power, and yet blind, bound in awful chains which no human hand could sever.

Amy, acutely aware of being, in herself, nothing more than a clay pot—ordinary, plain, fragile—knew that the pot held a priceless treasure which the old Hindu scholar had never seen: "the light of the knowledge of the glory of God in the face of Jesus Christ."[3] Would God give these people eyes to see that light?

---

3. 2 Corinthians 4:6.

Chapter 17
Blissful Work

Eighteen ninety-eight began with weeks of neuralgia which, combined with the heat, made language study even less of a pleasure than usual, but the *Scrap* letter of February 17 says, "Hallelujah! Hurrah! The exam is passed! I'm free for souls at last!" While the study of Tamil had certainly been a battle, and would continue to be, the fourteen months which had seemed so long were over, and she could join the *real* battle, the fight for souls.

Missionary work in a place where Christ has never been named is sometimes less arduous than in places where, though named, He has not been honored by lives of holy obedience. How were the heathen to see Christianity in action, how feel its force, when so many who went by the name of Christian were nothing more than the descendants of people who had "crossed over" during "one of those dreadful mass movements" of the early nineteenth century? They were for the most part from the lower castes, lured by the hope of worldly gain. They lived in a sort of twilight, far from the true Gospel light. As for the upper castes—the Brahmans, the Vellalas, and the trade guilds—their ranks were nearly unbroken, their homes veritable fortresses into which no unclean Indian, let alone foreign missionary, could enter.

"They smile at our belief in a Power they do not see at work, while the power they see is all but omnipotent." Amy pleaded in her letters for men. Where were the men with mental powers equal to those of the educated Indian, men who would count as refuse the success and acclaim they might have had and "lose" themselves in some out-of-the-way corner of the earth? Were there none like

Ragland, Tinnevelly's "Spiritual pioneer,"[1] whose life was lived on the lines of John 12:24, "Except a corn of wheat fall into the ground and die, it abideth alone: but if it die, it bringeth forth much fruit"?

To those who asked what they could send, Amy answered *books*. Missionary biographies. She was fortified and cheered to read of Gilmore of Mongolia, Henry Martyn of India, Judson of Burma, Coillard of the Zambesi. Their stories were "a sort of standing dose of mental and spiritual quinine."

"O to be delivered from half-hearted missionaries! Don't come if you mean to turn aside for anything—for the 'claims of society' in the treaty ports and stations. Don't come if you haven't made up your mind to live for *one thing*—the winning of souls."

Again and again Amy's hopes were raised as one after another responded momentarily to the Gospel. A caste girl declared that she wanted to be baptized. Would she have the courage to flee her home? If she did, what would happen? Would the missionary bungalow be stormed? "I hope so! I should like to see some real fight. This dead stagnation is worst of all," Amy wrote. A young wife sat quietly and listened to the story of Jesus, shivering with pain when she learned of the cross. But they were interrupted at that moment, and when Amy tried to visit again the husband forbade it. How could such a woman follow Christ? The words of Jesus came with terrible power: "If anyone comes to me and does not hate his father and mother, wife and children, brothers and sisters, even his own life, he *cannot be a disciple of mine.*"[2]

One day Amy went to the villages where old Saral had taught the Bible. She was disappointed to find that little seemed to have been learned. One woman who had heard the Word for five months did not know who Jesus was. Several who had shown an interest died, some of them mysteriously. A widow said, "My heart is weary, my friends cannot help me, nor can the gods I worship do me any good. Your God is God, the true God. I know He can help me. His way is

---

1. "The first Englishman to camp among the people of India as a missionary of Christ." Amy Carmichael, *Ragland, Spiritual Pioneer* (London: Society for the Promotion of Christian Knowledge, 1951). p. vi.
2. Luke 14:26 NEB.

the right way. I believe all that." But she could not be persuaded to act. It meant breaking caste, and to her that was suicide. Once, speaking long and earnestly with a woman who seemed open, Amy reached out her hand and touched her. The people were infuriated. She had defiled her, degraded her, was trying to drag her by force into the Way.

Someone sent an English magazine which stated that Indian women considered English women fairer and more divine than anything imagined before. That was "very nice to read," said Amy, but her own experience proved it preposterous. She was taken for a "great white man" because of her sun helmet. There was an argument over whether she was man or woman. All agreed that she was an "appalling spectacle." Questions were fired: What is your caste? Married or widow? Why no jewels? What relations have you? Where are they all? Why have you left them and come here? What does the government pay you for coming? Amy answered them all, then explained why they were there—to bring Good News. And what did the people do when they heard the news? They simply stared. They sat on the floor and chewed betel leaf and stared.

In one house an old lady leaned forward and gazed with a beautiful, earnest gaze. "Then she raised a skeleton claw and grabbed her hair and pointed to mine. 'Are you a widow too,' she asked, 'that you have no oil on yours?' After a few such experiences that gaze loses its charm. 'Oil! No oil! Can't you even afford a halfpenny a month to buy good oil? It isn't your custom? Why not? Don't any white Ammals ever use oil? Do you *never* use oil for your hair?' "

Patiently the Good News was repeated, with constant interruptions—two bulls sauntered in, a cow followed, somebody went off to tie them up, children wanted attention, babies cried. Rarely were there five consecutive minutes of quiet. "As the Father hath sent me," Jesus said, "so send I you." How much sincere attention was there when He preached to the crowd on the mountain? How many consecutive minutes of quiet had He in which to give His message? So Amy wondered, and went on with the work, "blissful work," she called it, remembering the answers to prayer in "my dear Hirosi."

Saral, who had been with Amy for more than a year, went to visit her family and did not return when expected. In answer to inquiry there were excuses. At last it was evident that she did not plan to return. Amy had lost another comrade in the fight, and suffered perhaps a deeper pain than that caused by the indifference of the nonbelievers. She began to pray for comrades who would endure.

Friends in England offered to provide a tent for the Walkers and Amy which would enable them to make longer visits in the villages. Unlike Japan where lodging could be had in something resembling hotels, there was nowhere in South Indian villages where a defiling foreigner could lay his head, let alone eat a meal. The tea basket Amy carried on her forays was always an object of curiosity whose beauties she was required repeatedly to display, and when she wanted to "perpetrate the barbarity of consuming a square inch of chocolate" she had to try to find a hidden corner in which she could retire. With the tent they would be ready for "a regular raid into the Kingdom of Darkness with the glorious Light." But were they truly ready for such an invasion? The tent was a mere physical provision. What about the readiness to be a vessel *broken for the Lord*, "continually surrendered into the hands of death for Jesus' sake," as the apostle Paul wrote in 2 Corinthians 4:11, "so that the life of Jesus may be revealed in this mortal body"? That was the crying need: the life—visible, tangible evidence of the truth of what they preached. Too much talk had been heard, too many professions made, without that unarguable revelation. Camping in the villages would give Christ's ambassadors the opportunity to show the life they talked about.

The Fight became intense in September when a girl, the first of her caste ever to do so, decided to follow Christ no matter what the cost. There was a tremendous row. The girl fled for refuge to the mission bungalow in Pannaivilai where Amy was living with the Walkers. The relatives pursued her, camped on the verandah, putting the household in a state of siege. The poor old mother threw herself on the floor, thumping her head, beating her breast, moaning. They made all manner of promises if the girl would renege—they would not force her to marry, they would let her go to church, worship God at home, anything, if only she would not break caste. "Only come! Come! We are your own people! Come back to us!" There was a breathless pause. Amy could do nothing but watch the girl suffer, wait for her answer. "I cannot go back," she said, and they began again. At last Walker entered. "You have had a fair field. You have done your best. She is free to go if she wishes." Then he turned to the girl. "Do you choose to go?" "NO!" she said, with all the strength left in her. That was the end of that interview, but not of the fight. For days there was palaver, threat of lawsuits, wheedlings, a deposition. The mission school was burnt to the ground. Rumor said someone would blow poison in the girl's face if she went to church. When the girl decided she had nothing more to say to them and would hear no more from them, Amy spirited her away to the mission house in Palamcottah where she was kept safe. She was baptized in October and given a name which meant Jewel of Victory.

In the same month the prayer for a comrade who would endure was answered. Ponnammal, whose name meant Gold, was a widow of twenty-three, a fourth-generation Christian who had taught Sunday school and attended Mrs. Walker's prayer meetings. She had been a trusted friend for some months,[3] "and we felt she was being trained by God Himself for some special service," but because of family control she was not free to serve the Lord as she wanted. She prayed for this freedom, and suddenly and strangely it came. There was trouble, the family took sides against her, and she was turned out.

"I think God wants to make me *pure* gold," she said, "so He is burning out the dross, teaching me the meaning of the fire, the burnt offering, the death of the self-part of me."

Ponnammal was one of the "Starry Cluster," the Tamil name given by the people to the itinerant band. Pearl was another one, an Indian "Lydia"[4] whose heart God had opened. She had lost an arm as a child, was treated as a disgrace to the family and lived in a "hole," the sort of place Englishmen rarely saw, or, if they did, never understood—"Indian India, the old, old India of legend and song." There was a widow named Blessing and a married woman,

---

3. *Ponnammal: Her Story* gives the date of her joining the itinerant band as June 1897.
4. Acts 16:14.

The Band and the bandy.

Marial. Amy hesitated to admit Marial because "husbands are so much in the way . . . an obstruction and a nuisance. Women need to escape them," but Marial's soldier-spirit was irresistible. Her husband was "hardly a man exactly." "I have spiritual needs—these I expect my God to supply. I have also physical needs—these I expect my wife to supply," he said, so they took him on as a cook, he being "incapable of higher things," and Marial was thus "free to fight the Lord's battles." Sometimes the women traveled with the Walkers, sometimes by themselves. They had a flag made of folds of black, red, white, and yellow sateen, "a most useful text for an impromptu sermon," like the Wordless Book.

Off we would go in the early morning, walking, or by bullock-cart, as many of us as could get in, packed under its curved mat roof. Stuffiness, weariness, that appalling sensation of almost sea-sickness . . . but one only remembers the loveliness of the early lights on palm, and water, and emerald sheet of rice-field; the songs by which we refreshed ourselves as we tumbled along in the heat; the pause outside the village we were to enter; the swift prayer for an open door; the entrance, all of us watching eagerly for signs of a welcome anywhere—for this was pioneer work, not work in prepared ground, and in scores of the places to which we went no white woman had ever been seen before.

Sometimes we would get out at the entrance of the village and walk on till we saw a friendly face—and we almost always found one. We usually separated then, and went two and two, and won our way past the men who would be sauntering in the front courtyard, and so penetrated to the women's rooms; or, if that proved impossible, we held an open-air meeting somewhere; or sat down wherever we could, and waited till someone came to talk, for we found—at festivals, for example—that if we waited in some quiet street, sitting apparently unconcerned, Indian guru-fashion, on a deserted verandah, or under a tree, that one by one people discovered us, and came and squatted down beside us and asked questions.

Sometimes the listeners were tall men in white loincloths with knives at the belt, "fearless, intelligent, with none of that undignified Englishism adopted by city men."

Later in the morning the Band went home, or back to the tent, breakfasted, and studied the Bible together, searching its pages "through and through for that without which our work would have

Camp scene with the Walkers.

been vain." Afternoons and evenings were spent much as the mornings, except when there was street preaching and music on the baby organ.

A typical campsite would be a bit of sandy jungle cleared of scrub and thorn, as near to a river as possible. Under the mimosa and palm trees three white tents—a tiny one for Walker, barely big enough to hold him and the irreducible minimum of necessities, one for the three servants (a servant to put up and take down tents and see that white ants didn't devour them, another to cook, one to run errands). The women had a twelve-by-twelve tent with two side-wings for dressing and for storing the beds during the daytime. There were folding tables and chairs, "a shocking number of belongings," including all food except milk, which was obtainable in the villages. Most indispensable of all were the books and pictures with which they told the old, old story.

Once in a while the Band believed God wanted them to ask specifically for one convert on a given day. On one such day they were on their way back to the tent without having seen a convert. Something the bandy-man said made Amy ask him when he would come to Jesus. "Tonight," was his answer. He came into the tent, "we all prayed, and he prayed too, and we think the Good Shepherd found him." A letter from England told them that people there had asked specifically on that date for a convert. What a cynic would call a coincidence Amy called a clear answer, and more than an answer—a sign of the love of the Lord.

Amy experienced a sense of evil worse than in Japan. Once a devotee of the temple, "very very old and very very bad," with not one "good line" in his ancient, wrinkled face, came to listen. "After the preaching I went to him, poor old man, so old, so bad. He just scowled and muttered some horrible thing and tottered away."

Never once were the members of the Band asked to come back and teach again. "Go!" said one woman, "We neither want you nor your book nor your way." An old leper called out, "Who wants your Lord Jesus here?" A devil-dancer with her hair matted and twisted, her face spotted and smeared with idol marks, snarled at them, "Your god is no god. If I come to him my devil-god will kill me. *He* is god. Yours died, you say—died and was buried. Your god is no god. Go away and tell your lies somewhere else. Who asks you to tell them here?"

Not all rejected the Truth. There were now and then occasions of tremendous joy when, at sunset, all the Christians streamed out to the nearest lake and the new believer was "buried with Christ in baptism." "A little to the right the devil shrines, a little to the left the devil temple, and we on the shore watching, praying, singing."

One boy stood straight and fearless as he told his story. His father was a sage. One day the boy said, "Father, I have a load, the burden of sin is heavy. What can I do to get rid of my sin?" "Learn the Thousand Stanzas and your sin will melt away." He learned them, but the burden was heavy still. "Is there no other way?" he asked. "You are young. Wait for a year or two, then you may find the way." But what if he should die? At last "a thirst like the thirst for water came, and I was thirsty, thirsty." He heard the Christians sing a gospel song, "Earnestly, tenderly Jesus is calling." Next morning he came to Jesus and drank. "Where was my burden then, where was my thirst? Gone—as the dew when it sees the sun!"

One day Amy had an encounter with a very unusual woman. She looked intelligent, could read, knew the classics, quoted poetry "in, for a woman, a most bewildering fashion." She scorned Blessing, the widow who had believed only a month earlier. "What could that ignoramus teach *me?*" the woman wanted to know. "You say you must not tell lies, and here is a regular big one! Learning indeed! Her very grammar is defective! She is the merest block of wood!"

"I am only one month old," said Blessing, "I have no wisdom to answer you, but I can read this Book of God and my name is in His Book and in my heart His peace and joy are dwelling. Is not joy better than much learning?"

Not till afterwards did Amy learn that the woman was a temple woman, a prostitute, "married to the gods," whose life was spent in the service of the priests and worshippers. Not one from among them had ever been converted. No one had ever been allowed to work among them. The discovery of this system was like a sword in Amy's missionary soul. Something must be done. Someone must find a way somehow to touch these women for God.

Chapter 18
The Cost of Obedience

The great passion of Amy Carmichael's life was uttermost love, which meant uttermost obedience. The prayer of Jeremy Taylor was always hers: *Lord, do Thou turn me all into love, and all my love into obedience, and let my obedience be without interruption.*

This was the spirit she sought to instill in the members of the Starry Cluster. The question of jewels illustrates their earnestness. *Jewels,* a word which embraced all gold or silver necklaces, bracelets, bangles, and rings (for nose, ears, and ankles as well as fingers), were, in Tinnevelly, by far the most important elements in a woman's appearance. "It is a pretty custom," Amy wrote, "and we thought nothing of it. Our Band members wore the usual quantity. It is considered part of their dress." Its significance, however, went far beyond prettiness. Women were more or less sold to their husbands for so many rupees' worth of jewels—a man with a B.A. could command so many, an M.A. so many, this caste so many, that one so many. In this way the quantity of jewels a woman wore declared her husband's honor as well as her family's wealth.

Amy herself wore no jewels of any kind. A strict Irish Presbyterian upbringing probably forbade such vanity, so her desire to identify with Indian style could not allow her to go so far. Nor did she oil her hair, a fact which made her startlingly conspicuous. She gave in once and anointed her head in order to avoid the inevitable remarks, but the "scent" she found "prohibitive." The very few photos we have of her reveal beautiful, soft, wavy, dark hair, in distinct contrast to the gleaming, sharply parted, satin smoothness of the Indians' hair. Her bun was not worn low on the neck as was theirs. It is doubtful that her upbringing included any special sanctions regarding coconut oil or the exact elevation of a hair bun. It is more likely that the flat, tight look did not strike Amy as particularly becoming to herself. Vanity (probably unrecognized) made her willing to differ here, as the notion of physical protection made her willing to differ in the matter of foreign shoes, sun helmet, and umbrella, things which identified her unmistakably with colonials.

"Gradually as we sought to know more of our Lord and the power of His resurrection and the fellowship of His sufferings, the conviction grew upon us that these things (i.e. jewels) were out of place in His own chosen workers—His separated ones—and that this conforming to the law of the fashion of this world was of the flesh and not of the Spirit." Hair oil, hairstyles, and shoes were not, in Amy's view, an indication of conformity to the world's fashion, any more than were topees and umbrellas, which were believed indispensable if foreigners' brains were not to melt.

Jewels, on the other hand, were in a separate category. "I love the old native customs. I cannot bear the foreignizing element so common in much mission work in India, so it was much against the grain that I faced this thing at all. But here God's Word ran one way and custom another. There was no help for it. We prayed that if God wanted the question raised He would raise it among our workers, apart from us, and He did."

A man had asked that his wife be allowed to travel with the Band for a while in order to learn to serve others. They consented, and he came one day to ask her to give him her jewels. He did not think them appropriate for the sort of life he desired for her. Ponnammal overheard his words with intense interest. Only the evening before she had heard a child (referring to Ponnammal) say, "When I grow up I will join that Band so that I may wear jewels like that sister." Ponnammal asked the Lord about this and the answer came, "Thou shalt also be a crown of glory in the hand of the Lord, and a royal diadem in the hand of thy God." The message was unmistakable. She saw herself as the Indian world would see her—unjewelled, a marked woman, an eyesore, an offense. To take off her jewels was unnatural, disgraceful, even hypocritical. But in the Lord's eyes? He would see the love that lay behind the action. She went home, took off the jewels, laid them at His feet.

"Lord, Thou didst empty Thyself for me. I empty myself for Thee." One by one the other women of the Band followed. The "outside Christian world" laughed them to scorn, but an English preacher, F. B. Meyer, came just in time to strengthen the Band in its conviction. He was the first they had ever heard mention the jewel question. Other women who heard him saw it as utterly impossible. "Where would my glory be if I took them off?" said one. "Where would my husband's be? Tinnevelly women never will!" So the Band became a "peculiar people," knit together in their desire to be "otherworldly, separate unto Jesus." When a teenaged girl escaped from her Hindu home and joined them, Amy had a talk with her about jewels. The child, with very bad grace, tore off two foot jewels. No, said Amy, Jesus was now her jewel—would she not give Him all? The girl took off all but one ring. She looked at the members of the Band, jewelless, singing "Jesus is my jewel." Off came the ring.

Years later the oddity appeared as an eminently practical thing when a watchman of the robber caste said, "If those girls, those hundreds of girls, wore jewels according to custom, not all the money in the world could hire a watchman to guard the place."

Financial provision for the Band came as it had come when Amy needed money for the Welcome Hall in Belfast. It was prayed for. Her own personal needs ever since she had left for Japan had been fully underwritten by Mr. Wilson, but money for the needs of the Band and for travel expenses (hundreds of rupees per month) came from other sources. The Church of England Zenana gave twenty-five rupees per month to hire a pair of bullocks, and readers of the *Scrap* letters sent money, which Amy called "the sinews of war." But she was scrupulous in her adherence to the principles learned in Ireland. She would not mention a need to any but God until it had been met. Even that had its hazards. "The mere telling of how a need was met is often like telling of a need, which is asking crookedly instead of straight out," she wrote in *Scraps*. "But this much I will say—with every fresh need has come a fresh supply." The Band women learned the lesson, and sometimes a little pile of change would appear on Amy's table with a note to say that it had not been needed.

They sought opportunities to speak to little children, coolies, educated men, women whose caste dictated that they must help with bricklaying, anyone at all who seemed the least inclined to hear, and often those who were not in the least inclined. The "pun-kah wallah" was a skinny old man who sat on a rattan stool and patiently pulled the rope which activated the huge ceiling fan. In the dead calm of midday heat it is not surprising that he sometimes fell asleep (Amy stitched into one of her *Scraps* a photo of him with eyes closed, his turbaned head leaning against a mat). Hoping to do the poor old soul some good Amy asked, "How do you pray?"

"Our Father who art in heaven."

"What does that mean?"

"How should I know? Am I a parson that I should understand?"

One day Amy stopped a Christian wedding procession to ask why they had idols on the corners of the wedding car. They were not idols, she was told, they were nothing but dolls. Indeed they were heathen idols, she protested, and had no place in anything that called itself Christian. There was a great argument but in the end she succeeded in trading some tracts and English-made dolls for the idols, which she took home for firewood.

Most of all the Band longed for contact with Brahman women, who were virtually unreachable and showed no interest whatever. One day some of them were sitting on a verandah, looking bored and weary. Amy asked if she and her helpers might sing to them. Yes, they said. A group gathered. They heard perhaps twenty minutes' worth of "plain Message-giving," illustrated with pictures. Amy stood on the bottom step of the verandah and begged the women to allow her to come nearer. They were horrified and refused. Men began to gather, hundreds of them, so she turned and asked them please to go away, for they could hear anytime. It was the women the missionaries had come for. But the men drew nearer and the women moved away. Finally Amy spoke to the men, "as straight as ever I could," trying to put things simply enough for the women to understand while at the same time holding the men quiet.

"You haven't an idea how hard it is to get a real chance with Brahman women. They *never* let us into their houses in these old Hindu towns. It is next to impossible to get any quiet in the street even if they will let us speak there, which they seldom will. Brahman women are as out of reach as if they lived in Central Africa, more so sometimes."

The Band visited the Village of Vishnu's Heaven where there was a fort which no woman had ever been allowed to leave. Men went in and out, as did a few Untouchable servant-women, but the women of the fort were prisoners. Once, it was said, a little girl of four had had the audacity to look out the door in the high mud wall. She was killed at once. Amy and her Indian sisters went to "view the wall" and to pray that it might somehow be breached. Along came a man who offered to escort them inside. They were given a few minutes to speak to the women of one of the houses. What hope had such women?

"No words of mine can give you any idea of the awful difficulty surrounding any Hindu or Mohammedan girl or woman who dares to take a stand. It is terrible for the men and boys, but infinitely more so for the women. Things no pen could write—at least mine could not—go on behind those prison walls. They are utterly in the power of ruthless relatives. Nothing but a miracle can bring them out." A girl who had shown an interest in Christianity was murdered; a boy was drugged, his intellect ruined for life. Because of bribery the police were often on the side of the family in whatever measures they chose to take. Anyone who wanted to follow Christ had to leave all in order to do so.

"Why the dreadful wrench of coming out and leaving all for Christ? Because it is absolutely impossible for a Mohammedan or Hindu to be a Christian at home. In a very tolerant house they may be allowed to read the Bible and pray. In very rare instances exemption from various idolatrous ceremonies has been allowed, but open confession and baptism—NEVER."

"She shall burn to ashes first," said one of the men. "She may go out dead if she likes. She shall go out living—NEVER!" There was nothing for it but obedience at all costs and at all risks.

For Amy, as for any true-hearted soldier, there was the element of thrill in battle. The reality of danger energizes and sharpens the faculties. "Will Gold [a high-caste woman who had shown an interest] come out? If so we shall be in the very thick of the fight again—Hallelujah! Will God move in Beautiful's heart so that she will dare her husband's fury and the knife he flashed before her eyes? If so, our bungalow will be in the very teeth of the storm, angry men all around it, and we inside, kept by the power of God!"

Miraculously another girl in addition to Jewel of Victory escaped. There was the same furor and consequent need for protection at Palamcottah. When the time came for the annual trip to the hills, Amy received permission from Mrs. Hopwood to bring the girls along. This was her chance to spend uninterrupted time with them, teaching them what discipleship meant. Amy Carmichael never sugarcoated the terms. They must learn to love the Lord and to forsake all—even their beloved Ammal (Amy)—to follow Him. She saw the danger of their becoming dependent on her, clinging to human love rather than to divine. They were desolate. One of them said she would be "like a withered stump in a field" if Amy sent her back to Palamcottah. The feeling was mutual. She felt for the girls what Paul felt for Onesimus: "my very heart would fain have kept him with me." But to them she was adamant. They must learn to stand. The one whose name meant Ladychild, when only four months out of the "horrible pit" of heathenism, confessed, "When I'm told to do what I don't like, something springs up in my heart which says, 'Don't do it! Don't! Don't!' and I listen and think, 'No, I won't do it.' " Amy saw that some of the "miry clay" was still sticking. A new heart was what the child needed, she explained.

Victory was overjoyed to receive a letter from her brother, but the contents brought tears. "Most beloved and cherished, most precious and most beautiful, as the apple of the eye, as the jewel among jewels, as the ruby, as the pearl, as our joy and delight, our immaculate and learned and advanced in all wisdom, yet all wisdom-despising younger sister. . . ." Then followed a string of pathetic stories—one member of the family ill, another weak with waiting for Victory to come home, another who had tried to see her but could not catch a glimpse "even with the extreme corner of the eye."

"In the Hindu Religion," the letter went on, "as you ought to understand, Caste and Piety are one and the same. Piety IS Caste. Caste is Piety. Why then do you defile your Caste? Have you entirely defiled it? If so, you have entirely defiled your family. If you choose to write, write, but not upon a subject with which my mind has no affinity."

One scene burnt into Amy's mind as never before the horrors of caste. She had seen a little boy of three or four who seemed to be suffering with his eyes. He lay in a swinging bag hung from the roof and cried piteously the whole time they were in the house. Two months later she visited the same house. There he lay, crying still, though his cries were weary and much weaker.

They lifted him out. I should not have known the child—the pretty face drawn, full of pain, the little hands pressed over the burning eyes. Only one who has had it knows the agony of ophthalmia. They told me he had not slept "not even the measure of a rape seed" for three months. Night and day he cried and cried—"but he doesn't make much noise now." He couldn't, poor little lad. I begged them to take him to the hospital at Palamcottah, but they said to go to a hospital was against their caste. The child lay moaning so pitifully it wrung my heart and I pleaded and pleaded with them to let me take him, if they would not. Even if his sight could not be saved something could be done to ease the pain, I knew, but no—he might die away from home, and that would disgrace their caste.

"Then he is to suffer till he is blind or dead?" and I felt half wild with the cold cruelty of it. "What can we do?" they asked. "Can we destroy our caste?" Oh, I did blaze out for a moment. I really could not help it—and then I knelt down among them all, just broken with the pity of it, and prayed with all my heart and soul that the Good Shepherd would come and gather the lamb in His arms. I can hardly bear to write it—but you have not seen the little wasted hands pressed over the eyes and then falling helplessly, too tired to hold up any longer and you have not heard the weak little wails. And to think—*it need not have been!* The last thing I heard them say as we left the house was "Cry softly, or we'll put more medicine in!" The little hands tightened over the poor eyes as he tried to stifle the sobs and "cry softly.". . . Oh friends, is it not a cruel thing, this horrid hydra-headed caste? Those women were not heartless, but they would rather see their baby die in torture by inches than dim with one breath the lustre of their brazen escutcheon of Caste!

For seven years, almost without a break, Amy worked in the country towns and villages. Her letters tell story after story of the battle—Hindu houses practically impregnable; an inquirer now and then who gives great hope, only to disappear again behind the thick walls; the drama of discovering one bright, eager face in a crowd, of having the breathtaking joy of teaching that one for a brief time and then the sorrow of seeing him turn his back.

Treasure was a girl apparently divinely prepared for the Seed of the Word. It fell into her heart as into "good ground," sprang up, was tended and watered and brought forth fruit. Then suddenly she refused even to look at Amy or the others. An awful change had come over her in a night, and she was beyond their reach. Prayers, embraces, Scripture reading, all the love she had received like a famished soul she now rejected, coldly, finally. There were only two possible explanations, Amy believed: She had been poisoned (mind-destroying drugs were well-known there) or she had sinned in such a way as to shut herself away from God.

Amy was like the sower in the Psalms: She went forth weeping, bearing precious seed. She prayed and she begged her friends at home to pray, pray, pray. "Oh, *will* you pray? Stop now and pray, lest desire turn to feeling and feeling evaporate."

Often she ministered to the professing Christians. But, they said, the kind of Christianity she presented would cost too much. To be consistent one must not quarrel, and they loved a good fight. "We know what it means now, and it is very inconvenient," said one, and another said, "If I am to be converted I shall have to forgive *her*, and I can't do that at present—so—!"

In addition to the crushing pressure of such work, she faced again the agony which she thought had been laid to rest: The D.O.M. asked her to come back to him. He quoted Paul's poignant words to Timothy, "Do thy diligence to come to me before winter,"[1] and sent money for her passage. There was no doubt in his heart that his child would come. "It was *agonia* (I use the word with care) not to fly to him. And yet I could not. Something held me fast." At last Wilson wrote to her, "The Master's word was brought to me this morning early: 'He that loveth son *or daughter* more than Me is not worthy of Me,' 'Bind the sacrifice with cords even unto the horns of the altar.' No drawing back. May it be so in

---

1. 2 Timothy 4:21.

the strength He gives. It is well to have some gift of value to present to Him who gave His all for our redemption. Praise Him."

"From that day on till the end," Amy told her children, "there was no drawing back. The date of that letter was July 1899. It comforts me even now to know that after that early morning time with his Lord and Master, that beloved old man must have read very tender words, for a small *Daily Light* always lived beside his little old Bible which is mine now: 'As one whom his mother comforteth, so will I comfort you,' and his mind would run on to the end of that promise, '*and ye shall be comforted.*' For six long years he waited in patience and then, on July 19, 1905, the last words on the page of that book were fulfilled, and his God wiped away all tears from his eyes."

Chapter 19
The Uninteresting, Unromantic Truth

Amy was relentless in her effort to describe precisely how things were, without artificial sweeteners or colors—"The God of Truth, it seems to us, does not ask for paint when the word comes to His servant. 'Write the things thou hast seen.'" How else could people know how to pray for the work? How could they begin to fathom what heathendom meant?

Toward the close of the nineteenth century a mission society asked Amy to write of her experiences. She wrote as she had always written in her *Scrap* letters—the straight truth. It would not do. The committee returned the manuscript as too discouraging. Could she make it a bit more palatable? She could not. It went into a drawer. In 1900 two friends from England visited her for several months, itinerating with the Band, seeing what Amy saw. When they learned of the rejected manuscript, they asked to take it home and try to find a publisher. They succeeded, and *Things as They Are* appeared, enhanced by photographs taken by one of the friends. Although the writer of the preface called them "thrilling chapters," many readers in England found them anything but thrilling. Could things be so terrible? Where were the dramatic conversion stories needed to draw crowds to missionary meetings? Years later Amy learned that a committee of Christians had met in India to ask that she be sent back to England because of the disturbance her book had created.

Because missionary reports generally included more about successes than about failures, Amy tried to shift the weight to the other side. "It is more important that you should know about the reverses than about the successes of the war. We shall have all eternity to celebrate the victories, but we have only the few hours before sunset in which to win them. We are not winning them as we should, because the fact of the reverses is so little realized, and the needed reinforcements are not forthcoming, as they would be if the position were thoroughly understood. . . . So we have tried to tell you the truth—the uninteresting, unromantic truth."[1]

In order to strengthen the credibility of the book the publishers felt it necessary to include in the second edition letters from missionaries certifying the facts.

"I am not surprised that anyone unacquainted with mission work in India should be staggered at the facts narrated in *Things as They Are*," wrote one. "But as one who has worked for nearly thirty years in the heart of heathenism, away from the haunts of civilization, I can bear testimony that the reality of things far exceeds anything it would be possible to put into print."

Indians also testified to the authenticity of what Amy had written. "I fancied I was living my old life among Hindus over again. I can honestly corroborate everything said in regard to the religious and social life of the Hindus," wrote Pandita Ramabai. An editor from Madras, Krishna Ram, added, "The question is often asked whether a high-caste Hindu convert can live with his own people after his baptism. It is only those who know nothing of the conditions of life in India, and of the power of caste as it exists in this country, who raise the question."

The incredulity of the mission-minded public did not alter Amy's resolve to present the unsweetened truth. After *Things* had gone to press the following story appeared in *Scraps:*

In the Flower Village there is an old Brahman widow who is dying of consumption. I took her cough mixture and stuff to rub on her head to ease the pain, and visited her again and again, trying new remedies (suggested by a medical missionary who is staying with us) and doing all I could think of, so far as she would let me, to help her.

As a rule a Brahman is very suspicious about anything given, and many a struggle this old widow had between her desire to get all she could out of

1. Amy Carmichael, *Things as They Are*, p. 158.

us and her fear of being given anything which would, as she put it, "draw her into the pit of pollution," our religion. I knew we could give her nothing which would cure her, and told her so; at first she did not believe me, and most greedily grabbed at everything, haggling over the bottles and corks (we don't give bottles as a rule, we give medicine, the people bring their own bottles) and trying to "do" me in every possible way, only always guarding herself from danger by refusing anything which looked powdery, for we are supposed to delude the unwary by getting them to eat, drink, or inhale some sort of powder. We put it into plantains for children (so we never can give plantains or indeed any eatables to children—often I want to give sweets to the dear little mites, but I never do). We put it in milk or medicine or simply sprinkle it on the pages of our Bibles; all this is believed except by those who know us well. So the old Brahman was careful. She would take a pill and crumble it in her fingers, "this is nothing but solid powder, I want a liquid!" She would hold the cough mixture up to the light— "There is powder floating in it. I want a *clear* mixture"—or else it would be, "I want nothing which has to be taken internally. I want external remedies. Give me something to rub on."

She was quite sure that if only she went on changing the remedies often enough I would get tired of bringing wrong ones, and would produce the one genuine article which she was certain would cure her. "Why don't you bring it?" she would say, after every fresh trial. "Don't you know that by helping a Brahman you will acquire great merit?" She never dreamed of being in the least grateful for what we were trying to do. She was condescending a long way down to let us do anything for her.

At last it seemed to dawn on her that if we could we would have cured her, and that as we had not, it was evident we could not. So she had no more use for us. But though she must have made up her mind about this before I went yesterday, she did not show it at first. I was allowed to sit humbly at her feet on the outside verandah, while she sat up on the doorstep. "Be very careful not to touch me," she reminded me as usual, and then let me read to her. "For ten rupees could one buy such a story?" This was about the parable of the Good Samaritan. Then, "As you have no medicine for my body, have you got a medicine for my soul?" and I gladly told her yes. "By means of this soul medicine will my soul regain its health?" Oh how gladly one said yes! "And how may one drink this soul medicine?" So I told her. "Then by listening to the Words of God and believing them one receives this soul medicine? So the medicine is received through the ear instead of the mouth, and absorbed by the heart, instead of by the digestive organs?" She seemed to have got it very clearly.

"There is nothing else to do? One has only to listen and let the words 'catch'? Then one understands them and one's heart believes them and so to the soul comes health. It is not difficult," she said.

Then she turned with a sudden twist and flung the two medicine bottles into my lap. "So that is how you delude us!" she said, but the words came with a sort of hiss. "First you tried to get me to eat your powder done up in a pill, then you tried to get me to listen to your Book's words which, it appears, by entering the ear, affect the mind and the heart!" Then, raising herself up and glaring at me like an old tiger cat at a mouse, she pointed with her skinny old hand to the street. "Go! Do you think I will allow your medicine to get to my heart? Go! You have no medicine that will cure my body. I want none to cure my soul. Did you ever know a *Brahman* drink your medicine? Go!"

She used the word used in speaking to a servant and then, addressing the onlookers, went on, pointing to me in a very disdainful fashion. "Does she think I bore the contamination of her presence—she who eats flesh and mingles with low-caste people—for the sake of her soul-deluding Book medicine? Let her go. I have no use for her. I have no use for her Lord Jesus. Let them both go!"

Were the *Scraps* accomplishing anything? Amy wondered. "Do not say, 'Oh, they interest us.' I do not care about 'interesting' you. One's being in India is costing too much to make it worthwhile to spend a day in a month, ten months in the year, in merely interesting you. . . . Nothing is worth doing at all, nothing is worth writing, which does not do something which will last."

A few lines from *On the Threshold of Central Africa*, by M. Coillard, spoke for Amy: "If those friends who blame . . . could see what we see, and feel what we feel, they would be the first to wonder that those redeemed by Christ should be so backward in devotion, and know so little of the spirit of self-sacrifice. They would be ashamed of the hesitations that hinder us. But we must remember that it was not by interceding for the world in glory that Jesus saved it. He gave Himself. Our prayers for the evangelization of the world are but a bitter irony so long as we only give of our superfluity and draw back before the sacrifice of ourselves."

Chapter 20
A Small and Desolate Mite

On March 7, 1901, something happened which "caused a new thing to begin and I was rooted for life."

Amy and the Starry Cluster had been itinerating in Tinnevelly District for about a year. One of the villages where they camped was Dohnavur ("Rhyme *Doh* with No, *na* with Ah, *vur* with Poor"). Dohnavur had been established in 1827 by Charles Theophilus Ewart Rhenius, a man of powerful influence in the missionary history of Tinnevelly. Although a Prussian Lutheran with pietist leanings, Rhenius had been sent to India by the (Anglican) Church Missionary Society in 1811 when English volunteers were few and far between. He has been called one of the ablest, most clear-sighted, practical, and zealous missionaries India has ever seen. He was the first to promote the education of women, establish Christian societies for charitable purposes, assemble the people of every Christian village for morning and evening prayer.

Wary of encouraging a merely nominal Christianity, Rhenius saw to it that every individual was drilled in doctrine, memorized Scripture, and was examined before being baptized. He helped to found organizations such as the Native Bible and Tract Society and the Native Missionary Society which sent local people to villages where there were no Christians. Congregations developed independence and a thoroughly Tamil, as distinct from colonial or European, cultural idiom. Perhaps most significant of all, he saw the caste system, on which India's entire culture and economy rested, as incompatible with Christianity and tried to influence believers to break it. Wherever the Gospel of Christ is preached, believed, and scrupulously obeyed, there is trouble. Rhenius's stand caused trouble. Christians were (quite justly) accused of intolerance, and became themselves simply intolerable. Persecution reached such a pitch that Villages of Refuge were needed. Some of Rhenius's friends in Europe sent funds to support such villages.

Suddenly, twelve years after his arrival, the CMS dismissed Rhenius and took over his work. The reasons for such a drastic step lay in his being a Lutheran who ordained Indians in violation of apostolic succession as defined by Anglicans. Not wanting to hinder in any way the work of God, he bowed out. Later, at his people's urgent request, he returned and struggled on, attempting to complete his Tamil grammar and his Bible translation, but died six years later before he was fifty.

Dohnavur was one of the Villages of Refuge. Rhenius named it in honor of a certain Count Dohna who had sent money for the persecuted Christians.

When Amy and her Band came upon it, it was "a bare sunburnt spot out on the plains under the mountains to the west, a huddle of huts and small houses round a fairly big, whitewashed church with, beyond low mud walls, an old ramshackle bungalow built of mud bricks and visibly falling to pieces." Many of the Christians there were nominal ones, descendants of those who had "gone over" during the sweeping Christian movements early in the previous century. This was not the sort of Christian Amy and her Band, any more than Rhenius, wanted to multiply. They were laying down their lives to see true faith born—in mere churchgoers as well as in Hindus, some of whom seemed to be earnest inquirers.

On March 4 the Band had left Dohnavur, traveling by night as usual, to return to their old "battlefield" in the east, the village of Pannaivilai. Not far from there, in Great Lake, was a Hindu temple. They had often tried to speak to the *devadasis*, women who served in the temples. Swami Harshananda, in *All About Hindu Temples*,[1] describes their function: "This system was opposed by the brahmanas. However, due to the pressure of the kings and no-

---

1. Swami Harshananda, *All About Hindu Temples* (Mysore, India: Ramakrishna Institute of Moral and Spiritual Education, 1979).

blemen it came to stay. The girls chosen to become *devadasis* would be married to the deity in the temple in a ceremonial way. Their main duties consisted of cleaning the temple, fanning the image, carrying lights, singing and dancing before the deity and devotees and so on.

"The system might have started some time during the third century A.D. It soon degenerated into prostitution, thanks to the notorious human weaknesses."

Sometimes the Band had seen little girls, bought as infants from their mothers and reared in the temple-women's house where, by precept and example, they learned the "trade." These children were "gracious little maidens, winsome in their ways, almost always more refined in manner than ordinary children, and beautiful."[2] Amy and her comrades longed to reach over the wall, but the procuring of these children was always a hole-and-corner operation, heavily guarded, and they could only pray that He to whom no wall is an obstacle would somehow show them a way.

The bullock bandies carrying Amy and her Indian friends rumbled up to the old bungalow in Pannaivilai on the evening of March 6. That very evening in the village nearby a strange thing took place.

Preena was a child of seven who lived in the temple house. Her father was dead. Her mother had been persuaded to devote her to the gods. Once she had managed to slip out and return to her mother, a twenty-mile walk to Tuticorin, "one of the Sodoms of the province." The temple women traced her, and the mother, threatened with the wrath of the gods, tore the child's arms from around her neck and gave her back to them. They branded her hands with hot irons, effectively burning into her young mind the heinousness of her crime. She had run away from a sacred calling.

One day Preena overheard a conversation about "tying her to the god." She imagined being bound with ropes to the idol in the dark recesses of the temple. Anything would be preferable to that, so she resolved to escape, no matter what the cost. Like the other little girls, she was under constant surveillance. She could think of

---

2. *Things as They Are*, p. 160ff.

only one way out. In desperation she went to the idol, threw herself down before it, and prayed that she might die.

On the same evening that Amy's bandy reached the bungalow in Pannaivilai, God sent an angel to the temple house. So Amy interpreted it. If He could send an angel to the prison in Jerusalem to deliver the apostle Peter, why not to a temple house in an Indian village to deliver a little girl? Amy wrote that the angel simply took her by the hand, led her out, across a stream, through the woods. There seemed no other possible explanation for her having eluded the all-seeing eyes and finding her way to safety. Preena's version was that she had heard the temple women call Amy "the child-stealing ammal," hoping to frighten her. The child made up her mind instead that that was the very ammal she wanted to find. The late afternoon of March 6 was the time she chose. (Was it God's angel who chose? Or perhaps both? For God works often through human choices.) A Christian woman named Servant of Jesus came upon the "very small and desolate mite with tumbled hair and troubled eyes" standing in front of the church in Pannaivilai. It was late, so instead of taking the child back where she belonged the woman kept her for the night, intending to return her next morning. But Preena insisted that she wanted to go to the child-stealing ammal.

Early the next morning Amy was having her *chota* (early tea) on the verandah when Servant of Jesus, looking astonished, suddenly appeared with Preena. "She did not know about the angel, I expect, and she could not understand it at all." The child ran straight to the white lady, climbed into her lap, and began to chatter away. "My name is Pearl-eyes, and I want to stay here always. I have come to stay."

Preena's memory years later of her precious "Amma" (*mother*), was of her taking her into her lap and kissing her. "I thought, 'My mother used to put me on her lap and kiss me—who is this person who kisses me like my mother?' From that day she became my mother, body and soul."

If it had not been late afternoon when Servant of Jesus found Preena, she would have taken her back at once to the temple house. If the Band had not arrived at the bungalow that night, there would have been no one to take her to. If Preena had succeeded in making her escape earlier, Amy would have been fifty miles away. Surely all this was a wonder of providential timing. When she told the story for the first time in *Things as They Are*, Amy began the chapter with David Livingstone's words, "It seems to have been a mistake to imagine that the Divine Majesty on high was too exalted to take any notice of our mean affairs. The great minds among us are remarkable for the attention they bestow upon minutiae . . . 'a sparrow cannot fall to the ground without your Father.' "

Slowly they grew to know the child and delight in her. "We watched her wonderingly. She was perfectly at home with us. She ran out, gathered leaves and flowers, and came back with them. These were carefully arranged in rows on the floor. Then another expedition, and in again with three pebbles for hearthstones, a shell for a cooking pot, bits of straw for firewood, a stick for a match, and sand for rice. She went through all the minutiae of Tamil cookery with the greatest seriousness. Then we, together with her doll, were invited to partake. The little thing walked straight into our hearts, and we felt we would risk anything to keep her."

Preena was followed, of course. The temple women ("We are servants of the gods!") came to the bungalow, crowds gathered, there was an enormous fuss. Preena would not go with them, and Amy would not force her. Amy dared not go near the child then lest they think she had some power to bewitch her. Arulai, one of the Band, took her away out of sight and the child clung to her and sobbed, imploring her not to let them take her. Their punishments were cruel—Preena had scars to prove it. Arulai managed to soothe her and took her back to the angry crowd. The little girl stood bravely before them all. Would she go with them? "I won't!" was her answer, and they went off, declaring that they would write to her mother who had given her to them.

For a while the Band continued their work as before, but when they returned to the bungalow in the evenings, there was a child to welcome them. "I remember wakening up to the knowledge that there had been a very empty corner somewhere in me that the work had never filled; and I remember, too, thanking God that it was not wrong to be comforted by the love of a child," Amy said. She was soon nicknamed the Elf. One morning the Elf asked Amy, "Can you be good without God's grace?"

Amy replied that she certainly could not.

"Well, I can!" said the Elf. "I want to pray now!"

"Now? It is eight o'clock now. Haven't you had prayer long ago?" Six o'clock was rising time.

"No. That's just what I meant. I skipped my prayer this morning, and so of course I got no grace; but I have been helping the elder Sisters. Wasn't that right?"

"Yes, quite right."

"And yet I hadn't got any grace! But I suppose," she added after a moment's thought, "it was the grace over from yesterday that did it."

Amy Carmichael learned things from this child that "darkened the sunlight." She heard firsthand of the secret traffic in the souls and bodies of little children, things unthinkable, impossible at that time to write about. Rumors which had reached Amy from time to time during their travels she had tried to dismiss as utterly preposterous. When she had (in the most delicate and circuitous terms, no doubt) tried to broach the subject to missionaries who might know the truth, she was squelched with remarks about her vivid imagination, "more ardent than informed." The rumors could not be true. They could not possibly be true.

There is some question as to whether the most elementary facts of life had ever been explained to Amy Carmichael. The word *sex* was unmentionable earlier in this century. A missionary who worked with her many years later insisted that Amy not only did not then know the truth about sex, but never learned. Whether her ignorance can be said to have been quite so abysmal is doubtful, but it is clear enough that her Victorian mind refused to admit thoughts which were so unpleasant and certainly unnecessary. Did she understand just what she was saving little girls from? "She did not know," said the above-mentioned missionary. "She only knew it was horrible."

Just how horrible it was she did her best to put into words. *Things as They Are* has a picture of a half-naked holy man. "This photo is from death in life," she writes, "a carcass, moving, breathing, sinning. . . . I knew something about the man. His life is simply unthinkable. Talk of beasts in human shape! It is slandering good animals to compare bad men to beasts. Safer far in a tiger's den than that man's monastery. But he is a temple saint—earthly, sensual, devilish. Now put beside him a little girl—your own little girl—and leave her there—*yes, leave her there in his hand.*"

The evidence for emotional and physical cruelty within sex, in India, whether marital or extramarital, has always been strong. The high rate of suicide among young women today supports this. Amy needed only to imagine the details. The overwhelming desire to save the children became a fire in her bones. "Sometimes the broad smooth levels of life are crossed by a black-edged jagged crack, rent, as it seems, by an outburst of the fiery force below. We find ourselves suddenly close upon it; it opens right at our very feet,"[3] wrote Amy, and Walker corroborated it, "We are skirting the abyss, an abyss which is deep and foul beyond description, and yet is glorified, to Hindu eyes, by the sanctions of religion."[4]

But how were they to track down these children? "The helpless little things seemed to slip between our fingers as we stretched out our hands to grasp them, or it was as though a great wave swept up and carried them out to sea. In a kind of desperation, we sought for a way. But we found that we must know more before we could hope to find it. To graze upon the tips (of herbage) is the Tamil synonym for superficial knowledge. If we were to do anything for these children it was vain to graze on the tips of facts; it took years to do more than that."[5]

---

3. *Things as They Are*, p. 188.
4. Amy Carmichael, *Overweights of Joy*, p. 35.
5. Amy Carmichael, *Gold Cord*, p. 22.

Chapter 21
Children Tie the Mother's Feet

Patiently they went on with their itineration, camping, seeking an entrance into homes, holding "Open Airs," with the usual disruptions—"a bullock cart rumbles round ... a herd of cows, perhaps fifty strong, with their calves, and as many buffaloes, each bent on making its way straight to its own habitation regardless of obstruction, tramples through the throng. One evening I was sitting on the doorstep of a house, with a dozen women round me, when suddenly a beast appeared, and without a moment's hesitation, walked straight over me and in."[1]

The *Scrap* letter for June of 1901 lists the members of the Band as Ponnammal, a widow, delicate, sensitive, highly strung, "a harp—God plays upon her and she responds to His touch"; Marial, "a dear, good, sturdy little soul with far more independence than any of the others"; Pearl, the one-armed, the only unmarried woman among them, tall, angular, thoroughly good and trustworthy; and Blessing, "a grand old muddler with a brave singleness of soul." Blessing had a singular habit of shaking down her hair and twisting it up again as she talked. Forty years later Amy laughed as old Blessing described Amy's singular habit, her manner of moving—not walking or even running, but "flying," always looking at her watch "lest we waste moments." As she told the story, down came the hair and, with a quick twist of the skinny old hand, up it went again. "And frequently," said Blessing, "yes, frequently you said to me, 'Art thou an elephant to walk so very slowly?' "

---

1. Amy Carmichael, *From the Fight*, p. 24ff.

Working with the Band and learning from them were five convert girls: Jewel of Victory, twenty, who had come in 1898, the first from a high caste, brave and steadfast; Jewel of Life, nineteen, who came a year later; Arulai (Star), fourteen, a girl of intense nature—"She has been won for some purpose, yet to appear"; Liberty, sixteen, fat, slow, with not enough energy to get into mischief, but she had borne great things for Christ, been beaten, had her arm torn with nails; and Jewel, who had held on to faith through thick and thin.

By June of 1901, only three months after Preena's arrival, Amy had become Amma (from Tamil *ammal*, "mother") to four more little children. They were not temple children, but for one reason or another needed care and were received for Christ's sake. The convert girls helped to look after these, who were nicknamed the Imp, Pickles, Brownie, and Tangles. (Poor little Pickles in a short time turned out to be "a fraud," though we are not given a hint as to why, and was sent home.)

"Children tie the mother's feet." It took rather a long time for the truth of this Tamil proverb to dawn on Amy. Driving herself as she had always done to buy up every opportunity for evangelism, she was now sleuthing for temple children as they journeyed and camped, and trying to be a part-time mother to the Band, the convert girls, and the babies. It was not a very satisfactory arrangement, but missionary life is full of unsatisfactory arrangements and Amy could not bring herself to believe that she should give up the work of evangelizing. Who would do it?

God has many ways of gaining His servants' attention. In July Arulai became desperately ill with typhoid. This girl, "won for a purpose, yet to appear," seemed to be dying. All journeyings came to a halt while Amy and her helpers, for three anxious and gruelling months, gave themselves to nursing. Arulai recovered, but the truth had not yet been borne in upon Amy that mothering is a full-time job and her family needed a home. She was a missionary. Mothering was not what she had had in mind when she answered God's call. And as for a home—had she not renounced all such earthly comforts? She had given up all thought, probably in the cave at Arima, Japan, of having a husband or a home. She wrote:

If Thy dear home be fuller, Lord,
For that a little emptier
My house on earth, what rich reward
That guerdon were.

The willingness to sacrifice that springs from a loving heart rather than the desire for spiritual distinction is surely acceptable to God. But, as in the case of Abraham's offering of his son Isaac, the sacrifice itself is not always finally required. What is required is obedience.

The Heavenly Father knew what the family needed and had been arranging an answer when the question of a home had not even been asked. "Before they call I will answer, and while they are yet speaking I will hear."[2]

The combination of events which had brought Preena and Amy together showed the "mysterious ways" of God's moving. Another event, no less remarkable for its mystery since it was in itself an evil, played its part in the group's settling down. At about the same time that Preena escaped, a man in Australia was murdered. A missionary named Storrs who was to teach a class of divinity students in Dohnavur "happened" to be in Australia just then, visited the murderer who had been sentenced to death, and led him to Christ.

It is not clear from Amy's account exactly what happened to Mr. Storrs next. He was "overstrained by this" (presumably by the man's having been hanged) and "lost his power to sleep." He could not return to India. Someone else would have to teach the divinity students. By the end of the year it was clear that there was only one possibility: Thomas Walker. Walker must go where the students were: to Dohnavur. The "Family," of course, must go with him.

So it was that they moved from the eastern side of the district to the western, "intending to move on when the cloud was taken up, according to the word in Numbers 9, 'or whether it were two days, or a month, or a year, that the cloud tarried upon the tabernacle, remaining thereon, the children of Israel abode in their tents, and journeyed not; but when it was taken up, they journeyed.' "

---

2. Isaiah 65:24 (AV).

Dohnavur, seen at first only as a center for evangelistic work (there were fifty or sixty villages within a radius of five or six miles), became home for the Family and, though she did not know it yet, Amy was rooted for life. From Ireland to England she had followed the Shepherd, then to Japan to China to Ceylon to England to India—Bangalore, Palamcottah, Pannaivilai, and at last Dohnavur.

The dilapidated mission bungalow had a leaky roof, a mud floor, and one small window. But "soon we found what a perfect place our Father had chosen for us, for at last children were saved, and moving about with them would have been impossible. If we had searched all over Tirunelveli we could not have found a place that would have been so safe and could be made so beautiful too."

Amy could not yet see that she must give herself entirely to the children, and in January of 1902 off she went again, this time for a six-weeks' mission with the Walkers in Travancore, leaving Ponnammal in Dohnavur to cope with the Band, the converts, and the "Lotus Buds," as they called the little children. As many as twenty thousand came to the Travancore meetings. The language there being Malayalam, two interpreters were needed for the speakers (Amy and Walker), as well as prodigious lung power, since public-address systems were then unknown. There is no report of spiritual results, but it seems that (through Amy's efforts?) the Indian minister, a Syrian Christian, was delivered from the outlandish getup which certain English missionaries had chosen for him—a suit of "violent checks" and a hat, in which "he looks exactly like a well-dressed monkey." A comfortable white robe with wide sleeves was a relief for him and very likely another black mark on the missionaries' list of Carmichael offenses. She had a propensity for upsetting things.

If it were possible to poll all the missionaries who have worked in all the world in all of Christian history, it would be seen that missionary work, most of the time, offers little that could be called glamour. What it does offer, as Amy wrote to prospective candidates in later years, is "a chance to die"—or, as Winston Churchill put his challenge during World War II, blood, sweat, and tears. It offers a great deal of plodding and ploughing, with now and then a little planting. It is the promise of rejoicing, given to those who "go

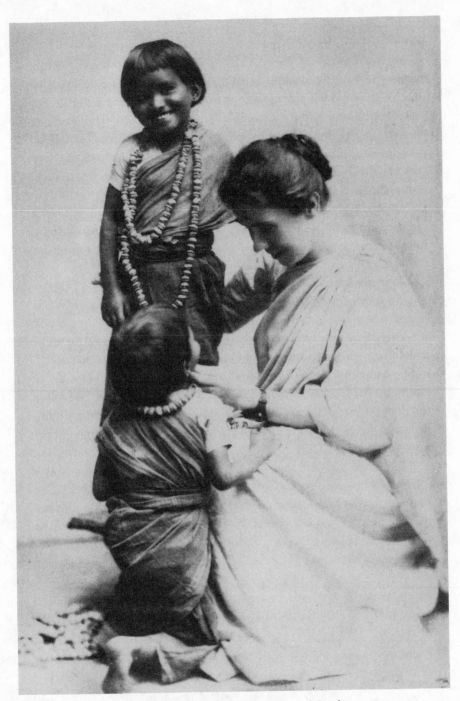

Amy, age forty-two, with Lola and Leela.

forth weeping, bearing precious seed" that gives heart. So it was with Amy. Her home letters are not triumphant accounts of people turning to God from idols, but little stories of the one or two children in a village who were willing to learn one Scripture verse, sing one little gospel song; the bored Brahman women who were diverted for a few moments by photographs Amy showed them; an occasional dialogue with an educated Hindu; a schoolboy who seemed interested in the Bible. But gradually the letters began to be lightened with stories about the children of her Family.

"Did you get caned in school today?"

"No, not exactly caned. I was standing beside a very naughty little girl and the teacher meant to cane her, but the cane fell on me by mistake."

Their questions were charming:

"Do fishes love Jesus?"

"Stones are young mountains, aren't they?"

When they saw an English lady wearing a veil: "Don't they like to look at God's beautiful world? Do they like it better *spotty?*"

She asked her English friends to send baby vests and lengths of cloth, but *not* frocks, for which they had no use whatever. She asked for dolls—"*girl* dolls, *please*. NOT boys—the games heathen children play are so terribly, unthinkably wicked that boys should *never* be given."

The Indian girls did their best to care for the children, but Amy's itineration became less and less feasible. By August she wrote, "Oh, I am getting so hungry for another child!" and was beginning to see that she must allow her feet to be tied "for the sake of Him whose feet once were nailed."

Chapter 22
The Vault Beneath the Meadow

The search for children in peril went on assiduously, but as quietly as possible. They found that there were five reasons for children being dedicated to temples. Sometimes it was because of a vow or obedience to a family custom. Sometimes it was in order to escape some social entanglement such as an out-of-caste alliance. When a poor widow or a deserted wife could not find a suitable husband for her child, she married her to the god. In some cases lack of money to perform the death ceremonies required by the caste tempted a mother to give up her child for her husband's sake.

It was three years before a second temple child was found, three years during which the Starry Cluster continued to travel and Amy continued to try to do the impossible. Her *Scrap* letters were fewer and further between, but she wrote many letters to friends in India, asking for help in finding the children. She investigated every possible avenue of approach to officials who might be of help in saving them, and pleaded with people at home to pray. Her book *Things as They Are* seemed of no use at all against the huge forces of the system which was Hinduism. One day, desperate to find words fiery enough to burn people's consciences, she cried out to God to give them. She wrote down the answer in an old exercise book:

Thou shalt have words,
But at this cost, that thou must first be burned,
Burned by red embers from a secret fire,
Scorched by fierce heats and withering winds that sweep,

Through all thy being, carrying thee afar
From old delights. Doth not the ardent fire
Consume the mountain's heart before the flow
Of fervent lava? Wouldst thou easefully,
As from cool, pleasant fountains, flow in fire?

Reformers were working in both Bombay and Calcutta, "but the subject bristled with difficulties and action at that time appeared to be impossible."[1] Once she was invited to meet with a group of men who might wield influence in the framing of a law to protect children.

Two of the ten men were in earnest, the other eight enjoyed the talk preparatory and attendant upon all action in India, but they saw no tremendous reason for immediate exertion of any sort. The evil was decreasing: education, civilization, these elevating influences would gradually and pleasantly permeate society. In the meantime, we asked, what about the perishing children? Ah, it was sad, doubtless; that they should perish was indeed regrettable. But after all, were there many imperilled? For his part one old gentleman doubted it, though doubtless, he added cheerfully, unaware of the force of his admission, "a change in the law is much required."[2]

Amy went out visiting some of the Indian women who had been mentioned in *Things as They Are*, hoping to find results from the wave of prayer she believed the book would have generated in England and elsewhere. She reported in her *Scrap* letter that she found little evidence. One old lady, so kind and hospitable in giving her coconut milk and sweets, said that she had chosen caste over Christ.

People in their kindness tried to distract us from this that could not be forgotten. To be with them, hearing their talk, so clear and friendly, reading their books, looking at their pleasant things, was like being in some clean green field full of blessed flowers. But every now and then the face of the field would fall in and discover a vault below; and in the vault chains and darkness and the souls of young children. . . . The desolation of the

---

1. *Gold Cord*, p. 29.
2. Amy Carmichael, *The Continuation of a Story*, p. 7.

children who had no deliverer, the wrong we could not redress, the fear, the cold deadness of forced sin, how little of this could be shown then or can be shown now.[3]

When she told of the child-wives, twelve or ten or eight years old, people said, "Oh, you mean betrothed! Another case of missionary exaggeration!" No, she did not mean betrothed. "We mean married."

Katherine Mayo's *Mother India* documents case after case of appalling physical destruction ("pelvis crushed out of shape," "so completely ravished as to be almost beyond surgical repair," etc.) which resulted from child marriage, which, "like its background of public sentiment, is deep-rooted in the far past of an ultra-conservative and passionately religious people. Anyone curious as to the fierceness with which it would be defended by the people, both openly and covertly, and in the name of religion, against any frontal attack, will find answer in the extraordinary work and in the all-too-reticent books of Miss Amy Wilson-Carmichael."[4]

One evening when the full responsibility of the compound rested on Amy (the Walkers were in England on furlough), she had what amounted to a vision. The tamarind trees around the bungalow were olive trees, and under them a man knelt alone. She knew it was the Lord, praying there in the garden for the children. So the burden was His, not hers. She need not ask Him to share it with her. He was asking her to share it with Him, to search with Him for the lost lambs. "Who could have done anything but go into the garden and kneel down beside Him under the olive trees?"

Her poem, "The Fellowship of His Sufferings,"[5] must have come from that evening's experience. She is "the lover." The masculine pronoun refers to herself.

> . . . Darkly distinct, he saw a vision pass
> Of One who took the cup alone, alone.
> Then broke from him a moan,

---

3. *Gold Cord*, p. 31.
4. Katherine Mayo, *Mother India* (New York: Harcourt, Brace, 1927), p. 48.
5. Amy Carmichael, *Toward Jerusalem.*

A cry to God for pain, for any pain
Save this last desolation; and he crept
In penitence to his Lord's feet again.
. . . Never an angel told, but this I know,
That he to whom that night Gethsemane
Opened its secrets, cannot help but go
Softly thereafter, as one lately shriven,
Passionately loving, as one much forgiven.
    And never, never can his heart forget
    That Head with hair all wet
With the red dews of Love's extremity,
Those eyes from which fountains of love did flow,
    There in the Garden of Gethsemane.

As she was praying, a pastor in the northern part of the district was traveling. He happened on a group of temple women with children, and prayed then and there that something might be done. Almost immediately he heard of a newborn baby just taken by a temple woman. He was able to rescue her. On March 1, 1904, the first temple baby, thirteen days old, was in Amma's arms—"the little old, tired baby face, the feeble, weary cry, the little hands moving restlessly as if feeling for a mother." She nearly died that same night, and "we hardly understood what we had undertaken." Preena was allowed to name her. She chose one of the precious stones from the wall of the Holy City—Amethyst. The second baby, also saved by an Indian pastor, was named Sapphire. She was a lovely, laughing baby, "a whole round gift of joy."

A girl named Lavana came, defying her parents' pleas to return to them. "I cannot possibly come," she said, "I am a Christian." They tried to lure her with jewels. "I don't want jewels. I have Jesus now." By June the Family had grown to include seventeen children, six of whom were direct answers to the prayer of so many years—they were temple children. The women of the Band were learning that if the Lord of Glory took a towel and knelt on the floor to wash the dusty feet of His disciples (the job of the lowest slave in an Eastern household), then no work, even the relentless and often messy routine of caring for squalling babies, is demeaning. To offer it up to the Lord of Glory transforms it into a holy task. "Could it be right," Amy had asked, "to turn from so much that might be of profit and become just nursemaids?" The answer was yes. It is not the business of the servant to decide which work is great, which is small, which important or unimportant—he is not greater than his master.

"If by doing some work which the undiscerning consider 'not spiritual work' I can best help others, and I inwardly rebel, thinking it is the spiritual for which I crave, when in truth it is the interesting and exciting, then I know nothing of Calvary love,"[6] Amy wrote after many years of such "unspiritual" work.

Facilities for the care of these children left much to be desired. A long, low mud room served as kitchen, dining room, night and day nursery all in one. Many of the children were frail when they came and needed mother's milk. They could find no one in the village willing to feed other people's children. It simply wasn't done. Later when a village woman consented to breast-feed one of Amy's babies in order to save its life, her husband killed her by slow arsenic poisoning for having thus sinned against caste.

Christmas Eve found Amma in the village church with a sick baby in her arms, searching for a Christian mother (surely a *Christian* mother would be willing?) to nurse it. There was no one. What were they to do now? Who knew how to prepare a formula? How should they know what formula would suit this child or that? Amy had nowhere to turn but God. She asked for wisdom and it came. He sent another blessing that year—Mr. Walker returned, bringing with him Amy's mother.

"An atmosphere of love and obedience pervades the compound," Mrs. Carmichael wrote to a friend at home. "In this large family of over thirty, ranging in age from thirty-four years to a babe of nine months, I have not seen an angry look, or heard an impatient word. A set of more loving, unselfish women and girls and children could not easily be found. . . . Since we came here a month ago I can truthfully say [Amy] has scarcely had leisure even to eat. She is mother, doctor, and nurse, day and night."

---

6. Amy Carmichael, *If* (London: Society for the Promotion of Christian Knowledge), p. 43.

One who specially loved this *Atah* (baby word for grandmother) was little Indraneela, "Sapphire." During one of the family's feasts, the children, dressed in crimson and yellow and blue, clapped their hands and called, "Indraneela! Indraneela!" and the baby danced and clapped with them and toddled to everyone who called. She clapped her hands when she saw the flowers, clapped them again with the music.

A few weeks later an epidemic struck. Two babies died, and Indraneela, the only baby left, lay very quietly on Atah's lap. She heard the sound of the children coming from school, and tried again to clap. Six children were ill then, and the nursing had to be divided. Amy and Arulai were with Indraneela in the early morning. "Just before dawn she called, and holding up her little hand as high as she could reach, pointed up. Then she pointed to a toy music box which we always kept beside her, and when it was given to her she turned the handle till the first notes came. She had often tried before, but never quite succeeded in turning the handle herself. Now she stopped and looked up with those joyous eyes, so unlike a baby's eyes in steadfastness of expression: 'Let me to my heaven go! A little harp me waits thereby . . . .'

"She held out her little hands to be kissed, and then, tired, fell asleep. In the few hours that followed we could not help noticing the other-world expression deepening in the baby's eyes. . . . Then there was a sudden breaking of the silence, one little cry, the baby's mother-word, 'Amma!' "

An angel came for her, Amy said—gently touched her so that she slept and woke to the music of heaven. Amy took the children to the garden and showed them nasturtiums and convolvulus which were not flourishing as they should have. But one beautiful lily, the first that had ever blossomed there, had opened that very morning.

"If Jesus came to our garden," she asked, "which flower would you give Him?"

They ran to the lily. "We would give Him *this*!"

Would she give Him her lily? Indraneela, Amy was sure, was the child of an ancient, royal race. There was something noble about her, something dainty and imperious in her ways. *We would give Him this! We would give Him this!*—the words kept repeating themselves to her mind. Would she, could she give Him *this?* As she was resting in her room later that afternoon, trying to gather strength for the baby's burial, she heard Mr. Walker's schoolboys reading aloud from the book of Exodus the description of the breastplate of the high priest, which had four rows of stones. In the second row was a sapphire. It was the word she needed. Her Sapphire was "set on His breast." The child would be safe there.

> Dear little feet, so eager to be walking
>   But never walked in any grieving way,
> Dear little mouth, so eager to be talking
>   But never hurt with words it cannot say,
> Dear little hands, outstretched in eager welcome,
>   Dear little head that close against me lay—
> Father, to Thee I give my Indraneela,
>   Thou wilt take care of her until That Day.

Three months later a telegram told Amy that her Dear Old Man had died June 19. Two months after that she wrote, "It has not got to the place where I can talk about it yet."

Chapter 23
The Impress of the Signet Ring

Dates had particular significance for Amy Carmichael—time was a creature of God, to be noted and served with prayer and care. Like the Israelites who, at the command of God, set up piles of stones to remind them of places where God had met them in a particular way, Amy established certain days to remind the Family of His providences. Because Preena arrived on the sixth of March (1901), and Indraneela died on the sixth of January (1905), a day of prayer was instituted on the sixth day of every month to intercede for children in danger. It is still kept. The Family gathers and kneels, one of the members reads out the names of villages, and the whole group responds, "Lord, save the children there." Amy made a Praise Box into which slips of paper giving reasons for thanksgiving were dropped. This was opened on the Day of Prayer and the Family gave thanks together.

The Indian workers were steadily deepened in their love for the children and consecration to work which was "not naturally easy to the flesh, especially Indian flesh." The nursery emptied by the epidemic was filled again, "but these tiny things' hold on life is very light, and I fear to say much about them." Even Mrs. Carmichael, who had reared seven babies, was at a loss to know what to do for some of the pitiful little scraps that came to them. She knew how to sew and embroider, however, and could teach English, so the older girls sat at her feet and learned whenever they found time between helping to care for younger children and babies. As a family, all were given to understand that each must share in what it takes to make a home.

One day in 1905 "Jesus came to Dohnavur." That was how

Amy described what happened in the little village church next to the compound. All were together—school children, workers, bungalow servants, some of the village Christians. What started out to be an ordinary meeting turned into "a hurricane of prayer" which went on for four hours. Amy saw it as a revival, a great answer to her constant prayer for a building made of gold, silver, and precious stones rather than wood, hay, and stubble. She was disappointed, however, that only the Family seemed to be revived while the church members went on as usual. When would the Spirit of God sweep over the nominal Christians of South India? She struggled to avoid criticism, yet she could not suspend the faculty of judgment. The church was not as living and vital an organism as it should be, and the impact of the little company that lived alongside was so far very weak. God chooses the foolish to confound the wise, the weak to confound the mighty, but nobody seemed to be confounded at all.

The need for medical attention for the babies led to the opening of a branch nursery in Neyoor, a journey of a day and a half from Dohnavur by bullock bandy, where there was a London Missionary Society medical station. Soon there were fifteen Dohnavur babies there. Ponnammal ("God's golden gift to the work") was put in charge, though she could ill be spared from Dohnavur since Mrs. Carmichael had gone home. At first the women under her, young nurses and older women who were recent converts, objected to doing work which was beneath their caste. Ponnammal had learned from Amy that "motherwork," like any other honest labor, is God's work—not to be despised, but offered up to Him. Amma had taught her the aim of the Keswick people: *nothing less than to walk with God all day long*. The nature of the work itself made no difference whatever. This was a shocking notion to those indoctrinated in caste, but Ponnammal set the example for the others by quietly doing what they did not care to do. Her spirit created a new climate in the place, and the time came when there was not one nurse who would refuse to do whatever needed to be done.

Amy arrived one day for a visit, finding the babies "out to air" while the nurses did their morning work. Some were laid on mats, some swung in hammocks hung from a tree, some were in swings.

"They seemed to understand it was useless to demand attention just then, and were very patient and contented. But the moment the nurses reappeared, each little infant began to protest. . . . They considered being put out to air a tiresome proceeding, only to be put up with when nothing better was in prospect."

The Family could not live without money. Where was it to come from? Other missions had their ways of raising it. But such methods were not a part of the Pattern Shewn in the Mount, as Amy called the principles she believed God had given her for the Family. He had given her money for The Welcome and for every need since. Why not expect Him to go right on doing it? Amounts were nothing to Him. Nor did He lack methods. If it took ravens to feed the prophet Elijah, God sent ravens. Why shouldn't He send ravens to Dohnavur if He wanted to? If He feeds birds and clothes grass and flowers, why not look for the same provision?

We do not tell when we are in need unless definitely asked, and even then not always; for often the leading seems to be silent, except towards God, and we fear lest our little children should seem to crowd in among the many claims to help which must press so heavily upon the hearts of givers at home, and intercept anything which should be sent elsewhere. We rely upon the verses which assure us that our Father knows our needs, and we take it that with such a Father, to know is to supply.

We remember a time of threatened famine, when prices were suddenly rising and £20 was needed to lay in a stock of paddy (unshelled rice). That week brought us a single gift of £20 from a friend in England, whose very name up to that time was unknown to us. So the paddy was poured out in a great heap on the ground, and measured, and we paid for it with light and happy hearts. Again we remember a day when a letter came telling us of a child in danger far away. Sufficient money to meet necessary expenses must be sent off that same afternoon, or she would be otherwise appropriated, and from that appropriation there would be no release. We had not enough money in hand to pay for the chief charge, the long journey of those who would bring her to us; and no money could possibly reach us, even if we sent a coolie with a cheque to cash, for two days from that time. While we were reading the letter, our good postman, who is a sort of visible Raven, came up joyfully with a roll of rupees in his hand. The older children, who are in our confidence, know the look and the meaning of such a roll of rupees, and there was a glad call of "Money order!" It was from Canada, enough to cover all the expenses connected with that little child's deliverance. We piled the silver on the floor and knelt down round it and thanked God. It meant the redemption of our dear little Puck.

This and other incidents showing God's supply were recounted in a little book called *The Beginning of a Story*, published in 1908. Here and elsewhere Amy wrote that no appeals for money were ever made or ever authorized to be made. On page 19, however, she did allow herself to say, "Naturally, our greatest need, next to prayer, is just the simple straightforward need of money—to feed our little ones and clothe them, and to provide for the long journeys connected with their redemption and all other expenses bearing upon the salvation of Temple children." It was a mere statement of fact, so obvious it hardly needed stating. Yet Amy later withdrew the book from circulation, fearing that that line might be taken as an appeal for funds. She did not mind listing other needs in her letters home: *prayer* first, last, and always; then sewing and writing materials, colored pencils, rattles for the babies, pink or white vests, yardage of sateen ("blue, white, mossy green, terra cotta, or bright golden, not orange or lemon—we have no use for ugly colors. They are not necessarily cheaper than pretty colors. If they were I would pray for grace. . . . I say very humbly, send us something pretty").

The Family was rapidly outgrowing the buildings, but to plan and finance expansion was a serious business. "Expenditure leads out into expenditure," she wrote a few years later. "The only expenditure, and all its outworkings, for which God can be held to be responsible is that which He directs." Questions about finances were asked again and again. Again and again Amy stated her position: Our Heavenly Father knows what we need and gives it to us.

There is no myth, no imagination about it: God does hear when we speak to Him; God does answer us. For money is a tangible, unmistakable thing; you cannot act when you have not got it as you would if you had it. It is not a case of "Believe that you have it, and you have it"—a kind of faith which has puzzled me from a child. Believe it will come, yes, if you are sure your order is to go forward and buy land or build buildings or save children. But woe unto you if you imagine you have been told to do such

The Cottage Nursery.

things and then find the order has not been signed above. But the sign, the very impress of the signet ring . . . is a solemn thing to see.[1]

Early in 1906 when it seemed that they must expand, they asked for "the impress of the signet ring" in the form of three signs:

1. possession of an adjoining field,
2. money for two nurseries, a kindergarten, and workers' rooms,
3. a marked increase in the Family.

Two answers came in a short time. The field was purchased. Seventeen children arrived between spring and fall of 1906. The money was not yet in hand, but because of the rains, building could not begin anyway.

No matter how crowded her days and nights, how many demands were made on her time, how impossible privacy or time for reflection might seem to be, Amy Carmichael managed to write. It was a necessity laid upon her. While itinerating and evangelizing and teaching and mothering, any one of which tasks might have ex-

---

1. *The Continuation of a Story*, pp. 35ff.

hausted an ordinary woman, she somehow contrived to make time and reserve energy for writing. By this time she had a typewriter, so that was the end of handwritten letters home. Although no *Scrap* letter survives from 1904 (it is not hard to suppose she was literally too busy to write), and only two from 1905, she wrote *Overweights of Joy*, a three-hundred page sequel to *Things as They Are*. It was published in 1906 with the hope that some whose spirits had sunk on learning the terrible facts of the first book would find "something of a cordial" here, although there was no attempt to tone down the facts of *Things. Overweights* was meant to be a song of praise out of the darkness which was the background of the work. In addition to many more stories of the powers of heathendom and its indifference to the message of Christ, the book contains happy stories and photographs of the children brought out of that darkness into light. Leela was one of those children. She had absorbed a good deal of theology.

"In the beginning," began Leela in unctuous tones, "the bad devil was good. He was an angel. He lived in heaven. One day all the angels came to sing to God. Then the devil was angry. He got angrier and angrier. He was very rude to God." Here Leela seemed to freeze all over, and her voice sounded quite deep and awful. Irreverence was far from her intention. "That bad, bad devil said, 'I won't stand before God's chair anymore, and I won't sing to God anymore. *I want to sit in God's chair, and make God sing to me!*' " There was a perfectly horrified pause, as the enormity of the transgression became evident. "So God took him and tumbled him down out of heaven, and he was turned into the devil."[2]

One night in a little crowded house in Dohnavur village in 1900 Amy had been asked to nurse a boy with pneumonia. It was her first experience of being in charge of one so ill and although she distrusted the method of treatment (hot oil poultices) she felt she could not add to the family's distress by suggesting any other. "By the kindness of the Lord, the Healer, he recovered, and so did all others nursed in the same primitive way, but I looked up [i.e. prayed] that first night and asked for a trained nurse." Nearly seven

---

2. *Overweights of Joy*, p. 264.

years later a young woman, believing God had called her to this work, arrived in Dohnavur. She was loving and unselfish, but stayed only a few months before leaving to marry a man she had met on board ship.

Cholera struck the village in December 1906. "Night after night we were in the little stricken huts, day after day, too . . . and what cholera can be no one can begin to understand who has not fought it alone, without a doctor, without modern weapons."[3]

The doctor and the modern weapons were a long time in coming. The work of God is done on God's timetable. His answers to our prayers come always in time—His time. His thoughts are far higher than ours, His wisdom past understanding.

Although cholera prowled around the Dohnavur Family many times, never once did it enter the gates, even though it was often necessary for Amma and her helpers to come straight back from the stricken village to the compound, stopping only long enough to change clothes. While God sent no miraculous medical assistance He seemed to put a hedge around His helpless children.

---

3. *Gold Cord*, p. 56.

Chapter 24
Strife of Tongues

Early in 1907 seven Dohnavur girls were baptized in one of the "shallow sheets of water that make our countryside so beautiful after rain. . . . Behind the calm, bright water, more present in a sense than even the hills whose shore that water washed, we saw the striped walls of the temples. There are joys that are unearthly in their power and in their sweetness."

Amy had learned to expect attack from the enemy of souls whenever an Indian took an uncompromising stand as a Christian. As the Assyrian king Sennacherib swept down upon Israel just after a time of feasting and gladness, so the enemy struck the little company of Dohnavur. This time it was a triple attack. Amy herself, thoroughly exhausted to the point of breakdown, was ordered home. Of course she disobeyed the order. Home? India was home. To leave it was not an option. But she did go to Ooty where climate and civilized comforts provided respite. While she was gone, a particularly virile kind of dysentery swept the nursery in Neyoor. One baby with dysentery is a full-time job for a mother. Ponnammal, with sixteen babies ill at once, wrote to Amma, "All is windy about us now, but the wind will not last always. The waves beat into our boat; but when the Lord says, Peace, be still, they will lie down. Let all your prayer for us be that we may rest in the will of God while the wind lasts." Ten of the babies died. Sometimes a grave had to be dug to hold two of them. "My little heart's joy, my own little jewel-of-the-eye has gone. But Jesus stays with me," wrote Ponnammal.

News of the worst of the three attacks came in a letter from

Scenery near the compound.

Walker, who was holding the fort at Dohnavur. The enemy had triumphed this time. What Amy called "a great wind from the wilderness" blew on a girl named Jeyanie, one of the convert workers, so that she was under serious suspicion of wrongdoing. It is not named, but in Amy's eyes was "worse than illness and death," and Jeyanie was sent away. Then another was involved in "a coil of trouble" which ultimately rendered her useless.

Ill and out of reach, Amy was assailed by some of the same enemy's fiery darts in the form of questions. The dysentery had spread rapidly because of overcrowding. There was only one Ponnammal, so to open a second nursery was impossible. Should they have refused the babies and sent them back to the temples? Unthinkable. Should they have waived the matter of gold, silver, and precious stones and settled for whatever help they could get? "But a constraint had been laid upon us. We could not have done that,"[1] said Amy, and Ponnammal wrote, "Let us work until we drop, but let us never lower the standard."

---

1. *Gold Cord*, p. 58.

At this time someone sent Père Didon's *Spiritual Letters*, a book which was not mere paper and ink to Amy "but force—wind and fire and dew."

"The roads are rugged," he wrote, "the precipices are steep; there may be a feeling of dizziness on the heights, gusts of wind, peals of thunder, nights of awful gloom—fear them not. There are also the joys of the sunlight, flowers such as are not in the plain, the purest of air, restful nooks; and the stars smile thence like the eyes of God."

Still the babies came, each one given in some way to Dohnavur when she might have been given to a very different kind of life. One brought by train from Bangalore was spotted by someone connected with a temple who made an offer. Another was found by a Bible woman who saw the mother standing on a street waiting for an offer. The "precipices" were indeed steep, and Amy felt all the more keenly the need for a comrade, one "who will be utterly other-worldly, utterly single-hearted, utterly consumed. Don't think I am that myself! I fall far short of my own standard. But that is what I want to be, and that is what we must be if we are to stand the strain and conquer."[2]

Occasionally other missions sent candidates to help Amy. Usually they had to be returned. They were accustomed to walking on the beaten track. The "little pile of red sand" which was Dohnavur was "off track" in more ways than geographical, and the standard insisted on was impossibly high. Amy began to pray that every obstacle might be placed in the way of candidates—any silly story about her which might put them off, every variety of test, all possible dissuasions, in order that those who could be kept back should be kept back. Not one person did she want who was not *meant* for them.

Two Indian teachers came who seemed to be the answer to prayer. Both foundered on the rock of truth and had to be sent back. "If our children were to grow up truthful they must be taught by those who had a regard for truth; and not just a casual regard, a *delicate* regard. On this point we were adamant."[3]

And so the parting of the ways began. Amy Carmichael was

---

2. *Scraps* No. 2, 1907.
3. *Gold Cord*, p. 66.

marching to a different drummer. There was no getting around that fact. She called herself "the least of His messengers," yet it was to her, as to God's anointed prophet Moses, that "the pattern in the mount" was shown. She stood, as it were, with her face to God and her back to the people, waiting to receive His word for the "chosen people." She had had a vision of holy living. She would not deviate from that no matter how well-established, rational, and practical the ways of older missions seemed to be.

Was love the Gold Cord of life in other missions? An older missionary once said to Amy, "But missionaries always do fall out with one another, and then make it up."

"We have never lived like that," Amy replied. "We could not bear to live for one minute out of love with one another," an answer which she supposed "sounded simply silly to the one who knew so much better than I did about missionary life."

Did not other missions sometimes hire evangelists? Were there not nominal Christians participating in mission work (not to use them was deemed "impractical")? Did they understand the motives which led Amy to eschew jewelry, Western dress, and the segregation of Indian and European? Most burning of all questions: was it the *Cross* that attracted them? Amy did not articulate such questions to them or, so far as one can tell, to anyone. But the questions were unavoidable. She avoided what could be avoided: condemnation—to their own Master they stood or fell, and she left them with Him. She earnestly tried to avoid what can never in honesty be avoided: the exercise of the critical faculty, in other words, judgment. "We seem to be judging when in truth we are only seeking humbly to obey," she said.

There arose during the early years of the Dohnavur work a fairly strong "Get-Amy-Carmichael-out-of-India" movement among missionaries and Indian Christians. She was a thorn in their sides. Why should she stubbornly refuse to accept the heretofore acceptable—nominal Christianity, for example, or the hiring of workers who hadn't the "single eye" for God's glory? Why must she persist in doing the unacceptable—wearing saris, doing work which was beneath her, refusing to pay salaries? The question asked years before by a Japanese, *Can you show us the life of your Lord Jesus?* was asked again by an Indian. Amy had no other purpose. This was the task

assigned: to make the truth visible. When it came to a choice between the good will of the missionaries of South India (and Christians elsewhere) and obedience, there could be no hesitation. She
would resolutely follow the Master who knew all about misunderstanding and opprobrium. Even as a little child Amy had known she
was set apart. Other children might suck peppermints in church.
She was forbidden. Were peppermints wicked? No. There were
rules for behavior in the Carmichael family that other families knew
nothing about. Never mind the others. "Is that your business,
Peter?" said Jesus. "You must follow me."

Writing years later about the principles on which the Dohnavur
Fellowship was founded, she said:

It matters that we should be true to one another, be loyal to what is a family—only a little family in the great Household, but still a family, with
family love alive in it and acting as a living bond. To those of us who have
lived this life for years it is inconceivable that one to whom this loyalty
means nothing should wish to be one of us. *It is not at all that we think that
ours is the only way of living, but we are sure that it is the way meant for us.*

We have one crystal clear reason apart from the blessed happiness of
this way of life. It is this: prayer is the core of our day. Take prayer out,
and the day would collapse, would be pithless, a straw blown in the wind.
But how can you pray—really pray, I mean—with one against whom you
have a grudge or whom you have been discussing critically with another?
Try it. You will find it cannot be done.[4]

Theirs not the only way of living? Yet, in the last analysis, was
there any other? "It cannot be done." The attempt to live strictly in
obedience to the Word of God taught Amy and her co-workers the
meaning of Jesus' stern words, "I did not come to bring peace, but
a sword." She expressed something of this lesson, stern though it
was, with gentle irony and humor in her poem, "The Calm Community of the Criticized."

> If, though all unawares, and not of ill intent,
> Thou steppest one inch outside the beaten track;
> If thou in deed or word or preference

---

4. Amy Carmichael, *Roots*, p. 55.

A Chance to Die

Depart from the Accustomed, or ransack
The unexplored, bright treasure-mines of life
And drawing forth their jewels make the House
Religious, as men call it, a glad place—
O then hide, hide thy face.
Or make quick pretence
Of suitable penitence,
For drum and fife
Are out against thee: perish thy mad *nous*
Or what it was that set thee grubbing where
A decent missionary never should be found.
They'll chase thee off the ground,
They'll harry thee,
Proclaim thee singular,
The while the truly sane and sober tar
Thy broken reputation for good sense.

At first, unconscious thou that things are thus—
Being innocent of all intentional wrong—
Thou wilt not know the fervent, general fuss
Pertains to thee at all; but gradually
It breaks on thee that various eyes are bent
Upon thy course, the lightness of thy gains
To scrutinize; and thou wilt see ere long
That certain hands hold firm a piece of chalk
To write thee up upon the wall. Advised
Be thou then, O my friend, in time;
Ponder the manner of thy careful walk;
See that thy very thoughts are close emmewed;
Tune all thy bells to play the usual chime,
Or brace thy spirit to be flayed alive
For its own good. The which if thou survive,
Thou'rt labeled one of that community
Who loving much can suffer woefully,
And yet mix laughter with their foolish pains,
And go on unsubdued—
The Calm Community of the Criticized.[5]

Rumors flew about this extraordinary woman, who at first had no idea that the "fervent, general fuss" pertained to her at all. Once an

5. Amy Carmichael, *Made in the Pans* (London: Oliphants), p. 37.

Anglican canon asked her to speak at a drawing-room meeting in Madras. The last thing Amy sought was the limelight. It had nothing to do with what she called "K.B.," King's Business, and it might hinder the work for the children. Furthermore—was she to appear before these Britishers in her sari? Courtesy to her host, however, won the day, and she stood up before the crowd in the bungalow. "The atmosphere was in the main frigid," said one who was there.

Her opening sentence confirmed one of the rumors. "I had a dream last night." She was reputed to be a dreamer of dreams.

"I thought I had come to this gathering, and an aged child of God with many years' service behind him was asked to pray. 'O Lord,' he said, 'here we are gathered together for yet another meeting, and Thou knowest how tired we are of meetings. Help us to get through this one.' "

The humor melted some of the ice on that occasion and her listeners allowed themselves to laugh. Perhaps the little sari-clad dark-haired dynamo was not quite so stuffy as they had imagined.

But criticism continued. Someone suggested that her efforts to save temple children were nothing more than a stunt, meant to draw attention to herself. The temple system was centuries old—what did she think she could do about it? Preposterous allegations found ready acceptance: She was a dictator, she opposed marriage, her Indian girls worshipped her.

No wonder she wrote,

> O Thou who art my quietness, my deep repose,
> My rest from strife of tongues, my holy hill,
> Fair is Thy pavilion, where I hold me still.
> Back let them fall from me, my clamorous foes,
> Confusions multiplied;
> From crowding things of sense I flee, and in Thee hide.
> Until this tyranny be overpast,
> Thy hand will hold me fast;
> What though the tumult of the storm increase,
> Grant to Thy servant strength, O Lord, and bless with
>   peace.[6]

---

6. *Toward Jerusalem*, p. 2.

Chapter 25
Place of Dragons

Eight years after Servant of Jesus and Preena had come to Amy's verandah in Pannaivilai, another woman and child materialized as unexpectedly on her verandah in Dohnavur. It was March 1909.

"Protect us!" the woman begged. Her relatives wanted to take the child from her and marry her to a man of their own choosing. "Muttammal is my only child. I cannot bear to give her up." Amy took them in, but found that the woman was "thoroughly wicked." She disappeared for two weeks, then reappeared, demanding the child back. They were forced to comply by order of the sub-magistrate. It proved to be an intricately tangled case, and Amy's letters were full of it for months to come.

In August Muttammal was released to Amy by the court on the condition that she keep caste. This was a great inconvenience to the Dohnavur family and a sore trial for Muttammal since it meant that she must cook her own food in a kitchen all by herself. The poor child fretted against this till she read the story of the meal prepared for the disciples on the shore. "Who cooked the fish?" There was a long pause. "Why, our Lord must have cooked it Himself! It doesn't say an angel came to do it." Another pause. Then, in awed and penitent tones, "And I didn't want to do my own cooking!"

Close watch had to be kept at all times, for if anyone succeeded in tying on her the marriage jewel, she was legally his property. There were repeated summonses to court, the relatives trotting out "proofs" that the girl was being illegally detained, and arguing among themselves as to whose were the rights. It was a cardinal principle of British rule in India that religious neutrality must be maintained. Amy's claim that she was protecting the child from danger, whether from marriage customs or religious activities that were iniquitous, was seen as a breach of that principle. A year or so before Muttammal's coming Amy had visited a temple child, "a little dove in a cage," and had seen the powers of the system at work.

I did not find that she minded her cage. The bars have been gilded, the golden glitter has dazzled the child. She thinks her cage a pretty place, and she does not beat against its bars as she did in the earlier days of her captivity. As we talked with her we understood the change. When first she was taken from school the woman to whose training her mother has committed her gave her polluting poetry to read and learn, and she shrank from it, and would slip her Bible over the open page and read it instead. But gradually the poetry seemed less impossible; the atmosphere in which those vile stories grew and flourished was all about her; as she breathed it day by day she became accustomed to it; the sense of being stifled passed. The process of mental acclimatisation is not yet completed, the lovely little face is still pure and strangely innocent in its expression; but there is a change, and it breaks the heart of the friend who loves her to see it. "I must learn my poetry. They will be angry if I do not learn it. What can I do?" And again, "Oh, the stories do not mean anything," said with a downward glance, as if the child-conscience still protested. It is worse with that little girl today; there is less inward revolt; and tomorrow how will it be with her?[1]

So it would be with Muttammal if the mother had her way. Amy would not give up the fight.

Life in Dohnavur was not "put on hold" while Muttammal's case dragged on. Day and night the babies were there. In Amy's Bible, on a card pasted inside the front cover, are these words:

"These children are dear to Me. Be a mother to them, and more than a mother. Watch over them tenderly, be just and kind. If thy heart is not large enough to embrace them, I will enlarge it after a pattern of My own. If these young children are docile and obedient, bless Me for it; if they are froward, call upon Me for help; if they

---

1. Amy Carmichael, *Lotus Buds*, p. 307.

weary thee, I will be thy consolation; if thou sink under thy burden, I will be thy Reward." The words are followed by a picture of the Shepherd, reaching for a lamb while a vulture hovers overhead.

Amy's children were growing, inquiring, needing to be taught. She must be more than a mother. As she walked the paths of the compound, worked in the nurseries and kitchens, lay on her grass mat at night and thought and planned and prayed, she was forming what might be called a philosophy of education. To name it as such would not have occurred to her, but certain principles began to emerge. Two things, both central to her character, her work, her writing, forbade the use of fiction in any form, including fairy tales. These were her concepts of truth and of soldierhood. She quoted from Plato's *Republic:* " 'War implies soldiers, and soldiers must be carefully trained to their profession. They must be strong, swift, and brave; high-spirited, but gentle.'

"But how must they be educated? In the first place we must be very scrupulous about the *substance* of the stories which they are taught in their childhood. . . . Truth, courage, and self-control must be inculcated by all the stories that are employed in their education."

She saw fiction, not as a powerful vehicle for Truth with a capital T, but as a waste of time and, much worse, a threat to the foundations of character. When "true fairy tales," far more magical than any of man's devising, were "happening" every day in field and garden, why lead the children into make-believe? What God made was Reality to her. Anything men made was a poor substitute.

"I do not think our little lovables lost anything of the silvery glamour that should make the first years of childhood like moonlit water to look back upon, or the golden sparkle either, that is sunlight on that same water."[2] It is possible, however, as one member observed years later, that they had lost something necessary: the capacity to discriminate between fact and fancy. The exercise of the child's imagination was limited to personifying the flora and fauna, but was not free to roam through castles and caves, the throne-rooms of kings or the workshops of elves. Perhaps Amy feared that the children might be drawn toward Hindu mythology or "wis-

---

2. *Gold Cord*, p. 67.

dom" writing, stories with a sometimes dubious moral, thought to be the source of Aesop's fables and other similar literature.

"We never suggested questions and never answered any that they did not ask (we had as much as we could do to find answers to those they did ask) but we, as it were, ran to meet their minds in welcome. It was a merry kind of schooling, and left many gaps, but it had some uses." They learned about color, and examined the chlorophyll in leaf cells through a microscope. They collected shells, abandoned birds' nests, stones, flowers. They went on a field trip to watch a refiner of gold at work. One especially bright girl began to study Greek while recovering from illness, so that she might read the New Testament in the original. The children were allowed to have pets, and were taught to treat them with gentle sympathy or at least with respect, even the termites, who were "trying to be good" by doing their job industriously, and the cobra and bandicoot, who had not "asked" to be a cobra and a bandicoot.

Besides hymns and songs of faith, Amy wrote hundreds of songs especially for the children, from the simplest little game songs ("Rabbit dear, do come here, we want to play with you") to songs embodying science lessons about the potter wasp, the rotifer and the animalcula, or a work song taken from words of the Apocrypha, "Hate not laborious work, joy, joy is in it."

Muttammal had been claimed again by her mother, but in December of 1909 she was once again released to Amy's care. The January *Scrap* letter tells of the journey home together, "in a dream."

At last the red roofs of the bungalow and nurseries appeared through the trees. Slowly the bandy crawled along the rutty lane leading up to the gate. Then there was a delirious rout, a rush and a shout and a sense of everyone everywhere—Muttammal's monkey, Tumbie, was tossed in upon us, a rolled-up ball of fur. . . . But that welcome, like some other best things, has to be left undescribed. It was an hour of perfectly unshadowed joy. My birthday had been spent in Palamcottah where the dear sisters made it as birthday-like as such a battle day could be, but now came the proper jubilations. After a welcome afternoon tea I was established on a stool in the compound. My room had been decorated during tea time, though as no one knew we were coming I could not imagine how the palm branches and other glories had been produced.

Then in a long line from the nurseries and Rooms of Love and Joy came the babies in blue and the children in white and yellow, all carrying flowers, such a pretty, pretty picture in the softened evening light. Nearly all the bigger people had a tiny packet wrapped in tissue paper. Each contained a pocket handkerchief worked in drawn thread by the giver.

Amy Carmichael loved celebration. If the Children of Israel needed feasts and celebrations and piles of stones to teach them the significance of life and death and sacrifice and the leading of God, why should not the children of Dohnavur need the same? Her deep sense of the importance of observance of special occasions pervaded the life of the compound.

In 1910 Suhinie, one of the loveliest of the convert girls who cared for babies, whose story is told in *From the Forest*, was taken with a seizure and died within a few hours. While Amy's grief was honest and human, she saw the Homegoing of a baby or any of the Lord's lovers as an occasion for joy. Her love of the natural and simple determined the method of burial which became the Family's standard. Clad in an old white sari, Suhinie was carried to the garden, later called "God's Garden," on a cane cot covered with flowers. "If the Lord Jesus does not come first, this is what I shall ask for," Amy wrote. "No waste, for the living are so needy, no fuss, only loving hands near, and only flowers between me and the good earth."

The schoolboys, led by Mr. Walker, were first in the procession, then the bier, followed by the women. "Coming home, I remembered Aristides: 'And if any righteous person of their number (speaking of Christians) passes away from this world, they rejoice and give thanks to God; and they follow his body as if he were moving from one place to another.' So we sang the happiest things we could."

In accord with this vision of life the first nurseries had been built of the simplest, most natural materials—sun-dried bricks with earthen floors and thatched roofs, like the ordinary Indian buildings surrounding them. They had not reckoned on the time it would take to maintain such buildings. Termites (the cute nursery song notwithstanding) were a constant nuisance, constructing their tunnels up the walls. The mud floors had to be treated each week with cow dung to harden the surface. Thatched roofs were the perfect target for any who might want to take revenge by setting them on fire.

Could it be right to spend the Lord's money on more expensive materials? If it was given specifically for that, they would accept it as His permission. As usual, they asked Him about it. The money came, specially designated, and they built a nursery and kindergarten with burnt brick for walls and tiles for roofs and floors. The rooms were Indian—unfurnished except for plain cupboards. There were brass vessels, kept bright with hand polishing, using wood ashes. The beds were grass mats, laid on the polished red tiles. The floor tiles in the schoolroom were the children's "blackboard" on which they wrote and drew with chalk.

The visitor today sees the same scrupulous cleanliness and order which was of such importance to the founder. She taught the children to keep their little world orderly—theirs was not a God of confusion. Paths were swept daily, floors scrubbed, gardens weeded, "because of the cloud of witnesses"—the communion of the unseen body of Christ and all His angels, who saw where no human eye might see.

And why should not the place be beautiful? Some years before, when Amy was in Travancore on an evangelistic tour, she had admired the ancient style of its buildings in contrast to the "hideous English style" of one of the rajah's palaces.

"Why people should build ugly buildings when they might as well build beautiful, is as great a puzzle to me as why they should go in for ugly colors when pretty ones are to be had. But we noticed wherever we traveled that the most graceful and beautiful things flourished best out of the sphere of English influence."

The style of the Dohnavur structures as they are today combines what she found in Travancore with certain elements brought by missionaries from China. All of the buildings are of the same red color as the earth out of which they seem to have risen. Earth-red, too, are the seven-foot walls which surround the property. A visitor cannot fail to notice these, and may question the wisdom of thus separating the Family from the world outside. To Amy the disadvantages, great as they might be, were not nearly so great as the necessity to protect the children. Occasionally a tiger found its way from the nearby hills, but there were other "tigers," far more to be feared.

All through the year 1910 there were rumblings about Muttammal. She was not out of danger. In January 1911, Amy was summoned again to court. In March came "the supreme hour of the long fight, the hour of utmost defeat, when for the first time we tasted public shame and scorn, and knew how little we had drunk as yet of the cup of our Saviour's agony for souls."

On the night before she was to appear in Palamcottah in court she lay on the cane cot on her verandah in the starlight. Her child Muttammal lay in her arms. We do not find the mother frantic with anxiety, or seeking, by sundry deceptions, to steer the child away from the reality of what might take place. Instead she speaks to the little girl, so lately introduced to Jesus, about His mysterious message to John the Baptist just before he was beheaded: "Blessed is he who is not offended in Me."

"I took her hands in mine and looked down into her upturned face. 'Promise me, whatever happens, by His grace, you will never be offended in Him.' " Muttammal promised.

Amy went alone to court in the morning. "We were as those smitten in the place of dragons." The clerk floundered slowly through thirty or forty pages, the voice droning through the heavy heat till he came to words which "stung like a whip-lash"—Muttammal must be returned to her mother, all legal costs to be paid by Amy.

At the moment of the verdict Amy experienced a sudden strange, triumphant joy, a shining, perhaps, of the Lord's face. She could not explain it, but it was worth all the subsequent hours which were "emptied of all conscious illumination."

What she did not know was that by this time Muttammal had disappeared from Dohnavur. No one knew where she had gone. Weeks of silence and uncertainty passed, broken only by an anonymous postcard with the words of 2 Chronicles 16:9,[3] suggesting

---

3. "The eyes of the Lord run to and fro throughout the whole earth, to show himself strong in the behalf of them whose heart is perfect toward him."

that Muttammal was safe. It was months before she learned the story. A guest, Mabel Beath, to whom Amy had confided, had dressed the child as a Muslim boy and sent her out of the compound by a certain gate. Two Indians met her with a bandy and by circuitous means she was taken to Colombo, Ceylon.

For Amy, of course, the situation could be far more serious than heretofore. Prison looked like a very real possibility. Other children might be endangered. But she clung in faith to the promises of God and went for her usual holiday to the hills. There she met an old friend whom she asked for help. He found the child in Ceylon, escorted her to Penang, Singapore, and Hong Kong, then six hundred miles up the West River to the home of missionaries. For six months they did not hear of her whereabouts. In October came the letter saying she was safe.

Four years later Amy had another of her dreams. She saw Muttammal being married to one of the young men of Dohnavur. She told him of the dream; they consulted Arulai, by then a trusted fellow-worker, who said she had been praying about this very thing for a year. For the man there was nothing unusual about an arranged marriage. It was the custom. So in due time letters were written, the two were engaged, married in Colombo (according to every detail of Amy's dream), and returned to Dohnavur six years after Muttammal's nighttime escape.

Chapter 26
Love Is Not a Sentiment

L et those parents that desire Holy Children learn to make them possessors of Heaven and Earth betimes," wrote Traherne, "to remove silly objects from before them, to magnify nothing but what is great indeed, and to talk of God to them, and of His works and ways before they can either speak or go."

Holy Children. That describes what Amy Carmichael as mother desired from the very beginning of the children's work. Many of those children are old women now, living quietly in the red brick bungalows of Dohnavur after years of self-giving. "Be the first," their Amma had told them, "wherever there is a sacrifice to be made, a self-denial to be practiced, or an impetus to be given." It was no empty pedantry. Her own life made the truth visible to her children. The word became flesh and lived with them.

"When we were very small we were on the wings of her love," said one, but that love had little of sentimentality in it. Nearly all her children speak of her love, but many mention their fear of her as well. She was strict. "No work that is set on following the Crucified escapes the Cross," she wrote in *Kohila*, the story of the shaping of an Indian nurse.[1] "It would not wish to do so. Sooner or later, if those who must give account to God do not weaken on some point of loyalty to Truth, they will find themselves bearing the Reproach of Christ." Always in her consciousness was the solemn charge that was hers as one accountable to God for these little ones. It were better that a millstone be hung round her neck than for her to cause one of them to stumble.

---

1. Amy Carmichael, *Kohila*, p. vii.

Amy with Lullitha, one of her "Lotus Buds."

The Book of Proverbs speaks of the need of the rod in the training of children. The parent who does not use it hates the child. Love, therefore, requires self-discipline, self-denial, and courage. It took all of those for Amy to use a cane or a leather strap on a child's wrists. Like her own mother, she expected the child to hold out her arm without flinching. Often the spanking was followed by a kiss and a piece of candy. Amy took the responsibility of administering these punishments herself rather than asking it of the *accals* (older sisters) or *sitties* (mother's younger sisters, the name used for European workers). She, after all, was the mother. If a sittie or accal felt that a caning was called for, she would send the child to Amma with a note. Those notes, it is reported, did not always reach their destination. At least one child arrived with a bright smile and the candid admission that sittie had sent her with a note. But where was the note? "I swallowed it!" was the answer.

Other punishments were more imaginative. A child who lied might have quinine put on her tongue or a sign that said LIE hung round her neck for half a day. One little girl who lied habitually had her mouth inked and was kept out of school for a day or so. After the second or third time she was taken to Amma's room. "I was shaking. She sent me to the bathroom for the strap, took me on her lap in front of a mirror, and read to me from Isaiah 53— 'He was wounded for our transgressions, he was bruised for our iniquities. . . . All we like sheep have gone astray; we have turned every one to his own way and the Lord hath laid on him the iniquity of us all.' Then she beat her own arm instead of mine and explained salvation to me. Without understanding I said 'Yes, Amma,' but I had not changed a whit. When I was thirty-three I was rude to one of the workers and was sent to my room without food to think. When I came out the worker was there. I kissed his hand, he kissed my forehead. That was heaven to me."

When two little girls quarreled, Amy tied their pigtails together so that they might be obliged to walk in harmony. A child of seven who could not stop biting her nails went to Amy with flowers one day. "Darling, I want to talk to you," she said, and took the child's hands. "You have beautiful fingers. What have you been doing to them? Aren't these the Lord's hands?" The child was terrified.

"Don't be afraid," said Amy, and kissed the hands. "Promise me and the Lord Jesus you will stop. Then come and see me again next week." It worked. The child kept her promise.

"I am reminded of how she suffered for her dear children in pointing out Nature as the Second Bible," wrote one of them. "I remember her rushing out of her house when she heard that someone was killing a beetle with a stone. She got hold of my tiny hand and hit me with the same stone, stating that the beetle had all freedom to live unless it came inside the house. I was only ten then, so I remember crying, but the lesson learnt was forever to be kind to any creature."

Amy's partiality to certain children could not be disguised. Of a five-year-old who died she wrote, "Lulla was perhaps the only child we had who would quite have satisfied the most critical taste. There was a delicacy of feature and creaminess of coloring which is rare in southern India, and her sweetness of disposition combined with a bright intelligence added something which made her peculiarly precious to us all." The most critical taste, of course, meant the most critical European taste. Indians with Aryan blood, of fair skin and silky hair, were, naturally enough, most appealing to the European in Amy, as indeed to the upper-caste Indian. The black Dravidians of the south find less place in the photographs she included in her books, though this may have been the photographer's choice.

"Because I was dark I was always put at the back," said one. "She loved the fair ones. I was caned. Tara, who was fair, was only put in the corner. When years later I asked Amma why, her answer was, 'You needed the cane. Tara needed the corner.' " To another who taxed her with favoritism she said, "Oh darling—I did not mean it!" and it was forgotten.

"Chellalu and Seela were clever and mischievous," said another of the older women. "Amma liked them for that. But I was a crybaby. I was dull and did not like lessons. I liked hard work. Even now I like it. I had no troubles with Amma. I always did things properly. But she did not love me much. She did not want a sulky child in front of guests. When I was ten years old I went to work in the nursery as a *tungachie*, a younger sister. Amma did get angry if she found a baby wet. 'But I have thirteen babies under eighteen months to care for!' I said. Oh, she was a dear, loving person."

Amy admitted that they were sometimes so shorthanded that the children who became "little helping nurses" were pressed into service before they were really old enough. But they learned "all manner of useful things," their devotion to the babies was remarkably constant, considering their immaturity, and they were "trained to look upon it as the most honorable as well as the happiest work."

When a child came to Dohnavur the date was recorded and celebrated yearly as her Coming Day, since exact birth dates were hard to determine. On that day, in the years before the size of the Family made it impossible, the child was allowed to go early in the morning to Amy's room and have chota with her in bed. Each child received a tiny piece of scented soap and a card as Coming Day presents, and then there was the wonderful gift cupboard from which she could select something else. Amy would talk to her of what she had been saved from— "a wicked, wicked place"—and of the story of how she came to Dohnavur. One baby, Piratha, arrived while a group were actually on their knees in Amy's room, praying for the salvation of babies.

Once Amy took a girl to the temple in order to show her what she had been saved from. The lesson was lost on the child. She saw how happy the temple girls were, what beautiful jewels they wore. But years later a temple woman who came as a patient to the Dohnavur hospital described to her the real life. "I was a rebel before," she said, "but I was grateful after that."

Tarahai remembers the earnestness with which Amy reminded them, year after year, of the meaning of the name she had given them. "Amma took hold of my hand and said, 'I gave you your name Star that you might be a shining star for the Lord Jesus.'" Karima meant "Singing Bird," Dayala "Grace."

As the children grew up she spoke of her hopes for them. Would they be willing to do what others had done for them—care for babies, wash bottles and diapers, lay down their lives in the nurseries? "I pray that you will be a warrior, and look after children," she said to Dayala. Amy was quick to see other potentialities. "She was a prophet" was the testimony of several. She encouraged some to be hospital nurses, teachers, bookkeepers, and evangelists. If, as often happened, a girl's ambitions were quite other than what Amy envisioned for her, the girl would be reminded of the "easy yoke"

Christ offers, "but if we make our own yoke we shall be miserable."

"Amma wanted me to nurse babies," said one whose name meant Well-Beloved. "I hated that. It was my will to teach. She gave me the Bible verse, 'Take this child and nurse it for me.' " A fourteen-year-old tungachie who seemed a hopeless case and could not control the children was given a whole day alone in a sittie's room to "listen to God." If He would give His presence and help, she decided, she would do anything, like it or not. By the second year she had not only learned how to manage her charges well but had found that the doing of humble work for Christ's sake transformed it into what she now calls "heavenly joy." Shanthie, who worked as a pharmacist for forty years, found that her greatest desires had been fulfilled. "Duty was my pleasure," she said.

Motherwork was relentless at Dohnavur as it is anywhere, and in order to oversee the work in schoolrooms, nurseries, milk kitchens, storerooms, weaving and sewing rooms, Amy whizzed from one to the other on a large tricycle. The picture must have been a startling one to a visitor who happened by—this dumpy little dynamo, careening around corners so enthusiastically that more than once she ended up in the dust. Sometimes she would collect a "set" of girls who ran after the tricycle to see a bird in the garden or to go to her room for an ad hoc prayer meeting. There were moonlight picnics, bandy rides, games when she would play bear. She was an arresting sight on horseback, trotting along the lanes, riding sidesaddle in her creamy pale saris, sometimes inviting a child up onto the horse's back to share the fun.

Although the children's firsthand knowledge was almost solely limited to the compound, their imaginations ranged far beyond its red brick walls. Early one morning Amy roused a houseful of girls to show them the stars for which, six months before, they had named their dolls: Andromeda, Aldebaran, Betelgeuse. When she took them to see the beginnings of a new nursery for which they had prayed, they named the stones for the mountains of Africa.

Loyal love was what Amy called the taproot of the tree that became the Dohnavur Fellowship. She never got away from the memory of that gray day by the gray sea in Shimonoseki, Japan, when a missionary spoke casually of the lack of love among missionaries.

"He that loveth not his brother abideth in *death*." "See that ye love one another with a pure heart fervently." These were the watchwords. Amy resolutely refused to settle for the usual. She would believe God to see a company of His servants knit together in loyal love.

"Never about, always to," was one of the rules. They were not to speak about another person but face to face. Trust was established on this ground.

Another rule: "It must be *Come*, never *Go*. We cannot ask another to do what we have never done or are not willing to do. That is why we ask for our fellowship only those who come 'without a but, an if, or a limit.' " It was a steep hill they were asking the Family to climb. The leaders must climb it first.

Chapter 27
The Lesson of the Weaned Child

The year 1912 was a year of stripping. The power allowed to the enemy seemed at times far beyond the limits the love of God might set.

On August 13 Amy Carmichael's spiritual mother in India, Mrs. Hopwood, died. She was the hostess at Ooty, the place of cool refreshment in the hills where Amy had spent every hot spell for fifteen years. To know that Mrs. Hopwood was there was strength and cheer to Amy. She counted on her continual prayers. She looked to her for sympathy, understanding, and godly, motherly counsel. The road was going to be steeper without that support.

On August 17 little Lulla, leader of kindergarten games and "all nursery joys," died. She had always been delicate, so Ponnammal had kept her in her own nursery. Her breathing seemed strange one evening, then there was a sore throat and low fever. In two days she smiled such a smile as none of them had seen before, kissed Mabel Wade, her nurse, flung her arms round Amy's neck, and was gone. "She was the sort of child who nestles into the heart and we could not help her slipping into that innermost place, which perhaps should never be given to any little child. And yet He said 'Love . . . as I have loved you.' We cannot love too much."

Nor could they help wondering about the possibility of something especially satanic in the "selection" of those who died and those who were left. Several retarded and other "utterly unsuitable" children rarely gave any anxiety and survived every illness. The real "temple child," on the other hand, the child who was their reason for being, "no sooner reaches us than something almost inevitably happens, sometimes an accident, sometimes an illness. Often, so often, the newly ransomed little one is snatched away by death. It cannot be a mere chance happening. It occurs too frequently for us to think so now. But if the devil has anything to do with it, thank God—after that there is no more that he can do, and his worst only sends the little life far out of his reach forever. It is a mystery, a secret thing, and the secret things belong unto the Lord."

Exactly a week after Lulla's death came the master stroke. Thomas Walker, leader, strong tower of courage and comfort, father and brother to all, died of ptomaine poisoning. Mrs. Walker was in England because of illness. He was holding a mission when the sickness struck, and so was "crowned upon the battlefield."

Kind people, wanting to console, made the usual observation: "It is very hard to see how this can be for the best."

"We are not asked to SEE," said Amy. "Why need we when we KNOW?" We know—not the answer to the inevitable Why, but the incontestable fact that it *is* for the best. "It is an irreparable loss, but is it faith at all if it is 'hard to trust' when things are entirely bewildering?"

Others, with a sigh and a shake of the head, observed that it is difficult for us human beings to escape bitterness, even dumb rage, when such things happen.

"It is indeed not only difficult, it is impossible," Amy wrote. "There is only one way of victory over the bitterness and rage that come naturally to us—*To will what God wills brings peace.*"

"But are such things the will of God at all?" Amy herself raised the question, and answered it:

The honest heart cannot be content with platitudes. "An enemy hath done this" is a word that reaches far and touches more than tares. If an enemy has done it, how can it be called the will of God? We do not know the answer to that question now. But we have sidelights upon it, such as the vision in Revelation: They overcame him by the Blood of the Lamb and by the word of their testimony (victory through apparent defeat). . . . And as we rest our hearts upon what we know (the certainty of the ultimate triumph of good) leaving what we do not know to the Love that has led us all our life long, the peace of God enters into us and abides.

The Lesson of the Weaned Child

Just before Walker left for his mission, a group of them had been sitting under the stars in deck chairs. Amy was seized suddenly with the thought of how it would be if she did not have Walker's strong arm to lean on in the work. She could not do without it, she said. "Well, you are not asked to!" said Walker with a laugh. But hers was still the soldier spirit, and when the wire came she was still under the same Captain. Her orders had not changed: Give up your right to yourself, take up the cross, follow. The Captain had been over the course before. Would she refuse to obey now? It was a lesson that had to be reviewed many times, for her as for any soldier. She wrote of that lesson in a prayer-poem:

> From prayer that asks that I may be
> Sheltered from winds that beat on Thee,
> From fearing when I should aspire,
> From faltering when I should climb higher,
> From silken self, O Captain, free
> Thy soldier who would follow Thee.
>
> From subtle love of softening things,
> From easy choices, weakenings,
> (Not thus are spirits fortified,
> Not this way went the Crucified,)
> From all that dims Thy Calvary,
> O Lamb of God, deliver me.
>
> Give me the love that leads the way,
> The faith that nothing can dismay
> The hope no disappointments tire
> The passion that will burn like fire,
> Let me not sink to be a clod:
> Make me Thy fuel, Flame of God.

"The searching forces of bereavement" were not abated. One week after Walker's death a little girl of eight died, and within a few months it was found that the beloved Ponnammal had cancer. Amy knew and fully believed that the touch of Christ still had its ancient power. She had seen it often, and had herself been given, for a short

Ponnammal, with Preetha and Tara.

time, the gift of a healing touch. But for Ponnammal she had no liberty to "claim" a healing.

"We hardly understand the use of that phrase; we know too little to 'claim' where temporal blessings are concerned." But they prayed. Amy prayed. The accals and sitties prayed. The children, one of whose songs told the story of the little girl who wanted blue eyes, prayed. Was the answer to be yes or no?

"We knew our Father. There was no need for persuasion. Would not His Fatherliness be longing to give us our hearts' desire (if I may put it so)? How could we press Him as though He were not our own most loving Father?"

Amy spent three months in the Salvation Army hospital at Nagercoil with Ponnammal, nursing her through two operations while she herself suffered from neuralgia and seventy children in Dohnavur (of the Family which by then numbered a hundred and forty) came down with malaria. In July of the same year, 1913, Amy's mother died. The *Daily Light* reading for the day the cable came was from the Song of Solomon: "Awake, O north wind; and come, thou south; blow upon my garden, that the spices thereof may flow out." If the life of a man or woman on earth is to bear the fragrance of heaven the winds of God must blow on that life, winds not always balmy from the south, but fierce winds from the north that chill the very marrow. It seemed a howling gale that had been let loose on Amy that year.

How was she to go on? She was an orphan. Her own parents gone, her spiritual father and mother gone. She had not known life without such support. Nor has the child, when weaning time comes, known life without its unfailing source of nourishment. Like the weaned child, Amy knew that the lesson assigned now was to learn to do without. She wrote another prayer:

> And shall I pray Thee change Thy will, my Father,
> Until it be according unto mine?
> But, no, Lord, no, that never shall be, rather
> I pray Thee blend my human will with Thine.
>
> I pray Thee hush the hurrying, eager longing,
> I pray Thee soothe the pangs of keen desire—
> See in my quiet places, wishes thronging—
> Forbid them, Lord, purge, though it be with fire.
>
> And work in me to will and do Thy pleasure
> Let all within me, peaceful, reconciled,
> Tarry content my Well-Beloved's leisure,
> At last, at last, even as a weaned child.

Chapter 28
Across the Will of Nature

Matthew Arnold's tribute to his father in *Rugby Chapel* was for Amy "one of the lights I steer by."

> If in the paths of the world
> Stones might have wounded thy feet,
> Toil and dejection have tried
> Thy spirit, of that we saw nothing.
> To us thou wast still
> Cheerful and helpful and firm. . . .
> Languor is not in your heart,
> Weakness is not in your word,
> Weariness not on your brow.

We are allowed to see a good many of the stones that wounded Amy's feet, but we hardly hear her say "Ouch!" The power of her passions breathes in every word she writes, but because her aim was always to tell only that part of the truth which in her view *mattered*, that is, would edify and strengthen, she often sidestepped a description of what today's reader would find most fascinating. Walker's death was without question a stunning blow. Even if it had not come in succession with so many other blows, she would have reeled under it. If she succumbed to as much as a few moments of self-pity, she did not permit herself the luxury of wallowing in it. She knew where to turn to regain a firm footing: first to her God, and then to the thought of others—Mrs. Walker, for example, whose loss, Amy told herself, was infinitely greater than her own. The lesson of the weaned child was learned far more quickly than it might have been because she set about at once writing Walker's biography, a task which would transform her own loss by giving to the world the story of a hidden life.

Although at their first meeting she was impressed with the jet-black hair, the earnest eyes, the wisdom and learning and, most of all, the utter absence of narrow-mindedness, she had decided that she did not like him. He seemed to take with less than proper seriousness her desire to burn out rather than rust out. Could he possibly understand such a motive? Later she knew how perfectly he understood. He understood as no one else in India could understand.

And Amy loved him. To read the biography is to know that she loved him. Her love had never been half-hearted for anyone. She was all that a sister could be for her own brothers and sisters, devoted to each. But Walker was what she had not had at home, an older brother, and far more. She was brilliant, personable, charming—more so, it is said, than his wife. The scenario could have been explosive if all three had not been soldiers under orders. Walker loved his wife. Amy loved and respected her, worked closely with her, although it was not easy for her to live with a couple so obviously in love.

By the time World War I began Amy had finished writing the biography, *Walker of Tinnevelly*. She held it back from publication until 1916, feeling that people would not want to read anything other than war news.

With the war came increased anxiety for the children. The thought of their future had always been of paramount concern. "What are you going to do with them all in the future?" people had repeatedly asked, sometimes with a tone which implied she had not given the matter a thought. "She lives in a Utopia," said one. "I pity her, I pity her with all my heart when I think of all that is before her when her children grow up!"

"Neither of these sanguine sympathizers nor one out of a hundred questioners has any idea of how their doubts appeal to the anxious part of us, for—

> Far in the future
> Lieth a fear,

Like a long, low mist of grey,
Gath'ring to fall in a dreary rain,
Thus doth thy heart within thee complain;
And even now thou art afraid, for round thy dwelling
The flying winds are ever telling
Of the fear that lieth grey,
Like a gloom of brooding mist upon the way.
But the Lord is always kind,
Be not blind,
Be not blind
To the shining of His face,
To the comforts of His grace.
Hath He ever failed thee yet?
Never, never: wherefor fret? . . ."[1]

There was not only the question about what the children were to do when they grew up but also the question of how their thousands of needs (there were nine nurseries now) were to be met in the process. The temptation to fear became very strong in the early years, "a gloom of brooding mist upon the way," and Amy was "allowed to taste of the cup which would be poured out for me if the money did not come." She recalled Allan Gardiner, missionary to South America, who was allowed to starve to death. As usual, her hyperactive imagination went to work on that one. "Suppose the children die and we all (of course) die with them, and the Christian world cries shame on the one responsible, what will it matter, after all? The children will be in heaven, and is that not better than the temple?" She took her questions as usual to the faithful Master who pointed her to the story of the feeding of the five thousand.

"And, as I believed, the promise was given to me then that there should be baskets over and above our daily supplies, and that, just as those men and women and their children were free to use the pieces of the loaves over from that great meal if they needed them before they reached home, so we should be free to use ours, should need arise before we too reached Home, we and our children."

More money than was needed then began to come in, so that by the time the British pound fell and the price of rice rose during the

---

1. *Toward Jerusalem*, p. 8.

war (sending the cost of bringing a child from the nearest station to fifteen times its former cost), the "baskets" were ready. "Standing on sure ground we can affirm just this: we have never lacked any good thing; and during the years of War, people in the towns and villages began to say, 'God is there,' for they could not account for what they saw except by saying that."

Life in Dohnavur was very like that of a cloister in many ways, and it is hard to see how it could have been otherwise, at least in those early days. The work which had to be done was all-consuming, there were few to do it and no time for extraneous activity. But Amy's sympathies were broad, her reading wide, and during the war she wrote "always with a sense of the sorrow in the homes to which this letter goes. What flaming fires of sorrow you are walking through these months! God comfort you all."

As one worker commented, "Amma went from crisis to crisis. She saw things as crises—but we had them, God knows, frightful ones!" Once a village lunatic got loose, came into the compound, entered the guest room where a lady was sleeping, lifted her mosquito net, gazed at her, and then sat down in her chair. She remained calm and the man left, but returned. Amy armed herself with a flashlight and a cane, "hoping he would prove amenable to the light and not require further incentive to disappear." She did not have to apply either, as the servants appeared and escorted him home. It was all in a night's work, however. "We have a tame lunatic always on hand who chops our wood and has scraps from the kitchen, but this was a new and not at all a pleasant sort to have about."

There were occasions when the mother was able, with a select group of her children and co-workers, to leave the cloistered life of Dohnavur. Often they made forays in the moonlight out to the plain, which necessitated passing through the village. Once they paused in front of the temple where the men were gathered and Amy spoke to them. "They were as attentive as the women, for they don't hear 'preaching' every day and always enjoy a novelty." Then little Chellalu, one of the more mischievous children, asked in a stage whisper if she too might speak. She "opened fire on those men, pelting them with facts as to their folly in worshipping some-

At Madras Beach.

body who did not love them and had not made them." Her hearers
stood amazed. Chellalu explained later to Amy: "When you were
speaking, a voice inside me said very loud, yes, *very* loud, 'Chellalu!
Tell those men about God!' and my heart said *pickapickapick!*"

Then there was a grand tour to Madras. Amy took fourteen
children, five helpers, one servant, and one sittie on the train to the
big city. They traveled third-class as always. Why? "Because there
isn't any fourth-class!" On the way they saw for the first time a
railway station, telegraph wires, signaling systems, the palace and
temple of Madurai, bazaars, motorcars, and then in Madras itself, a
motorcycle with a sidecar in which they rode, museums, a foundry,
a printing press, a cotton factory and—this was a first for Amy,
too—a movie. A friend arranged for a "good set" of pictures to be
shown instead of the "usual doubtful vulgarities." The children
thought the pictures alive, and were most astonished at the speed
with which the soldiers in the war pictures walked. Amy, tired of
the customary Oriental saunter, exhorted the girls to follow the soldiers' brisk example.

A clergyman took them to Madras Beach and, dressed in black

suit, clerical collar, and sun helmet, strode into the surf to take pictures of the girls, fully clothed in their white saris which were knotted up around the knees, wading. One of the rare photos of Amma shows her sitting in a beached boat, wearing her sari and helmet, surrounded by satin-haired girls with thick braids, her white hand resting on a black one.

It was during this trip that the issue of furloughs for foreign workers came up. Frances Beath was the sittie accompanying Amy. Her parents, who were in Madras then, wanted Frances to go home to Australia with them. Frances demurred. It was not the time. The parents and many friends thought this quite wrong, a decision not made in freedom but under duress—at least the duress of Amy's powerful example. She had never taken a furlough. The mother's feet, according to the Tamil proverb, were tied. Old Mr. Beath pleaded with her to release his daughter. There was no question of releasing her. The young woman was technically quite free to go, but Amy refused to persuade her.

"Supposing you knew the Lord Jesus was to return soon," said Amy. "What would you do?"

"Why, tell her to stay, of course!" said the man without hesitation. In a flash, he saw what he had said. He laughed. They gave their consent. The issue arose again and again in subsequent years when fellow-workers, feeling "a bit skeletonic," as one of them put it, raised the question of a furlough or even just a weekend off. All were given to understand from the first that the nature of the work made regular furlough plans impossible. If the doctors insisted on what Amy called "exile" for health reasons, it was granted. Otherwise she simply laid before them the principle that governed her own life: Ask not how little but how much can love give? She would allow them to choose the harder road, as she had written just after the Frances Beath experience.

If we would walk with an ungrieved Lord we must never let the fear of being thought "hard" or, far more subtle temptation, the fear of pain for a younger one whom we love, cause us to influence that one to choose the natural rather than the spiritual. If once a soul has entered the path where the Spirit, not the flesh, is guide, God does not lightly pass over such a lapse. Men may praise it; God condemns it; and those who know their Father know the bitterness of the hiding of His face.

She quoted again, as often in her writings, Tersteegen's poem:

> Across the will of Nature
>   Leads on the path of God;
> Not where the flesh delighteth
>   The feet of Jesus trod.
> O bliss to leave behind us
>   The fetters of the slave,
> To leave ourselves behind us,
>   The graveclothes and the grave.
>
> We follow in His footsteps;
>   What if our feet be torn?
> Where He has marked the pathway
>   All hail the briar and thorn!
> Scarce seen, scarce heard, unreckoned,
>   Despised, defamed, unknown,
> Or heard but by our singing,
>   On, children, ever on!

Chapter 29
Grey Jungle, Crystal Pool

Ponnammal, whose cancer had been discovered in April 1913, became very ill again in the following year. Several times she heard music when no earthly music was being played. Amy took it as one of "the many things of life which we may only know in part until for us too the curtain of sense wears thin."

The epistle of James says that the sick should call for the elders of the church to anoint them. Should they do that now? They were not sure. Amy was used to being given some sign to confirm a Scripture verse. So they prayed that if they should, someone who was earnest about following this primitive church custom should come along. He came, an old friend from Madras. It was a solemn meeting around the sickbed, the women dressed as usual in their handloomed saris, but white ones for this occasion. They laid a palm branch across Ponnammal's bed as a sign of victory and accepted whatever answer God might give, certain that whether it was to be physical healing or not, He would give victory and peace. It sounds like a simple formula. It was an act of faith, but certainly accompanied by the anguish of doubt and desire which had to be brought again and again under the authority of the Master.

The answer that came was that Ponnammal, from the very day of the anointing, grew rapidly worse. She lay for days without speaking, her dull eyes half-open, seeming to see nothing. The pain was violent, kept under only by large doses of morphia. "She has been walking through the valley of the shadow of death. I never knew how dense that shadow could become, for I never before watched anyone dying in this slow, terrible way. . . . Nothing was visible but the distress and depression of this most fearful disease."

Once when she seemed to be in unimaginable misery she told Amy how she had longed to be allowed to stay. She thought she could help a little "if the pain did not pass this limit." "It seemed to me the most unselfish word I had ever heard from human lips." Ponnammal touched the limit at last—the limit divinely set to pain—and her "warfare was accomplished" on August 26, 1915. She would never be replaced. She had been among the best. But "we shall have our best again, purified, perfected, assured from change forever." That was the ground of hope.

There was relief in September from the long strain when Amy took a group of children up into the forest near Dohnavur for a few weeks in a government bungalow. It was no longer possible to move such a family to the distant hill resorts, and Amy, always zealously protective of her children, feared European influences there that would contribute nothing to their spiritual welfare. There were worldly distractions which might sow discontent among her children. She saw the need for rest and change, however, and asked God for some provision.

It was an experiment, and the house was primitive. The floor was cement, there were no facilities, it was dank and cold when it rained. Everything but water had to be transported from the plain by coolies. But the weeks were glorious, full of flower collecting, swimming and diving in the pool of a rushing mountain river, hunting for animal tracks (wild elephant tracks by the hundred), bears' holes, tiger spoor. Amy and three cohorts gave the others "a shivering half hour" by hiding behind a tree and growling. "There was a wild rush up to the house, and then to our immense gratification we saw the whole household turn out with sticks, led by Sellamutthu, horribly alarmed but valiant."

What the holiday did for the children was salutary. What it did for Amy was something else. In October she was very ill, so ill that, according to a private note in a journal, she "gave way." To her friends at home she said nary a word about her health, but admitted that "various things happened which interrupted the even flow of life." (A biographer would be hard put to single out two days in a row when the flow of life in Dohnavur could be described as "even.") By giving way she probably meant that she let someone else know she was in pain. Perhaps she had to go to bed. "Distress of thought of doctor being called to leave far needier people for me. Distress of finding some dear ones overburdened because I had given way." She prayed, perhaps not for the first time and certainly not for the last, "Do not let me be ill and a burden or anxiety to anyone. O let me finish my course with joy and not with grief. . . . Let me die of a battle-wound, O my Lord, not of a lingering illness. Forgive this prayer if it be wrong."

In the same month it was discovered that Arulai, who had been pronounced cured of tuberculosis, now had Bright's disease, "another of those grave trials which give us a chance to prove the things we believe." Arulai, Amy's "Star," treasure of all treasures, the Elisha on whom Amy had begun to believe the mantle was to fall. On one of the worst days Amy was walking in the circle of nursery cottages called the Round, praying and thinking of Walker, Ponnammal, Arulai—"our three strongest spiritual influences, the three upon whom I could always count for strength of character as well as for spiritual power: Lord, must Thou take them all?" In early November the answer seemed to be yes. Arulai's pulse faded, she refused her medicine, and could not speak. Amy sent a message to a friend: *Come. Arulai dying.* She rallied and survived another twenty-four years.

Amy's determination not to draw attention to herself had not weakened since she first took the nom-de-plume "Nobody" in the little family journal in Belfast. When her biography of Walker was published, a blurb on the dust jacket—praise she was sure she did not deserve—made her "too ashamed to take any pleasure in the book. O my God, I am ashamed before Thee." The same motive of self-effacement must have been at least part of what inspired the periodic binges of "covering her tracks" by destroying diaries, a habit which creates tantalizing gaps in the story. Arulai once succeeded in rescuing part of a notebook before Amy had done away with the whole thing, but only God knows how much went into the fire, or into the maws of termites.

A few years later the governor of Madras sent a wire of congratulation on her having been included in the Royal Birthday Honors

List. Consternation was her response. A *medal?* For service in India, service to Him who had died for her? "I have done nothing to make it fitting, and cannot understand it at all," she wrote to Lord Pentland. "It troubles me to have an experience so different from His Who was despised and rejected, not kindly honored." She was persuaded at last that it would be ungracious to refuse the award, but she put her foot down when it came to attending the presentation ceremony.

The time spent in the government bungalow in the forest convinced everyone that such a place, though a more commodious one, was needed. The sign was asked for and given, and after several rugged and strenuous expeditions across the plain, into the thickets and up the steep ascents to three or four thousand feet, the perfect spot was found—a small, disused coffee plantation, the Grey Jungle. Money came in for a house, and building began. There were innumerable setbacks. Coolies quit working. Rains came at inopportune times and walls collapsed. Caste conflicts arose among the workers, so that the children took over the carrying of mud and bricks and tiles. At times the sawyers refused to saw so the carpenters were out of work. When the masons failed to protect the tops of walls and huddled in their huts while it rained, Amy and the children and Arul Dasan (who with his wife, Muttammal, had joined the work in Dohnavur) stood in the downpour handing up the mats to keep the walls from dissolving again. The house was finished during the last year of the war for five hundred pounds. They named it the Forest House.

"Green, green forest stretching as far as the eye can see on three sides, rising in mighty billows up the mountains, leaving bare only the rocky tops; high climbing, low dipping forest. A valley, like the trough of the wave of forest green. In the middle of the smother of green the red roof of a house, our forest house. . . . In front the trees drop sharply down, like a cliff dropping to the sea, the green, green sea of the forest." So she described the place in the opening chapter of *From the Forest.* And the pool, the joy of their ravine, "jade-green, clear, wonderful water-green, and when the angels are in a very kind mood they send a blue kingfisher to fish there. Then the pool is something quite too lovely for this everyday earth, and sets one thinking what the pools must be among the green woods of Paradise. Then, too, it is deep, deep enough for diving, and its floor of clean white sand, the powdered dust of mountains. In this pool we, the holiday children and whoever is up with them, daily turn into water-babies. . . . If you have troubles, the pool washes them off. Worries are just kissed away."

In the next few years a number of houses were built in the ravine, including the Jungle House and the Jewel House. They met the need for a place to "come apart," as the Lord called His disciples, to "rest awhile."

Amy loved the forest with a passion. She drank its beauty, literally caressed its rocks and trees, sang about it in countless children's songs. Here, for example, are a couple of lines she wrote to the elephant:

> His great big flat feet pound and pound
> With a rumpety—dumpety—crumpety sound.

and to the mosquito:

> Take good advice and promptly go,
> Abominable Mosquito.

Her long poems on the meaning of suffering, *Pools* and *The Valley of Vision*, were probably written here, as well as a number of other books, where isolation, quiet, and coolness made the task of writing less arduous than it was in Dohnavur where such commodities were in short supply. "There is so much sadness in the world, so many hearts ache, so many tears fall, it is rather wonderful to be away for a little while in a tearless world, left just as God made it. . . . these elemental things seem to carry one back to the beginnings, the fundamentals, the things that cannot be shaken, ancient verities of God."[1]

She explored every foot of the purchased land. Long-suffering servants toiled with her up steep cliffs, blazing trails wherever she

---

1. Amy Carmichael, *From the Forest*, p. 78.

wanted to go, lugging up crockery and food when the fancy took her to have a picnic by a just-discovered waterfall, or tea on top of a lookout rock. Children swept the paths daily, decorated the house with flowers, were taught not to disturb other forest dwellers—except for snakes and scorpions, and only if they came into the house. "Then I am afraid we must slay them, for they are where they ought not to be."

She was most insistent that the children learn to swim. She had learned in Millisle and Strangford Lough, but once nearly drowned in the forest pool when a child dragged her under. Never mind, she told them, the sensation of drowning was lovely. No need to alarm the family back in Dohnavur by mentioning it.

On a peaceful Sunday morning, in the midst of Sabbath quiet, "like a stone falling plump into a clear still pool," a fat Brahman gentleman arrived at the Forest House. Amy told the servant who announced his coming to send him to where she sat under a tree. He was a most unwelcome visitor with his retinue, and spoke to her cookboy in a tone "a badly brought up hippopotamus might conceivably use in addressing vermin." But she asked the servant to bring a cup of milk, and while the man poured it down his throat without touching the cup to his lips, she sat on her stone, reproving herself for disliking the intrusion of this man reputed to be "learned and cultured and full of public charities." Later reflection produced "A Song for One in Like Temptation":

> No, not for you He thirsted as He died:
> No, not for you my Lord was crucified;
> Woods, streams, and mountains, innocent are ye:
> Not yours, but mine, the shame of Calvary.
>
> And dear as ye must be to Him, ye trees,
> And running waters in your purity,
> To heart that broke to save them, dearer these,
> Sons of a poor undone humanity. . . .
>
> Give me Thy thirst: kindle, O Christ, Thy fire,
> Passion of fire, and love's sincerity;
> My wild wind-harp, take, make of it a lyre
> Whose music shall win men to turn to Thee.

Chapter 30
A Life Without Fences

What Amy Carmichael called "a new thread" was added to the "gold cord" of their life in 1916.

The world was still at war. Its depression lay heavy even in so far-off a place as South India. Dohnavur had twelve nurseries now, full of babies and toddlers to look after. There were dozens of children inexorably growing, seeking guidance, demanding more and more of those responsible for them. Arulai, the most responsible of the Indians, had nephritis. In the midst of all this, God seemed to be calling for a new decision of faith.

"I could not rise to it, the deadly truth had me in its grip: I was afraid." Amy's mind, filled with the military history she loved to read, was shaped by battle language. Of what use, she thought now, is a frightened soldier?

> Strength of my heart, I need not fail,
>   Not mine to fear but to obey,
> With such a Leader, who could quail?
>   Thou art as Thou wert yesterday.
> Strength of my heart, I rest in Thee,
>   Fulfil Thy purposes through me.

We are not told what the fearsome decision was, only that discipline was needed, for God had not given a spirit of fear (that spirit has another source altogether), but of power and love and discipline. She longed for comrades-in-arms who would share the disciplined life she knew she had been called to, who would gladly pay the price, forsake all, and live "a life without fences." She thought of the Lord, standing on the waves in the storm, with hand out-stretched to Peter. "Lord, bid me come to Thee, from any boat, on any water, only teach me how to walk on the sea."

There were seven young Indian women, including Preena, the first temple child, Purripuranam, Ponnammal's daughter, and Arulai, in whom the same spirit was found. Today some would say that Amy Carmichael was their "role model," a cold and sterile term which implies the mere assumption of a part or duty. Their Amma was far more to them than that. She was mother. They were mothered in every way a child can be conscious of being mothered—physically, emotionally, spiritually. She was a loving and powerful presence in their everyday lives, an older woman who did what the apostle Paul told his protege Titus to instruct all older women to do: teach younger women by example what godliness looks like.

"We shaped ourselves into a group," Amy wrote. They took the name Sisters of the Common Life, borrowing from Gerard Grote of Holland who in 1380 had formed the Brotherhood of Common Life, a group of men who worked with their hands and trained "such as sought, apart from the evil about them, a pure and godly life." Because in India, as everywhere else, a distinction was usually made between the sacred and the secular, the Sisters of the Common Life wanted to erase that line, remembering Him who took a towel. "Put on the apron of humility to serve one another,"[1] and "Come unto me and rest—take my yoke upon you"[2]—these were among their watchwords.

Amy wanted to share with these women the spiritual riches of books that had put iron into her own soul, so it was essential that they learn English. She gave them Richard Rolle, Raymond Lull, Suso and Tersteegen, Bishop Moule, Josephine Butler, Thomas à Kempis, Samuel Rutherford, Père Didon, Bishop Bardsley, "and the brave and burning souls of every age who had left torches." Such torches lighted the way of discipleship for these women. They were the ones ready to do whatever needed to be done. "Ask her,"

---

1. 1 Peter 5:5.
2. Matthew 11:28, 29.

it could be said, "she is a Sister of the Common Life. She will do it." For them promotion meant not more honor but more work, harder work.

The Sisters took no vows, it being understood that their orders were "whatsoever Thou sayest unto me." Marriage might be among the whatsoever, and several did marry, as Amy tells in *Gold Cord*. What she did not mention, Frank Houghton has told in his biography[3]: that if one of the Sisters married she ceased to be a Sister of the Common Life. During the early years all European women who joined the work automatically joined the Sisterhood, but later it seemed that not all were ready on arrival for that kind of commitment.

"There is nothing dreary or doubtful about (the life). It is meant to be continually joyful. . . . We are called to a settled happiness in the Lord whose joy is our strength."

When they had read together the books Amy gave them, "we" wrote what Amy called "a confession of love." Her customary use of the editorial "we" made it seem that all decisions were made in a body, all poetry received by simultaneous inspiration, all feelings harmoniously orchestrated. That, of course, was how she earnestly wanted things to be. She had no desire to be the chief. She saw herself as under orders, along with all the rest. But the confession of love was her work, given to the Sisters, and heartily accepted by every woman who wanted to be one of them:

My vow.
Whatsoever Thou sayest unto me, by Thy grace I will do
it.

My constraint.
Thy love, O Christ, my Lord.

My Confidence.
Thou art able to keep that which I have committed unto
Thee.

---

3. Frank Houghton, *Amy Carmichael of Dohnavur* (London: Society for the Promotion of Christian Knowledge, 1953).

My Joy.
To do Thy will, O God.

My Discipline.
That which I would not choose, but which Thy love appoints.

My Prayer.
Conform my will to Thine.

My Motto.
Love to live, live to love.

My Portion.
The Lord is the portion of mine inheritance.

Teach us, good Lord, to serve Thee as Thou deservest; to give and not to count the cost; to fight and not to heed the wounds; to toil and not to seek for rest; to labor and not to ask for any reward save that of knowing that we do Thy will, O Lord our God.

Chapter 31
Where Are the Men?

One of the features of village life in South India was the Car festival. The Car, or juggernaut, was a towering wooden structure on wheels which bore the Hindu idol. Its dark, carved surfaces, representing various aspects of worship, were covered with streamers, tinsel, and garlands of flowers. One day in 1909 Amy was standing in the blinding heat and smothering dust when, "with shoutings and flingings of arms in the air, the brown flood swept past." Thousands of men, stripped to the waist in honor of the god, strained and sweated at the ropes. "The flood grew denser, the shouts were frenzied, the Car moved round the corner, rocked for a dizzy moment, and stopped." There were policemen about, lest any devotee attempt to fling himself under the huge wheels. But it was not the Car or the crowd or the heat or any other aspect of the festival that riveted the attention of the missionary—it was little boys, acolytes, attending the god, one of them on the upper tier of the Car, wreathed in pink flowers.

Amy could not bear it. She believed that the gods of India, as depicted by their aggressive or seductive images, were satanic, and they who made them were "like unto them." The things she had learned about the character of Hindu worship, through years of study of the language and the mind of the Hindu, were for her quite literally both unutterable and nearly unthinkable. It was "slime, filth, sin," she wrote, but "books that whitewash Hinduism are turned out by the dozen now, and it's terribly unfashionable to feel as we do."

These things shaped and colored all Indian thinking. There were exceptions. "India has men to whom these evil things carry no appeal. The 'light that lighteth every man that cometh into the world' has lighted the mind and soul of some who have never heard of the Light of the World. They have not blown out that Light, and surely the Powers of Calvary have reached even unto them," she wrote. "But never has one ray of light come from the idols of the people, only a darkness which has defiled the mind of millions of India."

She could not bear the sight of those lovely little boys captured by that system. Neither could she forget it.

John Donne wrote, "Ignorance is not only the drousinesse, the sillinesse, but the wickednesse of the soule." She would vastly have preferred to remain in ignorance of this sort of thing. The vexation to her Victorian soul was nothing compared to the outrage to her Christian conscience. It blackened the sun. She refused to sit blindfolded. She began to investigate.

As before, she met with bland indifference and denial. But there were Indians who knew and deplored as she did this traffic in little boys, similar to that in little girls. Many were sold or given to temple houses where they became musicians and teachers of dancing and poetry to the girls. Others were adopted by Hindus or Muslims, sometimes for purposes she could only describe as "infamous," meaning homosexual. Others became the property of dramatic societies connected with the temples, and learned to act in plays which were "wholly unclean, soul-destroying."

She received a telegram from Simla urging her to provide the government with facts. She did so, asking that the information and its source be kept confidential lest her own work be hindered by publicity. The result was "much earnest movement" among both Indians and English to end this "black iniquity towards innocence." At last laws were passed, "thank God, which at least mean to help, but India knows how to evade laws. . . . So we go on."

Once an Indian friend, acquainted with the ways of the underworld, took her to a house with barred windows and verandahs and a heavy, bolted door. It was not different from the other houses in the street, but he knew what went on inside. In answer to their knock an old hag opened the door a crack. After the usual polite preliminaries the Indian asked if the children were well.

"What children? There are no children here."

"The boys, O elder sister, the boys who learn here."

"No boys learn here," and the door all but shut.

"Oh, say not so, sister. Do they not learn songs?"

"No boys learn songs here." And the door shut.[1]

Later Amy succeeded in walking straight into a house where the boys were taught. A white woman in topee and European dress would never have managed it. The boys swarmed around the lady in the sari, taking her hands, begging her to sit down, "friendly and lovable and keen to make the most of this welcome interruption to an apparently strictly enforced routine." After an illuminating twenty minutes the interruption was discovered. An angry man rushed in like a whirlwind, sent the boys off to their lessons, and, "too confounded for speech," returned Amy's calm salaam as she departed.

She bought a ticket for the drama, and found that the boy who had invited her into the house was the star of the show—a little queen, "robed in a shimmer of pink and gold jewels, playing a musical instrument, which showed to perfection the delicate sensitive hands. As he played, he turned his little head slowly from side to side and bowed in the approved fashion of beautiful queens." The crowd, boisterous before, was suddenly hushed, transfixed by the beauty of the child.

When she spoke to her comrades of the plight of the boys, they pointed out the impossibility of her doing anything about it—her hands were already more than full. Boys were more difficult to rear than girls. Boys' and girls' work should be kept separate in India. Where were the men they must have to help them? What about a doctor? No, it was unthinkable. Surely God would raise up someone else for the job. She listened politely. She did not settle for that verdict. Unthinkable? Not to God. She prayed and kept on praying, the face of the little queen indelible in memory, for years.

One day she knelt by a rock in the forest. There was a quiet pool beside the rock, on the floor of which lay sodden leaves. It was one

---

1. *Gold Cord,* p. 211.

of those "figures of the true," a visible sign of an invisible reality—life out of death. "Broken, battered, sodden leaves—these that were ready to sink out of sight and be dealt with in any way, all choices gone, they were near to becoming life to the forest. 'Learn to obey, thou dust, learn to meek thyself, thou earth and clay.' " She asked that God would either take away the burden for the little boys, or show her what to do about them.

Forbodings such as we had never known when we began to save the girls oppressed us. We knew more now than we did then of the inwardness of this to which we must set our hand. The fire shall try every man's work of what sort it is. Were we ready for that? Was our reputation ashes to us? This was a curious question that came again and again. What if our hopes fell in ruins about us like a child's castle of cards?[2]

The matter of where the needed men would come from was settled finally, in the forest again, this time not by the quiet pool but by a waterfall. Watching the ceaseless cataract pouring down from above she "heard a voice from heaven, the voice of many waters, *Can I who do this, not do that?* Spiritually, in that hour, the work for boys began."

Prayer and travail had to go on for a long time to come. She, "dust and ashes," was learning to "meek" herself. A doctor finally arrived, to Amy's joy and relief. She lasted only a short time. Health was the reason given for her return home. Dass, a friend from another town, made journeys in search of boys he had heard of. He was foiled again and again. One woman gave Dass her child, only to follow them to the bazaar and reclaim him. Later when he went to see her she said, "Take him, he's yours," and pointed to a bundle in the corner. He found the four-year-old, covered with smallpox, and blind. Back he went a few weeks later. There was no trace of him.

Late evening, January 14, 1918. A bandy jingles up to the bungalow in Dohnavur. A tired woman hands out a weary child who smiles and cuddles down on Amy's shoulder. Someone takes it to the nursery, and in five minutes Mabel Wade rushes back breathless: "It's a boy!"

---

2. Ibid, p. 220.

They named him Arul. He was "the first fruits of seven years' travail."

Amy swung into action—surveyed a field next to the girls' compound, "received the pattern" for the buildings, asked for a sign: one hundred pounds as a seal on the new endeavor, told the Family. On the next mail day it came—a legacy of exactly one hundred pounds.

Another boy arrived in June of that year, and by 1926 there were between seventy and eighty. Although Amy was not by nature suspicious, she had had to learn some lessons the hard way. Nevertheless she was duped by some who brought the boys to her. A trusted friend brought several, one of them a handsome Brahman whom he claimed to have "found." No doubt her eagerness to see the vision in the forest fulfilled caused her to lower her guard.

One prospective donor made it clear that his money would go for evangelistic work, not for buildings. The line between the secular and the sacred, long since obliterated in Amy's mind, in his was bold and black. "Well," sighed Amy, "one can't save and then pitchfork souls into heaven. There are times when I heartily wish we could. And as for buildings, souls (in India, at least) are more or less securely fastened into bodies. Bodies can't be left to lie about in the open, and as you can't get the souls out and deal with them separately, you have to take them both together. What then is to be done?"

It was a new mold of man required to train these boys, "so that the type of character evolved may be different from that which for so long has been the grief of every man and woman missionary who thinks deep thoughts." Where were these men? Amy knew they existed—somewhere. She had seen them. Her father, for instance: hard worker, a man of incorruptible integrity, generosity, zeal for the glory of God. Barclay Buxton. Thomas Walker.

But in India? There was Arul Dasan, faithful and true, though not endowed with the gift of strong leadership. Were there any others? Men with any notion of self-giving were not to be found when cholera swept again through the village. As before Amy went alone to the "black horror at our doors." She would not permit the sitties or accals to go. Their work could not be dropped. Amy sallied forth, armed with a dinner bell and a pail full of medicines, bottles, tins, rags, and disinfectants. She tried to get the local Christian leader, the catechist, to carry the heavy pail for her. He preferred to carry his Bible, he told her. He preferred prayer meetings to sanitary work. Once the headman asked her to help him clean out some of the deadliest houses. "I was thankful. When it came to doing it he had urgent work on his fields." Other men took an interest in the proceedings—to the extent of watching her at work.

When after two weeks the government hospital sent the sub-assistant surgeon, Amy was hopeful. He was "a dapper little youth with a long Brahman name."

"May I enquire of madam where you have obtained medical training?" he asked. Nowhere, alas, she said, but in the cholera villages themselves.

"But with 'excuses for importunance' he seemed very doubtful as to the propriety of this occupation 'for lay person.' " When he had delivered himself of a long dissertation on her unqualified practice, she heard herself saying "My dear boy, I was at cholera work when you were in your cradle."

"May India be pitied on the day when she is handed over to the tender mercies of such," Amy wrote. " 'We must put on turban or people will not respect,' remarked the Brahman as he replaced his very nice turban, the nicest thing about him, in fact; but I could not help thinking how truly (and quite unconsciously) he spoke. The people 'respect' the outward show of superiority and authority, but not in the very least the inward man of the topmost caste. The poorest peasant, however, respects to the innermost fibre the English Collector or Policeman or Doctor, and would if he were in rags. Take the salt of the land out of it, and what have you left? I don't often inflict politics on you, but for this once I do it."

The "salt of the land"—was it Englishmen only who were salty? Was there no such thing as a salty Indian? And of the foreign collectors, policemen, or doctors, were none saltless? Amy would have disclaimed such an implication, but within her own milieu, the evidence seemed to point that way.

The war ended in 1918. The day the Family heard of the Armistice "we had a most thrilling little service, with the Te Deum of course, and every praising thing that we could find." The school hall was made glorious with palms and yellow flowers, the children decked out in their "Sunday colors," white and yellow. For them it was all excitement. For Amy there was the dark backdrop.

"We could never for a moment forget the sorrowing hearts upon whom the clash of bells must beat with an almost agony, and the maimed men in hospital, blinded and broken for life, and we longed with a longing that hurt to reach them with our reverent affection. Sometimes it seemed almost unbearable that we should receive so much and give nothing. What we have to give is given in certain songs in *Made in the Pans.*"

This was a collection of her poetry and songs published in 1917, which included a section of war poems such as, "Battle-Burial," "Died of Wounds," "Missing," and "This Great Obedience," this last to a soldier dying near Ypres who instructed his soldier-servant to go on with his duty.

> . . . O English nurseries that trained such sons,
> O schools and playing fields that sent them forth,
> Where is your like? Decadent have we grown?
> Steeped in the spirit of the earth, consumed
> By lesser fires than the pure altar fire
> Of love of Duty? . . .

"Is There No Balm in Gilead?" touches the deep well of the meaning of suffering:

> . . . Today, upon the clan
> We call mankind
> Falls such a woe that hadst Thou, passionless,
> Spent easy days, O Christ, known only joy's dear kiss,
> Walked on safe sandalled feet
> In meadowlands—Ah, who that ever ran
> Naked across the plain,
> Scourged by the vehement, bitter rain
> And fearful wind,
> But turning to Thee desperate, would miss
> Something in Thee, yea, vital things? Tears were Thy meat,
> A spear-stab, Thy caress,
> Thou suffering Son of Man.

Chapter 32
Damascus Blades

Books not only about military heroes but about mountaineers (for example, Whymper of the Matterhorn, Somervell of Everest), explorers (Edward Wilson of the Antarctic), and great educators (Arnold of Rugby) strengthened Amy Carmichael's determination always to aim high in the training of the children committed to her care.

"Give them not only noble teaching but noble teachers," wrote Dorothea Beale of Cheltenham. Amy felt that the world had far too many run-of-the-mill Christians, cool, respectable, satisfied with the usual, the mediocre. Why bother to lay down one's life to multiply the number of those? Damascus blades, forged in extremes of heat and cold, were what India needed. For that she was quite prepared to pay the price. The training at Dohnavur—spiritual, intellectual, and physical—must be, as it were, the fire and the ice.

"It is worth *anything* to be able for the more delicate, difficult things of life and warfare," she wrote to an English recruit who was tempted to impatience at the long period of preparation needed before going to India. "So, darling, we shall think of these two or three years as given to forging the blade for what only a blade of that temper can do."

After Walker's death an Englishwoman who had been teaching in India for fifteen years offered her services and was gladly welcomed as God's provision for the family. Agnes Naish was one of those sterling spinsters, thoroughly dedicated, earnest, and possessing all the right academic qualifications. Though one co-worker called her "a *hoot!* three thousand years behind the times!" Amy saw her as a born educator, and—infinitely more important—one who had "the mighty Ordination of the Pierced Hands." What else would ever keep a foreigner serving where there was no glamour, no excitement, no recognition? Amy, whose general education had been largely informal and her special training only for evangelism, was relieved to be able to turn over to Agnes a job for which she thought herself to be far from fitted.

The decision had been made years before never to receive government funds. "We would not gain spiritually," Amy said, and "we did not want to run our little streamlet into the main stream and thus absorb its color." There were far more children now than Agnes could handle, and they were desperate for teachers. Where to look for Damascus blades? England was the only answer, Amy believed, for "English influence is required for India as it is now."

"Hopelessly impractical" was the charge laid against them, and not for the first time. They ignored the "dust of words," went on looking to the Unseen Leader for guidance, and did the best they could with what they had. Sometimes new workers who had come to do other kinds of work, even medical work, were pressed into service in the schoolrooms, for all agreed before they reached Dohnavur to help, regardless of their special training, wherever help was required.

Amy was a trailbreaker. Although in the early days of rescuing the babies she had no one to turn to for advice "for no one had walked this way before," she wrote in later years that none of her ways were new. Nevertheless they were new to many of her friends—and, we may add, enemies. Certainly no one had formed a family for this particular kind of child along these particular lines. Prevalent opinion to the contrary, she did on occasion ask advice— of those she trusted. The advice was listened to, at least. It was not always followed. Sometimes when it was followed she found herself in a tangle, and wondered why she had not gone directly to the One who had shown her the pattern in the first place. "I was troubled, and sorry of heart, for is there any need for those who walk with God to err in vision and stumble in judgment?"

God promises wisdom. Why not take Him at His word? With the Sisters of the Common Life she combed the Book of Acts for principles of guidance. They found that it came through circumstances, through careful thought, through the general feeling which followed prayer and fasting, by an impelling sense of duty, or a word from the Lord. This "word" might be something remembered at the crucial moment, or a direct command. Such commands, in the days of the apostles, came when the Holy Spirit spoke or when an angel appeared. Amy admitted that she had never been vouchsafed an angel visit, but all other methods of guidance she knew well. If there was neither inward assurance nor the visible opening of circumstances, a token was asked for and not refused.

As they went on facing the impossible time after time, she insisted that there must be "a word that cannot be mistaken." What she deemed unmistakable, fellow-workers sometimes deemed mistakable. That word which "doth in a way known to Himself twine and bind the heart which way He pleaseth" came at times to her but not to them. Taking an illustration from radio broadcasting, fascinating and new to her at that time, she wondered if the receivers were tuned to the proper wavelength. If not, no message could be received. She quoted Westcott's note on John 12:28, 29, "The apprehension of the divine voice depends upon man's capacity for hearing."

Then there were the "shewings" (she loved to preserve even the archaic spellings of the Authorized Version), things revealed in special ways, particularly when there was a very hard fight ahead. As for a "call," this was a matter of waiting at the Lord's feet for quiet assurance. "A call is just that. Then" (she was writing of a new recruit) "let her prepare her heart for temptations. . . . She will be instantly up against all sorts of attack and this will increase after she takes the next step."

All sorts of attack. Amy was a veteran of those. And no wonder. Her aims were otherworldly. The purer that aim, the more vehement the opposition, human and spiritual, "for our fight is not against any physical enemy: It is against organizations and powers that are spiritual. We are up against the unseen power that controls this dark world, and spiritual agents from the very headquarters of evil."[1]

---

1. Ephesians 6:12 (PHILLIPS).

Amy Carmichael's aim: to lead children out of themselves and into service for others, "untarnished by earthly thoughts."

This meant that Dohnavur workers must be of one mind about at least eight things:

following the Crucified;
loyalty towards one another;
continuing to be a family, not an institution;
being on guard against the foes of keenness and spiritual joy;
counting it an honor if they were made a spectacle to the world,
    to angels and men;
asking the Lord to mark His cross on natural choices;
unreserved renunciation of everything human beings generally
    love, and desire for what the Lord Jesus Christ loved;
willingness to be "set at nought."

Truth, loyalty, and honor were put first. " 'Truth once given form becomes imperishable,' but let the edges of truth be blurred, and that pure form is very difficult to recover."

Work was always mixed with play, even for toddlers. The smallest child could learn to tidy the bungalow or help peel palmshoots. Others husked rice, picked tamarind fruit, cleaned rice vessels. Songs helped:

> Jesus, Savior, dost Thou see
> When I'm doing work for Thee?
> Common things, not great and grand,
> Carrying stones and earth and sand?
>
> I did common work, you know,
> Many, many years ago;
> And I don't forget. I see
> Everything you do for Me.

This concept made the children "particular about the backs of places." "A little thing is a little thing, but faithfulness in little things is a very great thing."

Amy Carmichael offered no prizes. Why should a child receive a prize for what her patient teachers had given her? "The great reward was to be trusted with harder, more responsible work."

Nobody ever received a tip. If nothing else had ever done so, this would have put the Dohnavur Family in a class by itself. Everybody heard that they would help even those who had no money at all. People knew they could count on "not being fleeced in private."

Amy hated things cheap and nasty. No toy, no picture book reached the hands of her children without prior scrutiny. "Remove silly objects" was one of the watchwords, so anything that might pervert or even perplex was eschewed.

Music was never an accompaniment for conversation. The children were taught to sing, play, and *listen*. They learned the lesson of Ecclesiasticus from the second century B.C., "Hinder not musick. Pour not out words where there is a musician, and show not forth wisdom out of time."

Scripture and hymn memorization was an important part of the education. Amy took her cue from Arnold of Rugby: "It is a great mistake to think they should *understand* all they learn; for God has ordered that in youth the memory should act vigorously, independent of the understanding—whereas a man cannot usually recollect a thing unless he understands it." On Monday mornings everyone repeated together 1 Corinthians 13, the "Love Chapter," in Tamil and English. At least one child knew nineteen stanzas of Rutherford's hymn, "The Sands of Time Are Sinking," and several whole chapters of the Gospel of John and the book of the Revelation. The children had opportunity from time to time to teach Hindu children, by the Eastern method of sing-song repetition, what they had learned. There was power, they found, in "the merest thistledown of song."

The children had their own vegetable, fruit, and flower gardens. They sold the produce for the going market price to the housekeeper, kept the coppers in their own little clay banks, and once a year these were ceremoniously smashed in the presence of all, the contents counted, and a collective decision made about whom to give it to.

Remembering the long prayer meetings of her childhood, and her devices for passing the time (counting up in the hymnbook, for example, all the things a dying soul is supposed to say at the exact moment of departure), and the "firstly, secondly, thirdly, finally, and in conclusion" of those long Irish sermons, Amy arranged to spare her children such pains. Meetings, she decided, would be short. "The space of half an hour" sufficed in heaven for "the ultimate act of adoration"—silence—which followed the opening of the seventh seal (Revelation 8:1). It would suffice here, for "the human soul should not be drawn out like a piece of elastic and held so for too long at a stretch."

The training of a missionary should begin in the nursery; school should continue it; home should nourish it. All influences should be bent one way. That training should not be perplexed by a mixture of thoughts, but expressed in a single line of conduct, clearly recognized for what it is. In other words, till the life of a child has had time to root, it should not be exposed to various winds (confused or conflicting examples and ideals, different ways of making *t*'s). After it has rooted, let the winds blow as they will. *Then* they will only cause the roots to take a firmer grip.[2]

---

2. *Kohila*, p. 22.

Chapter 33
Rendezvous With Robin Hood

"N aturally, there was some pressure," was a remark which was somehow allowed to escape. Amy Carmichael's vocabulary rarely included words like "naturally" and "pressure." Life on the highest plane could ignore them. Twinges of the tension she felt between that plane and the one where her feet trod find expression in her prayers and poems:

> So let it be, Lord, when we know
>   The pressure of life's crowded street,
> The ceaseless murmur of its flow,
>   The mud that lies about our feet.
> O lift our souls, from star to star
>   We would ascend, until we be
> In heavenly places still, afar,
>   The while we walk life's street with Thee.[1]

The author of those lines was in a position, early in 1921, to sense keenly her need for supernatural assistance. Her lyric was no mere sentiment. Fourteen babies died of flu. Several of the boys were ill and Arul Dasan needed an operation. *Nor Scrip,* Amy's sixteenth book, was just off the press. Meant for "the innermost circle of friends," it told how God continually sent money to the Family, at the right time and in the right amounts. It was no surprise to her that, upon publication of an account of divine provision, faith should

---

1. *Toward Jerusalem,* p. 16.

come under fire on that very front. Financial supply dwindled as the work expanded. The supply of workers was critically short.

"Naturally, there was some pressure"—the understatement of the year, encompassing the thousand anxieties of the huge responsibility, the what ifs, the buts, the whys, the help-Thou-mine-unbeliefs. She had to live in the middle of this, to go on making decisions, leading the prayer meetings, writing her letters and her books and her journals, bearing on her mind and in her prayers the name of each individual child, accal, sittie, and *annachie* (elder brother), of which there were now two, Arul Dasan and an Englishman, Alec Arnot.

When the disciples returned from their apostolic travels the Lord asked them, "Did you lack anything?" Their answer was, "Nothing." Would Amy Carmichael give any other answer? She would not. If she had responded naturally, she would have had to say, "Yes, Lord. Money. Workers." God had promised to supply *all needs.* On that word, not on the sands of self-confidence, she built her house. Given the forces that battered her frailty she would have scorned any attempt to find an explanation for her strength apart from the foundation on which it rested—a Rock that never budged. When the (metaphorical) rains descended and the floods came, the house stood.

Pressure? Yes, *naturally* there was pressure. *Spiritually* there was always that higher view (not always clearly perceived), that purer air (not always deeply inhaled), which drew her. She saw the facts of life in her own torrid and dusty corner of South India as the very context in which God wanted to make her more than conqueror. Here and nowhere else she would prove Him, here, in the vicissitudes and exigencies of the work assigned. Her Lord too had "learned obedience." In a poor village home, in a carpenter shop, on the torrid and stony roads of Palestine, she found His footprints and kept following.

During one of the worst of the financial crunches a sum of money was sent to them under a misapprehension. Amy's conscience would not allow her to keep it. Twice she returned it, twice the secretary of the society that had made the grant sent it back to her. Finally he kept it, "as you apparently have more money than you know what to do with." They had no ready cash for the large quantities of grain and stores they needed. The logbook notes that they prayed for it on March 1. On March 2 a friend wrote, recalling that she had been about to take a nap when "something or someone" said, *No, you have put it off for two days. Go and do it at once,* and she sent off forty pounds in rupees. She had no idea she was mailing God's refund.

In the fall of 1921 a story began which held all the elements of drama so dear to Amy's heart—another sally into enemy territory, a struggle with forces of spiritual evil, contact with a human soul torn by moral contradictions. He was Raj, a famous outlaw, chief of a band of brigands. His name had been in the newspapers for his exploits—several escapes from police, the return of handcuffs: "Take these iron bangles back to the police," he told his guard, "for to that place do they belong." He was kind to children, old people, and the poor, brave and daring as Robin Hood, a sportsman through and through. What might not the energies of such a man, turned in a different direction, accomplish for the Kingdom of God? Amy's imagination was kindled.

She asked the coolies who worked for her in the forest if there might be a chance of meeting Raj. None whatever, they said. Nothing stopped her from putting Raj into her prayers, and one day she had gone to see some fields she thought of buying when suddenly, from behind nearby rocks, stepped three armed men. Raj was their leader, "a clear-skinned man of medium height, immensely strong apparently, and every inch an athlete. The great flashing eyes glowed like black fires under the bushy black eyebrows; but as the talk turned from point to point they lost their smouldering fires and softened or filled with humor."

"See, we have tea here, and bread," said Amy, opening her trusty tea basket, and they sat down together.

"There are unseen doors that lead out of the familiar landscape of life into another entirely unknown. Such a door opened then. And we walked straight through and did not know it."

For two years her letters were full of Raj. He had been falsely accused, had fled when he received a summons, returned because of his wife and children, found that he had been blackmailed, and fled again. His wife died of the shock. He asked Amy to care for his little children. When the police trapped him at last, Amy found herself in "a battle against the cruel powers of hell." She was allowed occasional visits. Once she dreamed that the gates opened of their own accord, and when she arrived at the Palamcottah prison the dream came true. She walked straight into the ward and asked, "Do you wish to be baptized?" His answer was yes, and a bishop friend, compelled by Amy's testimony of Raj's honesty and the miracle of the gates, baptized him and his cohort.

No more visits were allowed, so Amy was shut up to prayer. When she learned that he had escaped again she blamed herself—had she not instructed him clearly, had she failed him somehow? She prayed that he would "depart from iniquity." Apparently he did. Attacks were sometimes attributed to him for which impersonators were responsible. Would he come back, give himself up, lead an honorable life? She kept a light burning at night in hopes of his return.

By June of 1923 the police found themselves in a very embarrassing position. As many as three hundred armed men, under the command of two Englishmen, had searched for Raj. All efforts had come to nothing and the policemen's jobs were at stake. The last ditch was a humiliating possibility—might a woman succeed? They asked the missionary lady if she would try to persuade Raj to surrender. She had tried at every meeting, without success, and thenceforward had directed her energies solely to prayer. But the official request galvanized her to action once more. The challenge of seeing a notorious criminal not only choose to face justice but to be known as a Christian was worth any risk. A rendezvous was arranged. Thankful for the brown eyes she had once besought God to exchange for blue ones, she stained her face and hands, put on her darkest sari, and was led through the moonless jungle.

" 'There will be a sign soon.' The words came like a breath from a shadow on the outer wall of the little room where she waited." (Her book *Raj, Brigand Chief* is told in the third person.) "For an hour the shadow stood and did not stir, then from the jungle outside came a low call like the call of a night bird; a soft whistle answered. 'They are near,' breathed the shadow, and a silent guide led

Carunia through ways unknown to her, till, like a patch of denser darkness, she saw the two men."

Raj came toward her. She stretched out her hands. He took them both in his, fondling them "with the eager touch of a loving child." She pleaded with the men to trust God for protection for their friends, and to give themselves up. It was too late, they said. They would perish. "If only I heard that you had died without a weapon in your hands," said Amy, "I could bear it."

"Do not fear for us," Raj said. "Will God forsake us?"

Two months later the men were trapped. They fired on the police, intending only to scare them off. The police set fire to the house, the men burst out and ran through the village. Raj's cohort was shot. Raj leaped up onto a bank, swung his gun three times around his head, and flung it away. Then he tore the white scarf from his shoulders and, standing bare to the waist, shouted, "You whose duty it is to shoot, shoot here!" and pointed to his heart. They shot. The bullets missed. Slowly he backed toward a tamarind tree, faced his parents' graves to the west, did obeisance, returned to the tree and stood with his back against the trunk. Again the police fired—sixteen bullets into the bark around where Raj stood, more bullets in the branches above him and the sand beneath him. Not a bullet found its target. He sank slowly, as though to kneel. They fell on him then. One of them bit his neck to drink "the blood of such a man," another broke his arm. They dragged him toward the water before a bullet was put into his head at close range.

Amy was in the Grey Jungle when the news reached her. She had only one question: *Have they sinned?*

"No. They died clean."

Chapter 34
The Sword Smites Sharp

During the 1920s prayers for new recruits were answered, so far as concerns numbers, "exceeding abundantly." People were reading Amy Carmichael's books, prayer groups were being formed around the world for this unusual work, the *Scrap* letters, intended for an intimate circle of personal friends, became the *Dohnavur Letter,* no longer handwritten but typed, and even more restrained than *Scraps.*

It cannot be said that Dohnavur was guilty of false advertising. Never was it deliberately presented as an exciting, glamourous, or even an interesting place. While Amy's books are filled with descriptions of the beauty of the mountains, the plains, the forests, the rivers and lakes, the little children, and the love that outsiders seemed to observe ("It is as if you were all kin," said one man. "I see only love, I hear only words of love"), there are pages and pages which deal with the humdrum, the ordinary, the implacable daily round of plain hard work. While she never meant to make her lot look like a hard one (wouldn't that make it appear that she had a hard Master?), she did mean to be a realist wherever realism was not inimical to her purposes. She included in her descriptions the heat, the isolation, the primitive conditions; she wrote of calumny, disease, death. All these find expression throughout the writings of Amy Carmichael. It was discipleship she preached, and discipleship she practiced. Those who joined her must understand that it was discipleship, of the New Testament variety, that would be taken for granted. Wounds and scars also were taken for granted, as her poem "No Scar?" attests:

Hast thou no scar?
No hidden scar on foot, or side, or hand?
I hear thee sung as mighty in the land,
I hear them hail thy bright, ascendant star,
Hast thou no scar?

Hast thou no wound?
Yet I was wounded by the archers, spent,
Leaned Me against a tree to die; and rent
By ravening beasts that compassed Me, I swooned:
Hast *thou* no wound?

No wound? No scar?
Yet, as the Master shall the servant be,
And piercèd are the feet that follow Me;
But thine are whole: can he have followed far
Who has nor wound nor scar?[1]

"Not a word of attraction can I write to [a prospective recruit]. It will be desperately hard work, iron would snap under the strain of it. I ask for steel, that quality which is at the back of all going on, patience which cannot be tired out, and love that loves in very deed, unto death." Not of foreigners only was this expected. Some newly converted caste men were set to work hewing stones and digging foundations for the Forest House—in the presence of low-caste coolies. No sterner test could have been applied to prove the validity of their faith. "Grace in teaspoons would have sufficed for a preaching tour. It is honorable to preach," wrote Amy, who had seen enough of those who followed Christianity for its prestige. Ditchdigging lent dignity to nobody. "Grace in rivers was required for this. Day by day they grew in manliness."

Constantly Amy prayed, and asked her "prayer warriors" to pray, that those who joined them be sent by the Lord of the Harvest. No others would be able to "stem the tide, keep facing upstream," no others would "keep on fire. And truly on fire they must be if they are to set the native church on fire, for it is wrapped round and round in wet blankets of the devil's own weaving and soaking." Steel, tides, fires—every vivid metaphor she could think

---

1. *Toward Jerusalem,* p. 85.

of she employed to drive home the seriousness of the call. Stones they must be, shaped and fitted by the Master Stonemason, like the stones prepared in the quarries to fit perfectly into their places in the great temple of Solomon.

There was no psychological grid for missionaries to pass through in those days. Dohnavur asked twenty-five simple questions, among them:

- Do you truly desire to live a crucified life? (This may mean doing very humble things joyfully for His Name's sake.)
- Does the thought of hardness draw you or repel you?
- Do you realize that we are a family, not an institution? Are you willing to do whatever helps most?
- Apart from the Bible, can you name three or four books which have been of vital help to you? Apart from books, what refreshes you most when tired?
- Have you ever learned any classical or continental language?
- Have you ever had opportunity to prove our Lord's promise to supply temporal as well as spiritual needs?
- Can you mention any experience you have passed through in your Christian life which brought you into a new discovery of your union with the crucified, risen, and enthroned Lord?

In a statement written a few years later, Amy Carmichael put it briefly: Do not come unless you can say to your Lord and to us, *The Cross is the attraction.*

It might be enlightening to investigate whether the psychological screening applied to missionary candidates nowadays selects truer (more "successful"?) disciples than did Amy's set of simple questions. Neither is a perfect sieve. Recruits wrote, were interviewed in London by the earnest and dedicated but deaf and nearsighted Mrs. Streeter, corresponded with Amy, answered the questions to her satisfaction, and eventually appeared at the Dohnavur bungalows in a bullock bandy with bells jingling.

They came, it seems, in droves, during the twenties. At least one turned up completely unannounced. But they did not all stay. The crucified life did not look quite the same to them in Dohnavur as it had looked on paper. As one famous Christian wrote when a newspaper editor asked what is the trouble with the world, "Dear Sir: I am. Sincerely, G. K. Chesterton." The trouble with Dohnavur was people.

The reasons for the many departures from Dohnavur were diverse. Some were asked to leave, some peremptorily dismissed. Some left of their own volition, some because of poor health. This last being a fairly respectable way for a missionary to quit the field, the reasons which fell under this heading were sometimes specious. There were personality clashes which all the prayers for oneness in Christ and efforts toward unity did not resolve.

Several women, received in all good faith "in spite of social background" (a matter taken into at least some small account) failed to find a niche. One of them, poor soul, "behaved like a kitchen maid" and was asked to depart.

When the cause was failure of the man or woman concerned, Amy's lips were sealed. Love covered a multitude of sins. Questions raised were answered with "The full story cannot be told." More than once a dismissal which she refused to explain to the public brought severe censure on Amy herself, and gave rise to ugly rumors that she was an autocrat who would tolerate no one who refused to obey her implicitly and without question.

The home in Millisle was a place of principles. Compromise was unthinkable. The home she established in India for her children was likewise a place of principles. She could brook no compromise there. Those who could not bring themselves to subscribe to the standard Amy believed she had received from God were, in her view, turning away from Him. She suffered for them and because of them, yet continued to believe absolutely that the lady who did the "vetting" was called by God to that task in England as surely as she herself had been called to hers. They were one in mind and spirit. Prayer was the very heart of it. They asked for the right people. God knew who they were. God answers prayer. Would He not direct the lady, who seemed to be of a rather sanguine temperament, to those she should accept? The principles were sound enough. A sovereign God, however, works through flawed human instruments to whom He has given the power of choice. Sometimes the choices are mistaken. Divine sovereignty permits those mistakes.

Probably no recruits were more promising than a family of four who arrived in 1924—the parents, both of them physicians, along with their daughter and their son, a twenty-four-year-old Cambridge graduate. It was said that if Stephen Neill was a candidate for a university prize, then no one else would compete. With a fellowship from Trinity College which gave him every prospect for a brilliant career in the academic field, he opted for missionary work—to the astonishment of at least one of his classmates, Malcolm Muggeridge. The presence of the Neills in "little Dohnavur" lent a new respectability in the eyes of some who thought of it as an eccentric backwater. There must be more than met the eye if it attracted such distinguished people as the Neills.

While one contemporary of Amy's claimed that the Neills came with the idea of "doing a take-over," Amy Carmichael could not but have been overjoyed that the Dohnavur Family now had two doctors and two *men*. She was suspicious, however, of the credibility others prized so highly (is not the wisdom of the world foolishness with God?), and, fearing a mistake, perhaps in his motives or his grasp of the true picture, had written more carefully and straightforwardly to Stephen than to any other who had offered. He was not deterred. "He seemed to love *all*, and feel with us about all."

Her fears were not unfounded. Perhaps Neill had expected a more visible recognition of his exceptional gifts. One co-worker thought he had somehow hoped to become Dohnavur's bishop, although he was not yet even ordained as an Anglican priest. "I gave my whole soul to Dohnavur," he said, but before long he began to see the place as a world of illusion, insulated from the outside world by the high red walls within which love never failed. He could agree that love never dies away, but that it was always victorious? No, that simply was not the case.

As for the woman responsible for the whole phenomenon, "young recruits came to South India and found a myth," he said, a woman who had infallibility "pushed on her." "No smallest disagreement was admitted," yet he remembered peaceful hours spent over breakfast on Amy Carmichael's verandah as they worked together on the editing and revision of her book *Raj, Brigand Chief*. He perceived her as one living in a hushed atmosphere of awe and veneration, keeping a finger on everything, fearing an alien world. The compound, completely detached from village life, was "flooded with Europeans," who ate in a separate dining room. "Amma" had no Indian equals, feeling none to be as qualified as Europeans for leadership and responsibility. Her stock-in-trade was crises. Life in this lovesome garden spot was a perpetual ferment of crises and deliverances.

The Neill family succeeded in churning up even more turbulence. Dr. Neill, the father, "made a hit with the girls," according to one observer, something no man within those precincts had ever presumed to do. To Amy this was a serious threat to the strict separation she felt was necessary in the midst of Hindu society. It is conceivable that this threat was exacerbated by a (perhaps unwitting) feeling of rivalry, not only with the dashing father but with the scintillating son, who far outdistanced all other struggling students by learning Tamil in six months. To make matters worse, the Neills saw ways to improve "the pattern shewn in the mount." Stephen, who had no idea of the perils of mingling with "the outside," introduced interscholastic sports. The two doctors suggested that the medical work ought to be entirely separate from the compound so that the villagers could get at it, and Stephen told Amma she ought to move the boys away a bit too.

Amy stuck to the pattern. It had been "shewn." Who could gainsay it? She did not give in on either of the Neills' points.

It was a bad mix. Within six months the senior Neills left, and before a year was up Amy was in a state of anguish over Stephen. Apparently reports were carried to her by those Neill called her "spies." He claimed that he was never given a hearing, though this is vehemently denied by some. In Amy's view the matter was of the gravest nature: "the spiritual fortunes of the work hung by a thread."

"A dreadful time of distress," says her diary. "Never such known here before. I am beginning to sink. Lord, save me." All the years of prayer for clear guidance, for God's sole selection of workers for Dohnavur, the pattern shewn, the letters written, the assurances given—had it all come to nothing? How the enemy would be gloating! How those who scrutinized the work for evidence of the life of the Lord Jesus would shrug!

Beside the date of May 30 in her *Daily Light* she wrote, "1925—most painful night of my life." A prayer "pressed out of" that night was:

> O Savior, must the sword
> Smite sharp, nor spare?
> Then come, O loving Lord,
> Give strength to bear.
>
> O Lord of thorns and nails
> And piercing spear
> The coward in me quails.
> Come near, come near.

Later she called May 30 the night of decision, but no action was taken and things went on for months. In July there was "a strange and dreadful" prayer meeting, in which someone "prayed distressingly about *friction.*" Friction? It was a word never heard, never used, never thought about in Dohnavur, not by Amy, at any rate. If the word was unthinkable to her, to how many—perish the thought—was it not only thinkable but speakable, and in a prayer meeting at that? She could not be sure the prayer was unnecessary. In August she wrote to a close friend, "I do trust no one will ever know how difficult things are now—not even you, you dear!"

Stephen Neill was, according to one laconic colleague, "temperamentally unsuited to the situation." Dohnavur was a long way from Cambridge. Working under Amy Carmichael was at best difficult for him (he remembered his first meeting with her as "an impression of power"). Apart from her oracular mystique, she had been influenced, he believed, by strong Plymouth Brethren nonconformism, a bitter pill for an Anglican to swallow. She made veiled reference later to this time when "English worship services became impossible because—no, I must not embark on the reasons."

Neill was known to have given way to several violent explosions of temper during which he beat some of Amma's boys, yet in his opinion some of the punishments customarily used in Dohnavur, which he did not name, were "rather severe." No European or Indian worker who was there at the time seemed to know the exact nature of the problem. One suggested that his writings were perhaps not always in theological harmony with her beliefs, but it

seems unlikely that Neill wrote much in Dohnavur. He categori-
cally stated that theology had nothing to do with his dismissal, but
declined to mention any other reason.

The night of November 28 was "one of the saddest nights of my
life," Amy wrote in *Daily Light*, next to the words, "Let not your
heart be troubled."

Biographer Frank Houghton covers in six words what happened:
"Next day, the severance took place."

"I long over him still, miss him and want him and long to be one
in affection. The stab is not even beginning to skin over. It's just
red raw," Amy wrote to a friend nearly a year later.

Stephen Neill went on to become bishop of Tinnevelly, the district which included Dohnavur, but his name was hardly ever mentioned again. Years later he visited the compound. "Amma refused
to see him," said one who was there at the time. Not true, says the
one who showed him round the compound. In fact Amy spoke with
him kindly.

"Poor, poor S.," she wrote to one of her few confidantes just
after the visit. "It was his spoiling mother and the silly Christian
public chiefly. My heart is all one ache for him. . . . This visit has
been a burden on our hearts for months. . . . It has deepened our
understanding of what we stand for and want to be and by God's
grace must be."

Chapter 35
The DF Is Born

One day a Dohnavur boy who was visiting Madras was asked whether he was Church of England, Wesleyan, Baptist, or what.

"I am a Christian," he answered.

"But what sort of Christian?"

"I am just a Christian."

Nobody had prepared him for such a question. Until 1925 Amy Carmichael had belonged to the Church of England Zenana Missionary Society, but many who joined her in the work had other labels. Like those nicknamed "Plymouth Brethren" she wanted to practice as literally as possible whatever she found in the New Testament. She found no denominations there. "We can do far more for the Kingdom by being as we are," she wrote to an Anglican priest who was thinking of joining her, "loving all, belonging to all who love our Lord Jesus in sincerity. . . . We have a welcome everywhere—all societies all over South India welcome anything we can give, for all know that we are not out to harm any." When the mission in Ceylon had asked her to stay and join them she took Psalms 119:63: "I am a companion of all them that fear thee, and of them that keep thy precepts" as the word given to her then. She had held onto that ever since.

The boy's reply, "I am a Christian," was just what Amma would have wanted him to say. It was what Peter the Fisherman surely would have said, she thought, and who could improve on that? They belonged to the Household of God. Any who belonged to that belonged to Dohnavur. What else was needed? "The least intrusion of the 'I and mine,' an overemphasis on 'my views,' would be like a pebble striking a pane of glass," shattering the love that made them one. One way, wrote Amy, is shown to be eternally right—that of 1 Corinthians 1:10, "be perfectly joined together in the same mind and in the same judgment." Any other way is eternally wrong.

For years the Family had attended the Church Missionary Society's church next door to the compound, but things got too crowded (perhaps not only physically?) and the pastor asked that they arrange their own services. The arranging was according to Amy's eclectic tastes, incorporating some of the silence of Quaker Meetings the D.O.M. has taught her to appreciate, some of the liturgy which she selected from the Anglican service, and some of the freedom of the Free Churches. In early years an ordained man was usually in charge. Later it was more often someone who had received only "the mighty Ordination of the Pierced Hands."[1]

The break with the Anglican church was timely. When Stephen Neill went on to become the bishop of Tinnevelly, the thought of his being in a position to influence the children growing up under Amy's care was distressing. She explained things later: "When the local bishop has been a friend whose coming we felt would help towards the spiritual life of our company, we have asked him to come to us from time to time, and when he was not we have not." Had they been a part of the Anglican mission they would not have had that choice.

Among things that did not matter to Amy Carmichael were the method of baptism and the interpretation of certain Bible passages which scholars disagreed on. "Of one mind" need not mean identity of opinion, but "a community of sympathetic kindness." Three things mattered: the verbal inspiration of Scripture, the power of God to deal with His enemy, and loyalty to one another.

The "living bond," or gold cord which held the Family together was love. Always remembering that bleak walk along Japan's coast in the fog and rain with one who seemed to take for granted the lack of love among missionaries, Amy never slackened in her efforts

---

1. F. W. H. Meyers, *St. Paul.*

Amy, at fifty-seven, in 1925.

to see that Dohnavur was different. She succeeded. Not that all who lived there demonstrated what she called "Calvary love." She herself, as her little book *If* so piercingly shows, felt sometimes that she knew nothing of that love. Some of the Family were openly rebellious. But Amy succeeded in creating a different climate in the place, odiously different to some. Did she think *her* way was the only way for Christians to live? No, she said, not at all. "We are sure it is the way meant for us," because prayer "is the core of our day."

It was a charitable effort, meant to thread its way delicately between condemnation of all other ways and the view that one way is as good as another. Where prayer is not the core, unity is not required—but of course Amy would not have called that Christian. There was no getting around it—"her" way was the only way that could be called Christian. "How can you pray—really pray, I mean—with one against whom you have a grudge or have been discussing critically with another? Try it. You will find it cannot be done."

The committee of the CEZMS in London was responsible for the guidance of their missionaries. The board had asked questions she could not answer: How much did they plan to expand? What financial liabilities would they incur? "We soon passed the place where we could look to any for counsel except the One who was near enough to us to tell us what to do from hour to hour. It was His word which had caused the work to begin and only He (we write reverently) knew what we should do." So it was obvious that London was simply too far away. Geographical distance made communication difficult. Other distances made it impossible. There was her temperament—mystical and impractical it must have seemed to the men trying to monitor her activities, her disclaimers notwithstanding. And there were the less definable spiritual differences, such as an amorphous ecclesiology and a do-it-yourself creed.

On July 6, 1925, the group in Dohnavur severed all ties with the societies to which they had belonged. They needed a new legal identity in order to hold property, so they were officially registered in 1927 as the Dohnavur Fellowship. The "Memorandum of Association" states its object: to save children in moral danger; to train them to serve others; to succour the desolate and the suffering; to do anything that may be shown to be the will of our Heavenly Father, in order to make His love known, especially to the people of India.

That the break was a friendly one is indicated by the Church Missionary Society's having donated both the original bungalow and the guest house to the Dohnavur Family.

There remained the serious question of who was to be the leader. The constitution of the Dohnavur Fellowship made no bones about who was the supreme Authority. It was the Unseen Leader, the Lord Jesus Christ. The human leader, Amy Carmichael herself (who was not named), "seeks, in cooperation with the other members, to carry out the mind and will of the Divine."

They had been praying for years for a hospital, and for a leader for the boys. The arrival of the Neill family looked like the beginning of the answer to both prayers, so the disappointment was keen when they left. In 1924 a young missionary en route to China with the Children's Special Service Mission, Godfrey Webb-Peploe, had visited Dohnavur. He was the grandson of one of the great Keswick speakers Amy had known, a strong point in his favor, and she could not help thinking of him as a possible leader on whom her mantle might fall. She wrote in the margin of her *Daily Light*, "Goodbye to G.W.P.—A broken day," and added these lines from Alfred Noyes' "The Torch Bearer":

> Let me not live in vain, let me not fall
> Before I yield it to the appointed soul.

Some months later Godfrey's older brother Murray, a physician, decided to go to China as a medical missionary. His widowed mother was to accompany him and wrote to Amy that they would like to stop in Dohnavur en route. That letter was "like the moss rosebud of old home gardens that is hardly to be recognized as a rosebud at all." It was to blossom in unimagined blessing.

There were now seventy boys in Dohnavur. The thought of their training, education, and spiritual guidance had lain heavy on Amy's mind for eight years. Questions tormented her: Where were the leaders they needed? What if they were never found? She took her questions to the Lord, and He asked her a few of His own. "Are you prepared to perish with Me, to be counted a fool and worse than a fool by your own world, your missionary world? May I deal with every shred of your reputation just as I choose, and will you be silent? Are you willing to obey in everything, every time, everywhere?"

Five years before this time Amy had stood in the sunset with eight of her fellow-workers, looking over the plain, wondering how to reach the many scattered villages where there was no Christian witness. The towns were shut to the Gospel. But if there were a hospital?

"It was as though there swam into our view a Place of Healing, furnished with all that was required for the help of the people, and we saw the work of the place led by one in whom were the instincts and convictions and the glad abandon of the spiritual pioneer."[2] They went home and wrote down their hope in the logbook and signed their names under the date, January 30, 1921.

Three years later the Neills came, and a doctor from Ireland named May Powell. When Murray Webb-Peploe came he threw his energies into the medical work with Dr. Powell, in makeshift rooms of the old buildings. Amy began to see the two brothers as the very men they needed, Godfrey as Saint Francis for the boys, Murray as Saint Luke for the hospital. She tried to banish the thought—those men were called elsewhere. For the first time in her life she understood the power of the temptation to covet. The command against coveting included "thy neighbor's manservant." These two servants were called not to India but to China.

On the night of October 8, 1926, Amy was sleeping on the sand at Cape Comorin when she had a vision. With a sense of light and joy she saw Godfrey and Murray at Dohnavur. But "dreams have no conscience," she said, and she was not troubled by thoughts of China's loss. Later, in spite of her wide-awake conscience, it seemed to Amy that God was telling her to pray that they might join the Dohnavur Fellowship. A discipline problem arose shortly after her

---

2. *Gold Cord,* p. 279.

vision which gave special urgency to the need for men. A boy had said "a very bad thing before the younger boys, too deadly to speak about to Helen, so they came to me." After prayer for guidance, she shipped him off to Muppanthal, a place they had bought for people with special needs. She furnished him with paper and envelope on which he was to write to her when he had "got through this thing, seen its badness, and hated it." Then and only then would he be allowed to come back.

"Poor little lad," she wrote to Murray, "he sobbed as if his heart would break, but it had to be, and will do all the other boys good. All over five know this mire, and the Canaan ways of this land." She emphasized the need for a "brother, strong and fine and jolly with them as their own. The older men are all married. Helen does all a woman can do."

The impression that she was to ask for the Webb-Peploes was so strong as to be unmistakable. Yet—as usual, her mind wrestled with the question—might she be mistaken? What if the command were not divine at all, but the human in disguise? How could she ask for what would mean loss to others? Wasn't such prayer treachery? *Ask now* was what she believed she had heard.

She asked. The prayer of faith was bombarded again. One day, alone in the woods, her courage collapsed. She waited, "drinking from wells of bitterness and fear."[3] Then "came a question, tender, poignant: 'You fear to cause loss and hurt to your fellowservant; would I ask you to do so? You fear to intrude into the life of another; would I ask you to intrude? Have I been so long time with thee and yet has thou not known Me?"

Even then the fears did not entirely subside. Assurances alternated with doubts. "There is a place where the human fails, breaks down, turns to ashes. Hope has not a single foothold. In such an hour there is a perishing of everything unless the soul waits in silence for God only."[4]

Silence. Amy was silent. God was silent. But He had heard. Godfrey was already on board ship, headed for India with his

---

3. Ibid, p. 359.
4. Ibid, p. 360.

mother. He had rheumatic fever and needed a rest. Two weeks after the vision at the Cape, they reached Dohnavur, and a few days later he believed God called him to resign from the CSSM and join the Fellowship. Two months went by before he was free to reveal his decision to Amma.

She was overjoyed. Half of her prayer answered! She went on praying. Would not God bring Murray as well? It looked impossible. He had finished language study in Nanking and begun work in 1927 in a CMS hospital in Hangchow. Political events soon squeezed him and all British nationals out of the area. Soviet Russia offered to help Dr. Sun Yat-sen organize an expedition to crush the military governors of the north. An officers' training school was established in Canton, an army was raised, and the British were ordered to evacuate. Murray spent a few months in Shanghai.

For Amy the battle went on . . . and on. "Unless the Lord and Master of us all, blessed Captain and Pilot, turned the helm this way, *we don't want you,*" she wrote to Murray. "I cannot pretend that if He did turn the helm I should be sorry, wretch that I am!" Later she told Murray, "There was a day when I did not know how to bear it. The powers of darkness closed down upon me." Two years after Stephen Neill left Dohnavur, Murray Webb-Peploe arrived. Those two years were to Amy "the age-long minute," as she noted in her *Daily Light.* She expressed her prayer of that time in a poem:

> Thou art the Lord who slept upon the pillow
>   Thou art the Lord who soothed the furious sea,
> What matter beating wind and tossing billow
>   If only we are in the boat with Thee?
>
> Hold us in quiet through the age-long minute
>   While Thou art silent and the wind is shrill:
> Can the boat sink while Thou, dear Lord, art in it?
>   Can the heart faint that waiteth on Thy will?

Neither she nor Murray knew then that he was to stay, but Amy dared to go on hoping, and felt that God was giving her strong reason to hope. She sat up in bed that evening—it was May 31,

1927—and read *Daily Light:* "Blessed is she that believed; for there shall be a performance of those things which were told her from the Lord. . . . For all the promises of God in him are yea, and in him Amen, unto the glory of God by us."

On August 25 came the first gift for the building of a hospital— one hundred pounds.

Chapter 36
A Secret Discipline

D ear, dear Mother of Murray," wrote Amy Carmichael to Mrs. Webb-Peploe in the summer of 1928. "He's *sonthum* (our own). You know it—you know what it means of heart's joy too deep for words just now. I have tried to write but cannot. I can only say this and leave you to understand.

"In joy, the greatest that could have come on this side of heaven, and in grateful, grateful love, Amma."

Events in China had led to Murray's release from his commitment there. On July 13 he wrote a note to Amma, "May I stay here? Murray."

"It is all beautiful, the sure leading . . . I ponder it all, turn over every step in the wonderful ordering of events and worship God—I don't know anything as humbling as an experience like this. We had a thanksgiving service at 11. None of us found it easy to put our thanks into words, I least of all. I blundered through somehow but so poorly that I could only look up and say, 'Lord, please understand without words, for they won't come.' "

Amy's vision at Cape Comorin became reality. Her prayers for leaders for the men and the medical work had been answered precisely as she had hoped. These men exemplified for Amy a quotation from Dean Church: "Manliness is not mere courage, it is the quality of soul which frankly accepts all conditions in human life, and makes it a point of honor not to be dismayed or wearied by them." Would the pathway be more level and smooth from now on? Could she breathe a deep sigh of relief and turn over the reins, as it were, to the two strong men?

Not by any means all the reins. The Dohnavur Fellowship was a family and Amy Carmichael was, of course, the mother. Whether she had ever thought of Godfrey or Murray or any other man as the father is unlikely, but she began to try to think of Murray as father, at least to the boys. For years she had been grooming her beloved Arulai for the leadership of the whole family. It asked for a certain spiritual intensity and perspicacity she had not found in any man. Barclay Buxton in Japan—"My ever-beloved chief. There will never be anybody quite like him"—had come closest to the ideal. Thomas Walker ran a close second. But there was no such giant around now. In old times God used weak things to confound the mighty. Why not now? Arulai, a woman who had been learning for years to breathe the same heavenly air Amy breathed, seemed to Amy to be the one on whom God had laid His hand.

In one of his letters Murray called Amy the "skipper." There was no question of her authority. "Under God there was only one boss and that was Amma," wrote Hugh Evan-Hopkins, who joined the Fellowship later. "She wouldn't proceed with any course of action until everyone had agreed, but who dare oppose her? We were awed—perhaps excessively so—by her wisdom and experience. She was a remarkable woman, alarming to a raw recruit, with a sort of aura about her."[1] To another there was nothing of the sort. He spoke of her "absolute humility. You never felt she was someone superior."

When Murray decided to stay, Amy asked May Powell, who had been with her for several years before his arrival, whether she preferred medicine or surgery. Surgery, was her answer. "I'm so sorry," said the skipper, "because Murray will do the surgery." Case closed.

Then there were the babies. Dr. Powell had cared for them up to this time. Amy decided that would be not hers but Murray's job from now on.

"When Amma had seen a thing very clearly she expected the rest of us to see it as clearly. It was all wrong," says Dr. Powell now. "He lived outside the compound—they couldn't get at him.

---

1. Katharine Makower, *Follow My Leader*, p. 127.

But I broke Amma's rule by not going to her. *I* was all wrong—be sure to put that in!" So I have put it in.

During the next two decades some interesting and capable men joined the Dohnavur Fellowship. Alec Arnot, the first foreign man to join, put in years of solid work in agriculture and building. His contribution seems, however, to have been undervalued, or perhaps he was outshone by his successors. When he left for furlough he was not invited back, even though his wife, Gwen, whom he had acquired in Dohnavur, would be greatly missed as a teacher.

Harrie Scott-Simmons, a young Anglican priest from Australia, took what Amy warned him would be "a big step from the cathedral to the missionary scrap heap." Like other clergy before him, Hugh Evan-Hopkins and Bertie Berdoe, he found himself, ecclesiastically, in an awkward limbo. He was put to live with small boys, teach handcrafts, and train a choir. It was what he bargained for. In one of her earliest letters to him, before he had been accepted, she wrote, "I think of you in all the beauty and dignity of cathedral life, and with opportunities to broadcast and so on, and then I think of you as a buried seed. Is the contrast too tremendous? No, because the called and chosen can by God's grace be faithful, and to follow the Crucified is all that matters to the true lover and disciple. I magnify your office, I magnify your calling, only it does mean, for it must, *death,* that life may abound." She had tried scrupulously to give him an honest preview.

He came. The difficulties were as real as predicted. "She gave me a thorough scolding because I was not pulling my weight," he said, "told me my heart was divided between the work I had left behind (I was precentor at St. Paul's, Melbourne) and this work. We prayed together. She had a very special care for single people. Always thought of others, wanted to know if *their* experience spoke of the love of the Lord." After much hesitation he reluctantly returned to Australia.

The necessity of working under women put a severe strain on some of the men who came. One, at least, a man with military experience, did not have to work under women—except, of course, under Amy herself. She appointed Ronald Taylor medical superintendent over the heads of three doctors, Angus Kinnear, Christian

Rogan, and Nancy Robbins. Taylor's authoritarian approach, particularly to the Indians, was a bit overwhelming. Totally unable to conform to the Dohnavur way of working, he could not stay.

I inquired of an Indian who had spent many years in Dohnavur if most of the men found it difficult to work under female authority. "One hundred percent of them," was his reply. "But the women? Never, in all my wanderings, have I seen thirty or forty women live together in such harmony as I saw in the DF."

Sex complicates things. It complicated things enormously for the DF. In the early days of the work things were freer for the boys and girls of the DF than for Indians. Mixed bathing was allowed in the Forest, and as late as 1936 boys and girls went together for bird walks with Godfrey Webb-Peploe, starting out as two separate groups, returning home boy and girl hand in hand.

Later, because of her knowledge of the Indian mind rather than because of any Victorian notions, Amy felt that the rules must be tightened. Their Indian neighbors could not bring themselves to believe that men and women, boys and girls, could live and work in the same area and not indulge in sexual relations.

"We would gladly have had boys and girls study together in our school," Amy wrote in *Roots* (an unpublished paper giving the principles of the DF and what underlay them), "but though by this time this was beginning to be possible even in this very orthodox part of India (though sometimes with grievous results) such children had parents who had probably arranged their future partners already, or at any rate soon would. Family connections, Caste, Clan, and certain Caste rules decide Indian marriages. We were outside Caste and Clan and had no family connections. It would take too long to explain why and how this affected the question of co-education, and the free life of the West. . . . We had to be careful to give no cause of offence or lead any into temptation in this as in all else."

One of the bizarre rumors which was circulated in spite of all precautions was that Dr. Robbins, while living in a tiny village house, had "invited a man" into it, and that he had "undone his veshti." The truth was that he needed surgery on a finger. Although there was a dusty wind blowing, she took the tattered sacking which served for a curtain off the window so that the crowd of villagers might see the whole show. She had him lie on the floor and, with the help of her Indian nurse, operated. Not for a moment were the three of them hidden from the eagle eyes of the spectators.

So there was always "the men's side" and "the women's side," "the boys' side," and "the girls' side," with walls and gates between. Members of the Fellowship (often called DFs) were expected to maintain what seemed to European outsiders unnecessarily strict segregation between the sexes. It was not as strict as sometimes reported. DFs had meals together and there was consultation and discussion on matters concerning the work—always, of course, "in public," in and around the bungalow.

While maintaining that members of the Family were to follow the leading of their Lord, Amy took responsibility for approving and often for arranging their marriages. When Murray Webb-Peploe began to take an interest in a new missionary from Holland, Oda Van Boetzelaer, every conversation had to be chaperoned— "In Dohnavur you don't speak to a woman unless she's your wife," he said, so they chose "the blindest and deafest old lady in our family and parked her at the end of a long verandah."[2] The courtship, slowed not only by rules but by illness, was strung out over many long months. It was Amma who suddenly decided on the wedding date. Murray needed a long rest in Australia. Who could accompany him if not Oda? So, at Amma's behest, they were promptly married and off they went.

Amy's description of the wedding gives no hint that she was conscious of any ambivalence. The blessing of God was on the couple. "In the quiet light of the Unseen Presence standing very still in reverence are Murray and Oda, he in his Indian white, she in her mauve sari, a single rose in her dark hair. . . . There is a sense of shining." Everyone sang "O Splendor of God's Will," and "it was all solemn and sweet beyond words, and *real.*" But Amy had strong private reservations which she did not admit until years later when subsequent events seemed to vindicate them.

Because the work of the DF could not be carried on at all without a number of single helpers free from family responsibility, there was

---

2. Ibid, p. 128.

criticism that Amy Carmichael was opposed to marriage. She did her best, as did the apostle Paul, not to oppose it in principle, though Paul made it crystal clear that singleness was, in his opinion, the better way.

It is a good principle for a man to have no physical contact with women. . . . I wish that all men were like myself, but I realise that everyone has his own particular gift from God. . . . each man should live his life with the gifts that God has given him and in the condition in which God has called him. . . . as far as young unmarried women are concerned, I must confess that I have no direct commands from the Lord. Nevertheless, I give you my considered opinion. . . . amid all the difficulties of the present time you would do best to remain just as you are. . . . those who take this step [of marriage] are bound to find the married state an extra burden in these critical days, and I should like you to be as unencumbered as possible. . . . The unmarried [woman] concerns herself with the Lord's affairs, and her aim is to make herself holy in body and in spirit. . . . I am not putting difficulties in your path, but setting before you an ideal, so that your service of God may be as far as possible free from worldly distractions.[3]

This states exactly the ideal that Amy had held since before she left England, and it was the ideal set before the Sisters of the Common Life. The old women still living who grew up in Dohnavur say that it was the crème de la crème who were especially encouraged to remain single. For those less gifted Amma was not so reluctant to arrange marriages.

Psychology would find more than one explanation for the silence Amy herself kept as regarded her own love life. If we choose to accept the psychologists' rather than her own explanation, we know nothing which would distinguish her from the rest of the race—she was human, she was a woman. But a woman who purposes to live for God may be distinguishable from others in at least some ways. Her own explanation of her silence is more interesting (and possibly more important) than the psychologists'.

"There is a secret discipline appointed for every man and woman whose life is lived for others," she wrote in the story of *Kohila.* "No

---

3. 1 Corinthians 7 (PHILLIPS).

one escapes that discipline, nor would wish to escape it; nor can any shelter another from it. And just as we have seen the bud of a flower close round the treasure within, folding its secret up, petal by petal, so we have seen the soul that is chosen to serve, fold round its secret and hold it fast and cover it from the eyes of man. The petals of the soul are silence."

She broke her silence a little when, late in life, one of the Indian women who worked and lived most intimately with her asked why she had not chosen "the other life."

She told Neela then that a letter had come on the eve of her sailing for Japan. She did not say who wrote it. She did not say it was a proposal. She said merely that it "looked towards what you call 'the other life.' " She "waited quietly. Deep down in me a voice seemed to be saying, 'No, no, no, I have something different for you to do.' " She held to that word when her woman's heart longed for a man's love. That day in the cave in Arima, Japan, was one of those days, a day full of fear of a lonely future, when the Voice spoke again: "None of them that trust in Him shall be desolate."

Again at Ooty, she confessed, there was another proposal, or at least the overture to a proposal. She gave Neela no details. She did not use the word *proposal*. It was, she said, the last time the "other life" pulled. She added, "It was not a question of giving up His service. It never had been that. And now what was (as others would have told me) such a good thing would have led out into wider opportunities than ever before had been mine, but it would have led out of India. Lord, what wilt Thou have me to do? Shall I do this? And all I heard in answer to that was, 'No, no, *no*. I have something different for you to do.' " Shortly after that the work she would never have done if she had been married began. Small wonder she wanted comrades in singleness.

"One thing more," she added, as Neela was taking dictation of the autobiography meant for the children. "Remember our God did not say to me, 'I have something greater for you to do.' This life is not greater than the other, but it is different. That is all. For some our Father chooses one, for some He chooses the other, all that matters is that we should be obedient 'unto all meeting of His wishes.' "

In the end Amy decided to delete from her autobiography all that part of the story. The pages were put away somewhere. The Family did not need to know.

This poem may refer to this particular secret discipline:

O Prince of Glory, who dost bring
    Thy sons to glory through Thy Cross,
Let me not shrink from suffering,
    Reproach or loss.

The dust of words would smother me.
    Be all to me anathema
That turns me from Gethsemane
    And Golgotha.

If Thy dear Home be fuller, Lord,
    For that a little emptier
My house on earth, what rich reward
    That guerdon were.

And by the borders of my day
    The river of Thy pleasure flows,
The flowers that blossom by the way
    Who loves Thee knows.

Chapter 37
Place of Healing and House of Prayer

One day in 1900 Amy had been asked to help nurse a boy with pneumonia. She went, and did what they asked her to do, but the treatment was appallingly primitive, and it was then she "looked up and asked for a trained nurse." So it was that in a little crowded house in the village of Dohnavur the medical work—spiritually speaking—began. Then there was the prayer of 1921, on the evening when she and her comrades had looked out over the plains at sunset, thinking of all the suffering shut up in the little shut-up towns. The vision of the Place of Healing came, a place "served by a company something like the early Franciscans in the gaiety of their spirit. They were lovers of their Lord and servants of His sick."

When Murray Webb-Peploe came, he named his first hospital ward Buckingham Palace. It was nothing but an old hen house. This was expanded by the addition of four mat huts and then an Indian house which was called the Door of Health. The first installment on the purchase of land for a hospital was paid in February 1928. In the following year Amy believed God wanted them all to trust Him for a specific amount for the building—the staggering sum of ten thousand pounds. They agreed, and settled their faith on these words: "This is the confidence that we have in him, that, if we ask any thing according to his will, he heareth us: and if we know that he hear us, whatsoever we ask, we know that we have the petitions that we desired of him."[1] Taking the promise quite literally as meant for them in this particular instance (as nearly always,

---

1. 1 John 5:14, 15.

Amma's conviction that it was according to His will was accepted by all), they assumed the money was "received." Four months later to the day came a gift of one thousand pounds, and eventually the rest followed.

Medical work was the first "mission field" for the Dohnavur Family. The children were being trained to do everything, anything, however menial, measuring it not by hours or by rupees but by love. They were to learn to be grains of wheat, falling into the ground and dying, and what better field for that "dying" than a hospital where they could give themselves to people from whom they would receive no benefits in return?

It is a high calling, one that appeals strongly—in theory—to more than a few. It looks, from a distance, rather glorious. Living out that calling, one day at a time, in the same old place, with the same old co-workers, doing the same old humdrum jobs, is another matter altogether. Those who tried to offer this selfless service for the love of God found themselves daily open to challenge. Was it really worth it? Would it prove in the end to be really gold, silver, precious stones? They were powerfully tempted by "subtle love of softening things, easy choices, weakenings."[2] Bribes were sometimes offered, jewels or anything that could be turned into money, with the hope of obtaining "first-quality medicine" or whatever might not be given without a bribe. It took time for word to spread that bribes at Dohnavur got the briber nowhere.

The Door of Health, and later the Place of Heavenly Healing, provided private kitchens for each patient's family—minute cooking cells where Hindu or Muslim might have to smell another's fish cooking, but would not be defiled by contact with him. The Indian instinct for privacy was respected, and people were made to feel as much at home as possible. Live poultry in the sickrooms, however, was a bit much. The people had to learn that chickens were not welcomed, even if tied up tidily in a corner or under a bed.

The smaller children sometimes went to the hospital in the evenings, carrying colored lanterns, and, standing outside, sang the patients to sleep. This was an "Avenue of Gratitude," an early

---

2. *Toward Jerusalem,* p. 94.

opportunity for them to practice the lessons of unselfish service which their accals and sitties were daily trying to teach them by precept and example.

The devil does not care how many hospitals we build, any more than he cares how many schools and colleges we put up, if only he can pull our ideals down, and sidetrack us on to anything of any sort except the living of holy, loving, humble lives, and the bringing of men, women, and children to know our Lord Jesus Christ not only as Savior but as Sovereign Lord.

Every work undertaken in obedience to a divine command, whether the work be that form of conflict with the powers of darkness that we call prayer, or whether it be the action that follows, leads sooner or later to a new demand on personal devotion to our Lord Jesus Christ.

Murray Webb-Peploe expressed the purpose of the hospital: "a place where people may come, not to be preached at, dosed, and dealt with as cases, but to feel at home, to watch, to thaw, to allow those who take their names, and wash their bandages, and dress their wounds, to share with them what the Lord Jesus Christ has done and can do for them."

The House of Prayer.

When they were praying about building a hospital, the thought had come of having a House of Prayer. An old carpenter, the only Christian in his village, had given two months' pay for "a temple for our God." It seemed to him indefensible that every smallest village had its shrines, every town its walled temple, while the Christian Family of Dohnavur had no building for worship. Amy received some birthday money—small change and a few gold pieces—and asked the Lord how He wanted it spent. The answer seemed to be for a House of Prayer.

"But Lord Jesus, what about the hospital?"

"When My House of Prayer is finished, I will provide for a hospital."

They prayed, then, for the money. They did more than pray. The children sent notes to Amma:

"1. We wont waste soap, and put the soap to desolve in the water and sun.

"2. We wont put our seelies (saris) to the white ants, and we will try to keep our seelies without tearing.

"3. We will keep our lantern chimney without breaking, and we wont put our lantern on the floor.

"4. We wont give our food to the crows and dogs and we wont spill milk.

"5. We will try not to spill oil.

"6. We will try to keep our buckets carefully and not bang our buckets and crack them.

"7. We will try to keep our pumps without breaking, and try to pump carefully."[3]

They did coolie work. They dug, they carried lime and sand. Prayers were answered. Money came.

"Each gift has its story," Amy wrote.

Here is one of the last: On the morning of Monday, May 3, 1927, Alec Arnot and I pondered over the problem which in India is pressing, how to keep birds, bats, and squirrels out of the House. Birds (sparrows, chiefly)

---

3. Amy Carmichael, *Meal in a Barrel,* p. 40.

make such a noise in some churches that the speaker's voice is drowned and the quietness, so much valued here, is quite impossible. Squirrels chirrup in piercing tones—they are inimical to peace. Bats are dirty beyond belief. A domed roof does not encourage such creatures, but ours has rafters. There is no glass in any window, and four of the doors are open spaces. What could we do?[4]

All the money they had been given for the House had been spent. But surely God would want the House properly finished? Alec figured up the cost of the needed screening—about two hundred sixty rupees. Then the mail arrived. A letter from the States, dated March 26, said, "Something had impelled me to send you this further small sum with the word *that it is to finish something.*" Enclosed was a draft for one hundred dollars, worth two hundred seventy rupees.

The House was finished, a beautiful building standing in the middle of the compound, covered with flowering vines. The architect who designed it took its style from an old palace in Travancore, a city where the influence of Chinese carpenters had been felt from ancient times. There was hesitation about one feature of its architecture, lest it be a mere luxury, an unjustifiable spending of money sacrificially given, but a specially marked gift came for that very thing—a prayer tower. On its roof are two pointed shafts, symbol of the unity of spiritual and secular in the life of holiness—the men and women of Dohnavur lived a common life, but they lived it *with* God *for* others. In the tower are tubular bells, "things we should never have thought of buying." Morning and evening a hymn is played on the bells, and each hour they ring for a moment of stillness for prayer and recollection.

The tower windows look four ways over the compound—nurseries, schoolrooms, medical buildings, farm, moon gates (another feature of Dohnavur architecture, borrowed from China), the Path of Quietness—to the plains and mountains. Around the four sides of the room in the tower runs a handpainted frieze with four stanzas

---

4. Ibid, pp. 47, 48.

of an old hymn by Edwin Hatch which begins with the words:

> Breathe on me, Breath of God,
> Fill me with life anew. . . .

Heavy carved and brass-studded doors lead inside, where there are pillared arches and a smooth, polished red tile floor without furniture, except for a few chairs for the decrepit (the sick and the elderly, as well as foreigners, otherwise perfectly healthy, who have no idea how to sit on the floor without a backrest). A small raised platform at the east end has banks of flowers and a blue Persian carpet.

The visitor today is awed by the hush and order of what takes place in the House of Prayer. The children file in silently and sit crosslegged in rows according to age, the youngest nearest the platform, wearing bright flowered dresses. The next age group wears skirts and blouses, the next, skirts, blouses, and half-saris, the oldest, saris—crimson and cardinal, blue, purple, mauve. In their oiled hair they wear flowers which match the colors of their dresses.

Amy did not believe in keeping little children "stretched out like a rubber band." It was hard for them to sit still with nothing to do, especially if they were too young to know the words to hymns and prayers. So she gave them colored flags, and during the singing of certain songs, to this day, they stand and wave their flags while older ones accompany the singing with maracas, bells, cymbals, tambourines, brass bowls struck with a knitting needle, and drums (big narrow-necked clay pots with a leather flap which is thumped over the mouth). When they pray they kneel.

Sometimes the sick are carried into the House. Amy wrote of one little boy whose wounds had been mishandled at home. He lay in the services for many Sundays fastened to a frame on a cot. "He used to watch eagerly for the moment when a psalm or lyric set to an Indian tune was given out, and the band played and there was a flutter of flags all over the House; for in the flutter he would join with a happy triumph. In his hand, clasped tight all through the service, was his own blue flag."[5]

---

5. *Gold Cord*, p. 297.

On Sundays there were three services, one English and two Tamil, led by the annachies, Indian and English. There were special services, New Year's, for example, when toys for sick children in the hospital were collected in baskets. Today there are often special thanksgivings in the House of Prayer—a pause when the leader thanks God for the birds, so that the "dear birds" may be heard; thanksgiving when a girl "graduates" from the skirt and half-sari to the full sari; thanksgiving for needs met, people brought home safely, children saved (the child is carried by its accal to the platform so that all can see it).

The communion service is "an hour full of silence, broken only by the voice of our Tamil pastor, and by versicles of adoration and worship, sung kneeling. The House is white then, and the whiteness of the Indian garments and the stillness, and the very gentle movement and the singing, have a ministry of their own, and often there is a sense of a Presence manifest and all but visible." This service closed always with the same hymn, "Jesus, Thou joy of loving hearts," followed only by the soft whisper of the bare feet as they left the House.

Chapter 38
The Road Less Traveled

Great-grandmothers are said to have pursed their lips a century ago at the sight of an exposed table leg. Queen Victoria once remarked to a maid-of-honor that when she came to the throne young ladies did not have legs. They still hadn't, so far as Amy Carmichael was concerned. Amy was offended by the English word *leg* but not by the Tamil word *kaal,* so even the doctors found themselves inserting *kaal* into an English sentence when it was necessary to refer to the unspeakable limb.

Amy was appalled at the idea of missionaries playing tennis, and it seems that at one time games for the older Dohnavur girls were absolutely forbidden. Admittedly a sari makes less than satisfactory sportswear, but the possibility that an ankle might be glimpsed was probably the primary reason for the prohibition. While nothing in Indian culture forbade the showing of an ankle, Amy's idea of a lady's modesty did. The custom has been conscientiously perpetuated as the Dohnavur women walk around the compound. Even in the rain it is rare to see the hem of a sari lifted.

Games have been part of life in Dohnavur for many years now. Older girls play rounders, netball, and a species of hockey. All swim and dive. Those so inclined climb trees. With Amma's approval they began country dancing, "most energetically." In all of these activities plenty of ankle is revealed.

Amy usually wore beautiful voile saris—creamy yellow, white, lavender—with blouses of coordinating colors. While Indian widows and the poorest women wore only the sari without a blouse, the women of the Dohnavur Family wore not only blouses (with a prescribed sleeve length) with their saris, but underneath them tight breast-binders and petticoats. Amma would have nothing loose and transparent on her girls. When four visitors came dressed in Western style in the mid-twenties—"short-frocked Paganism"—Godfrey and Alec refused to allow them into the boys' compound. Amma borrowed some clothes, dressed them up decently, and prepared herself for a "whole new crop of stories" to be told about what a strange place Dohnavur was.

Amy earnestly tried to eliminate anything which might stir up sexual desire. While village boys wore only shorts, Dohnavur boys wore shorts and shirts, as Amma believed it helped toward purity. The men of the Family wore *veshtis,* the standard long Indian skirt which could be tucked up for greater mobility, and shirts of Indian design, collarless because of the heat. Amy, of course, found a Scripture verse to corroborate the shirt style: "There shall be an hole in the top of it, in the midst thereof: it shall have a binding of woven work round about the hole of it."[1] Colors were always significant to Amy—blue for love, purple for service, so the doctors were decked out ("can you imagine it!" one of them said) in violet veshtis with mauve tops. Dohnavur people could hardly be anonymous in a crowd. This, Amy felt, was not by any means a disadvantage.

As we have seen, the program for the Family had nothing approaching sex education except a few discreet references to the birds and the bees. If the many dogs in the compound ever engaged in any instructive performances, the lesson was apparently lost on most of the girls. The boys were initiated by having access to the cattle farm.

When a girl reached puberty, she was given a supply of blue and white cloths, but no explanation was offered as to exactly what the process was all about. Indeed, the accals themselves who mothered them had no idea. It was simply something women put up with. Although sex plays a central part in the life of Indian villagers and in their religion (the villages are full of phallic symbols), a girl in a strict Indian home might know no more than a Dohnavur girl. One who was married at the age of twelve later asked her mother why

---

1. Exodus 28:32.

she had not prepared her. "It is the husband's duty to teach his wife" was the answer.

And all these babies who appeared from time to time? Where, exactly, did they come from? "We thought the Lord laid them in the mother's bed," one of the "Old Girls" told me. Their ignorance is not quite so incredible as it may sound, since Dohnavur women seldom went out where they might have seen a pregnant woman.

It was not until the hospital was built and the accals began to care for patients that they were initiated into the astonishing truth. Since it was not a matter to be discussed among themselves, many bizarre distortions were believed. When one of the accals married an anna-chie, she was so poorly prepared for what he expected that she felt she was sinning grievously. It was not until the 1940s that sex education was introduced, and that only because younger missionaries insisted on it and were willing to teach it. Someone sent a book for children about how babies are made. Amy gave permission to one of the Indian women to show it to another, if her sittie consented.

"I shall never forget the first time I saw the pictures of a little baby in the [Tamil word for cradle] God makes for it—the first cradle, I mean," wrote Amy. "It helps one to understand what the words mean, 'He humbled Himself.' "

As late as 1946, according to one of the doctors, the ignorance was extraordinary. She spoke to Amma about it, suggesting that even the married couples led a monastic life. She listened, admitted failure, and promised to try to make amends.

There were some strange separations. Not only did Amy Carmichael condone the separation of husband and wife, she was at least partly responsible for arranging it when she felt the work required it. She moved one Indian couple, who had been with her in the work for years, away from their own children to Muppanthal, the place where the retarded were cared for. There was no adequate housing for them, and the wife finally returned to Dohnavur while the husband went off to live in the forest with a ranger. They were never all together as a family again. A Syrian Christian man lived and worked in Dohnavur, visiting his wife, who lived in Kerala, only once a year. One couple who left Hinduism to join them was kept separate for a time. When allowed to be together again, they produced more children than Amma thought fitting. Contraceptives were unknown to her, but why not practice continence? Long walks, the husband found, did not always "cool him off." When one of the sitties married, she was separated not from her husband but from the girls she had been caring for—marriage was "too exciting" for them. Amy preferred that they not hear things which might arouse desire.

Marriages within the Family, Indian or European, were few and far between. The Europeans, of course, had come to India forsaking all, which Amma took for granted in nearly all cases included the desire for marriage. As for the Indians, she had difficulty believing that her boys were good enough for her girls. It was often said that the men's work was spiritually at a lower level than the women's. "Men always are," said an English doctor who worked there, "but the corollary was not drawn!"

An Indian who had come to Dohnavur as an adolescent was particularly close to Amma. She used to ask him his innermost thoughts. "Have you any girls in mind, my dear boy?" she said one day.

"Well, maybe so-and-so."

"Oh no, she doesn't fit into your life."

He accepted her judgment. Later he chose another who had Amy's approval, but the girl rejected his proposal.

"Wait until she agrees," was Amy's advice. People in Dohnavur usually agreed. He waited six months, during which he says no pressure was applied. When Amy asked again on his behalf, the girl consented.

A sittie in her early twenties longed to be married but did not dare to mention her feelings. Surely Amma had no such temptations, no idea of the torture of desire others experienced—how could one broach such a subject to her?

"Oh, but she would have understood," said another, "although one would have hesitated to speak of it." Why? "Well, because she was so . . . No, if a person felt it right to be married Amma would have accepted that."

A young Englishman went to Dohnavur, leaving his fiancée, who had also been accepted, to follow him to India later. Health and family difficulties delayed her arrival for years. During this time Amma wrote to her as though she were the most beloved of daughters, "ownest own," as she often called her, though of course they had not met. Never did a mother pour out tenderer sympathy and deeper understanding on a daughter than Amma poured on this girl on the other side of the world. "The Lord, who is your Dearest of all, can satisfy. He can, He will; but He understands, and I do, those fierce aches for J. I am quite sure that He has you both in His most tender hands, so I am not anxious."

It would be unfair to attribute Amy Carmichael's attitude toward sex and marriage to mere Victorianism or mere ignorance. That she was a Victorian is not open to question. Proof of the degree of her ignorance does not exist. It is clear that she took the "road less traveled by"—in this matter as in many others. And "that has made all the difference."

People sometimes insisted that Englishmen might remain single but Indians could not. This Amy vehemently denied. Paul, she pointed out, was not a Western man. On his authority she defended her reasoning:

In our spiritual position towards our Lord and in His enabling power towards us, there is no difference (between East and West). See Galatians 3:28. "There is neither Jew nor Greek, there is neither bond nor free, there is neither male nor female; for ye are all one in Christ Jesus."

So it follows that if for Christ's sake and for the sake of souls for whom He died any one of us, man or woman, gives up what he or she would naturally desire, a home of our own, the resources of His power flow equally to each. To say there is a difference is to say His inspired word is not true, and that is a serious position to take.

This comes close home to us here. We know that unless many Carunias (the family surname given to all Dohnavur girls) are free to give themselves to the work of caring for the children, those children must go to destruction. This means that it is impossible to find wives from the best of the Carunias, for all Anandas (the Dohnavur Indian men). So we believe that to some Anandas love enough will be given to do without that which they would naturally desire. . . .

But is not such a life contrary to nature? Yes it is. But look at the plane. It is contrary to nature for tons of metal to rise above the earth and soar like a bird. What makes it possible? The presence of a Power within which enables it to fly "by its speed and pressure against the air." So with us. "It is God which worketh in you both to will and to do of his good pleasure."[2]

Once, in an hour of need, these words helped me:

> Across the will of nature
> Leads on the path of God;
> Not where the flesh delighteth
> The feet of Jesus trod.

Do I regret now that for your sake I chose to do without that which nature desires, what was pressed upon me, so that I might serve "without distraction" as Paul puts it? No, indeed I do not. "You will never regret it," an old missionary said to our Sisters of the Common Life. And to those who by God's grace are, and to those who will be Brothers of the Common Life I say the same. You will go through hard days, but *you will never regret it. You will never regret it.*

---

2. Philippians 2:13.

Chapter 39
No Milk Biscuits

Bring to India a strong sense of humor and no sense of smell"
was Amy's advice to an accepted candidate, along with warn-
ings of the temptations shipboard offered. She had known
many prospective missionaries who were "wrecked on the first voyage and arrived quite useless so far as the kind of thing I look for is
concerned." She usually sent instructions for spending the time—
exercise ("the time-honored way of walking hard"), prayer, wit-
nessing, reading. She included passages of Scripture, especially the
first three chapters of Ephesians, and book lists, but "keep off
novels, even good ones."

The apostle Paul described himself as "the filth of the world, the
offscouring of all things." The latter was a phrase Amy liked. "We
want the offscouring sort." It fit her idea of the scrap-heap that was
Dohnavur. But she made it clear that she did not mean *just any* sort
of offscouring or scrap. "We must have gentlefolk for reasons you
will understand later. We want educated, thoughtful minds . . . refinement, character, an inborn loyalty."

What she did not want was *biscuits*. "I don't pray for milk biscuits
for the DF, all cut to a pattern and stamped with a single decorous
pretty stamp. So many places, to judge by the results, seem to be
great biscuit manufacturers and they turn out tidy boxes of biscuits.
I pray for *soldiers*, not biscuits!"

A new arrival might at first see only flowers and babies and
bright faces, "and you will feel, I hope, a general sweetness and
happiness. . . . Under the sweetness there is a real Cross."

We follow a stripped and crucified Savior. Those words go very deep. They touch everything—motives, purposes, decisions, everything. Let them be with you as you prepare your spirit for the new life.

Dear, you are coming to a battlefield. You cannot spend too much time with Him alone. The keys of the powers of the world to come are not turned by careless fingers. So few are willing to pay the price of the knowledge of God. They play through life, even Christian life, even missionary life.

Here I have stopped. Am I asking far too much? Does it sound too stern, too earnest? I want to be sure you understand. The last group came out rather quickly, and I had not time to make all this plain.

I need not say anything about what people call "the other side"—the side of life that is full of joy and fun. We have any amount of that and I don't call it the other side at all. It's just part of the whole.

When a young woman doctor arrived in Dohnavur for the first time, she was taken to the bungalow to meet Amma in her room. "There was a lightness, brightness, and joy about her. She was loving, lovely, and warm. Not much over five feet, I suspect, with gray hair, wearing a blue sari. She had a twinkle, a gentle sense of humor."

In the first few minutes of greeting another new one Amma nailed her with the question, "Do you know your Bible well?" No, was the answer, "and I thought to myself, 'That's it. Next ship back.' But I was allowed to stay."

Amma was an actress. She loved to imitate a Tamil bus conductor. One young missionary remembers her coming into a room bent over a stick, the end of her sari over her head like a shawl, mimicking in a conversation with one of the children the dialect of uneducated villagers.

It was a stimulating atmosphere Amy Carmichael created. "She had tremendous *oomph*. An English accent, yes, but *not* one of those *plummy* public school accents. She could talk on any subject to anyone. You could throw in any question at the supper table. Amma read like lightning," read widely, and was able to "take the wheat and leave the chaff" of a book. She read George Herbert, George MacDonald, John Donne, William Cowper, Samuel Taylor Coleridge, Alfred Tennyson. Her bookshelves held Trevelyan,

Ruskin, à Kempis, Keble, Savonarola, Kingsley, Florence Nightingale, and Saint Augustine. She would bring things to the table to read. "Listen to *this!*" she would say.

When a newcomer needed help with a Tamil letter or short word, she would spill a little salt on the plain teak table and write with her finger. "Eating came last in her thinking at such times, and there would be a quiet word from someone, 'Amma dear, do eat a little chicken!' " She encouraged them with tales of her own struggles in Tamil study when the Lord reminded her that He had once made an ass speak.

In the early days all workers, Indian and foreign, ate together. Then they separated. Accals and anandas ate according to Indian custom, from brass vessels and banana leaves, using their fingers, as they sat on the tiles in the bungalows with their children. The food was carried to them from central kitchens. The missionaries had tables and chairs, flowers and candles, crockery and flatware, and were served by people hired from the village. Of course the dichotomy was puzzling to outsiders, and among the insiders there were many wrestlings over this decision. One reason for it was obvious—the family grew. There was no room large enough for everybody. That was a minor reason. Amy explained the major one, the health of the foreigners, in her paper, *Roots:*

"It seemed wiser to do what would keep us well than to do as we wanted to do. After all, we are not here to please ourselves but to serve India in whatever way our Lord directs." Foreigners did not seem able (though most were certainly willing) to subsist on curry and rice. They needed their tea and bread and butter. On feast days all ate outdoors together, and often the foreigners were invited to the cottages for a meal.

Nobody in Dohnavur ate beef. The reason was simple: "If meat make my brother to offend, I will eat no flesh while the world standeth, lest I make my brother to offend."[1] If anyone had objected that this passage refers not to such as Hindus and Muslims but to weak Christians, Amy would have replied with Romans 14:15, "Destroy not him with thy meat, for whom Christ died." That cov-

---

1. 1 Corinthians 8:13.

ered everyone. The force of the Brahman taboo against beef eating can scarcely be overstated. At Dohnavur they felt they could eat lamb, goat, and chicken without offending, so the curries were not strictly vegetarian.

Why the hired servants? When Indian members of the family served the missionary table, they sometimes found that guests treated them *as servants,* which Amma would not tolerate. She tried to treat all members of the Family as equals. "She made us work very hard," an Old Girl said, "We were all servants. Amma was a servant too, but we treated her as children treat their mother."

"Never eat anything you've seen a fly on" was supposed to be one of Amma's rules for new recruits, but they soon saw the impossibility of obeying that one and were exonerated when they found that "Amma didn't go by that in the least herself!"

Amy Carmichael had no compunction about throwing a new arrival in at the deep end. May Powell told of going to evangelize a village with Amma, expecting to stay quietly in the background and watch the others in action. Amma sat her down on a verandah with a group of women, handed her the Wordless Book, and told her to give a testimony. May had never given a lesson in English, let alone Tamil.

Many so-called "faith" missions require members to raise their individual support. Amy wrote to a candidate for the DF: "For those who have no means we make provision as He enables us. But there never can be any promise even of that. Each one must lay hold on the promises, on God, rather, the Faithful One. . . . I like those who have a private income to keep it and use it (if it is over and above their own needs) as led, from time to time, rather than to join the capital to a common fund. I do this myself (the D.O.M. had provided Amy's full support) and I think it is the better way. No one draws anything from any society." That particular candidate had an inheritance which she was willing to turn over to the Fellowship. Amy advised her to keep the principal "to use for Him year by year." Unhappily, Amy's policy was not to the liking of all, and more than once foreign DFs probed the private financial status of certain Indian members, pressing them to donate to the Family. When they acceded, a glossy report was carried to Amma of the "willing offering" made. She rejoiced that one more disciple had learned the lesson of giving all. The thought that the gift might not be entirely voluntary never crossed her mind.

Once a year a notice was sent around giving food costs in rupees per month, and those who had private means were expected to pay their share.

Allowances were not given to the children during Amy's lifetime. Some of them grew up without ever having handled money. Pin money was given automatically to workers when God provided it. When one man returned his allowance, Amma said, "Harrie, make sure it is not your pride which makes you refuse. God is not responsible for what He has not commissioned," meaning, one would assume, that it would not do for Harrie to expect God to supply his needs miraculously.

There was one very great luxury for DFs. "Above all luxuries a bathroom to yourself is to my mind the greatest," was Amy's comment. She saw to it that each missionary had her own small room with a large storage jar for water, a basin and dipper. A declivity in the floor with a drain provided a place to stand to pour water over oneself. There were both chamber pots and outhouses, the latter with a footboard on each side of a hole in the ground. Whatever served as latrine was given a polite name, "The Place."

A life of poverty was the ideal Amy had longed for. "I wanted to have no possessions except what I could carry in a big handkerchief!" Her comrades in the Starry Cluster had understood the desire, giving up their jewelry and their money, living the simplest life as itinerants. But it was a different life that was required now because there was a family. Amy wanted to have things to give them—books and paintings, music and microscopes, the things that had made her own childhood so rich. So, like everything else that was hers, she laid down the desire to have nothing and took up family life and all that family life meant. She was a mother. She lived for her children.

The time came when there was a good deal of pressure to change the Pattern in the matter of payment for work done. While Amy acknowledged that it was indeed much easier to have everything settled by contract, such a system was wholly out of harmony with the principle of family life. The Dohnavur Fellowship was patterned after the traditional Indian family, which had nothing to do with wages or salaries. "There is much done every day in Dohnavur that no caste person would do for pay, however much was offered," wrote Amy, who mentioned to one of her trainees that she had no doubt cut thousands of small toe- and fingernails—"I who said I would never do any work but 'preach the gospel.' It takes some of us years to learn what preaching the gospel means."

The Pattern was a costly way of doing things. She never disguised the fact. "We ask far more than the usual of our boys and girls, and this way of working *asks far more of us.*"

Chapter 40
Scrub-Land

Early in 1931 Amy gathered the members of the Dohnavur Fellowship in God's Garden and the decision was made to ask the Webb-Peploe brothers to be the leaders of the men's side and May Powell of the women's. Very likely the state of her own health helped Amy to see the importance of planning for others to take over. The headaches that had plagued her for years had become so troublesome that she occasionally took a glass of port mixed with quinine—port to help the headache, quinine "so that I won't take the wine for its own sake!"

May Powell was called to bring forceps to the Forest one day when Amy had a toothache she did not want anyone else to know about. May arrived to find her in a semikneeling posture on her bed, in too much pain to kneel up, praying for some girls who had a special need.

The tricycle on which she used to careen around the compound had to be given up. She was sixty-three, overweight, less mobile, and needed more rest. She had, since the beginning of the children's work, made a valiant effort, if not to kiss each child good-night, at least to see every face every day. One evening when she came past the dispensary on this mission May stopped her. "Amma, do go back to your room," she begged. "Get thee behind me, Satan!" said Amma.

Her diet had been far from ideal. Protein, with the exception of eggs, milk, and "elderly" fowl, was hard to come by. The strains of thirty-eight years, the devastating bereavements, the terrific emotional demands of the fights for Muttammal and Raj, had taken a greater toll than anyone realized. Insomnia, heart trouble, hypertension, tic douloureux (for which she had surgery) and iritis, which fairly blinded one eye, were among other "adversaries" she was trying to fight.

The last thing that occurred to Amy was any slackening of missionary zeal. The greater her own weakness, the greater the opportunity to prove divine strength. She continued to pray for a wider outreach from Dohnavur, the collapse of the "walls of Jericho" which were Hindu and Muslim strongholds. In August she took the commands of Isaiah 54:2 as meant for the DF: "Enlarge the place of thy tent, and let them stretch forth the curtains of thine habitations: spare not, lengthen thy cords, and strengthen thy stakes." Within a day's drive there were 100,000 Muslims. Couldn't they "lengthen the cords" to include them?

Mere business sense would have seen it as a poor time to advance. Funds were very scarce. In July there was a four-thousand rupee deficit. But when did Amy Carmichael ever operate on the basis of mere business sense? This, she declared, was "the very time to look for an advance!"

She liked to give picturesque names to places. Eruvadi, for example, she prettily translated "Song of the Plough." The great hump of a mountain seen in some of the pictures in Dohnavur books was Tiruvanna Malai, which she called "The Holy Washerman," mistakenly reading the Tamil word for washerman into a word which meant "holy elder brother." Indians were too polite to call attention to her error, and foreigners adopted the name in ignorance, as they did the Village of Uncrowned King, which was actually the Village of Crowned King.

Kalakadu was a town a few miles from Dohnavur whose name meant scrub-land—not very auspicious, but, in Amy's view, spiritually descriptive. "No faintest willingness was ever shown by anyone in that town to listen to the Gospel." It seemed an impregnable town, therefore one for which they prayed mightily and hoped tenaciously. God willing, it would not remain a spiritual scrub-land. Amy gave it what she hoped was a prophetic name, Joyous City, with no idea of the irony that name would one day hold for her.

In 1926 she had gone to Kalakadu with a small group from Dohnavur to preach outside the huge temple fastnesses. Finding a drama company about to make a presentation nearby, Amy forthwith went to the manager and, to the amazement of her companions, made her first stage appearance. It was an opportunity not to be missed of telling the strange story the crowd had never heard before—of Jesus and His love. A week later back they went and this time found lurid magenta handbills being distributed to the crowds:

SPECIAL ANNOUNCEMENT!

From 9.00 to 9.30 this evening the respected Carunia Ammal and the respected Mr. Proctor of Dohnavur will lecture on the Great War in Mesopotamia and on the story of Raj the Brigand. Because of this definite feature tickets will be on sale. . . .

So Ronald and Amma stood in the blazing lights and told the announced stories, bringing them round to another Great War, the war they were fighting, and what it meant. While the actors were making up backstage, the manager did his best to persuade them to remain for the show. The answer was no, thank you.

Apparently there was no indication in Joyous City of "ears to hear," nor would anyone think of renting a house to these Christians. But after five years there was a slight break. A house that had stood empty for three years was offered to them for rent. It was haunted. They were warned of the danger—something would happen, a curse would fall. They took the house for the dispensary two Dohnavur women wished to open.

Amy, to whom the special dates of her life were always fraught with deep significance, had no inkling on the morning of October 24, 1931, that this date would be another life-changer. She was visiting the Dohnavur dispensary in Song of the Plough that morning, and praying for guidance about money. For a long time she was silent. Then she prayed this: "Do *anything*, Lord, that will fit me to serve Thee and to help my beloveds."

That afternoon she was driven to the "haunted" house in Joyous City to make sure that all was as she wanted it to be for the women who were to live there. At first the key could not be found, so it was twilight before they were able to open the door. Amy went to the newly built palm-leaf shed which was to serve as "The Place." The coolies had dug the bore hole just inside the door instead of at the back where it belonged. In the darkness she fell across the opening of the narrow pit, broke her leg, dislocated an ankle, and twisted her spine.

Hadn't she been warned? The curse of Allah was on any who would challenge Islam.

She was in much pain. The car went back the four miles to Dohnavur to bring May and two others in a lorry to act as ambulance. May put a splint on the *kaal* and, making her as comfortable as they could, they took her to the hospital at Neyoor. One of the women described it as a "cyclonic" night, wild and stormy, pelting with rain. They could not rule out the possibility of demonic interference. Who knew what powers might have been released by that curse? Yet their confidence in the One who sets limits to those powers remained unaltered.

The lorry jerked and bumped its way for forty-six excruciating miles over gullies and washouts. A nurse named Mary Mills who was with Amma said she wished she could take the pain from her. "I knew that she meant to bear it herself instead of me. Then I heard myself answer, *Your joy no man taketh from you.* . . . a certain heavenly word given to me for whoever should want to do that loving thing."[1]

The morphine May had administered was wearing off before they reached Neyoor, where they turned Amma over to her friend of many years, Dr. Howard Somervell.

---

1. Amy Carmichael, *Rose From Brier*, p. 18.

Chapter 41
The Toad Beneath the Harrow

When Amy Carmichael was brought home from the hospital, no one foresaw that for the rest of her life her world would be the room in the main bungalow which had been her bedroom, sitting room, and study. Called the Room of Peace, it became for her what the apostle Paul's prison cell was for him. Her chains were of a different kind than his, but she saw herself, like him, "a prisoner of the Lord," having paid a price for the beginnings of a witness in a closed town.

In the Dohnavur letter, which by then had become *Dust of Gold,* Amy described the room:

It was not built to be a personal room at all, but a general home-room, with a wide verandah so that many girls could sleep here with me. A teakwood partition divides the room in two, a great convenience in long illness, and as you come in through the blue curtains near the door you see on the right hand teakwood panelling and on the left the bookcases to which the household come when they want biography, missionary and otherwise, and books of other kinds too; for all through my life friends have sent me books. They are my great luxury, my mental change of air.

Facing you as you come in are three big windows looking out on greenness where a pair of blue kingfishers continually fish for minnows in large vessels set under the trees.

The visitor today finds a mounted tiger head on the left wall of the entrance corridor, then a picture of a snow-capped mountain, painted by her friend Dr. Somervell, who had climbed high on Everest. Then a pendulum clock and something that certainly was

The Room of Peace.

never there in her lifetime, one of the rare photos of her. There is a little room off to the left where the precious logbooks are kept, then a door opening onto the verandah with its nearly zoo-size birdcage which she used to fill with brightly colored birds. Bougainvillea in shades of pink, purple, and salmon, and scented white jasmine grow up the pillars of the verandah. Her writing table stands before the three unglazed windows. The teakwood partition makes a dressing room which leads to the private bath, still with its primitive stone fixtures. Over the mirror are the words SERVANT OF ALL.

As she had put up texts in her cabin on shipboard and her rooms in Japan, China, and Ceylon, she put up texts in the Room of Peace. A very large one reads, GOOD AND ACCEPTABLE AND PERFECT.[1] On three separate plaques, hung together, are the words I KNOW, FEAR NOT, ASK HIM. There is a quotation from the *Confessions* of Saint Augustine, "By one who loveth is another kindled." On a wood cabinet are painted blue letters, "A purpose sustained Thou wilt guard. Then He said unto me, Fear not. Despairing of no

---

1. *See* Romans 12:2.

man." The largest textboard of all says GOD HATH NOT GIVEN US THE SPIRIT OF FEAR.

The bookcases have been reorganized by now. One of them holds her favorites, which include *The Cloud of Unknowing, The Spirit of St. Francis de Sales, Little Flowers of St. Francis, The English Liturgy,* William Penn's *No Cross, No Crown,* Richard Rolle's *Book of the Lover and the Beloved,* Francis Paget's *Spirit of Discipline, Hymns of Tersteegen and Others, Companions of the Way, The Oxford Book of Mystical Verse,* St. John of the Cross's *Spirit of Flame,* Bishop Handley Moule's *The School of Suffering,* Brother Lawrence's *The Practice of the Presence of God,* and books by Evelyn Underhill, Julian of Norwich, Père Didon, and many others.

While old books were to Amy "wells," from which she drew cold, pure refreshment, modern books were often "sawdust," "thin," "skimmed milk and tepid tea." With more time to read than she had had in Bangalore when she declined Aunt Annie's offer of novels, she loved those of John Buchan, "clean as sea wind," which carried her far from her surroundings.

Amma's complete healing was taken almost for granted at first. The injuries, after all, were not serious in themselves. For months after the accident the logbook meticulously followed her progress. "Amma walked six steps," "Amma walked ten steps," "A. carried to prayer room for meeting," "A. stood for short spells," "went for a drive," "first night without pain." In August 1932, it notes, "A. walked out to verandah quite well," and on December 4, "walked down steps into Prayer Room. . . . Almost too much JOY. We sang 'Praise God from whom all blessings flow.' We thank Him who promised us this."

Again and again the expected recovery appeared to have been given. Again and again hopes were dashed. When cystitis struck, the whole Family (not informed, of course, of the nature of the infection) gave itself to prayer, dividing the day into fifteen-minute watches, cabling to England and Australia (without Amma's knowledge) for prayer help. Help came. Then healing. But it was only a reprieve, not a pardon.

She began to write letters to the ill, in pencil, a little at a time, from her bed. Then they were typed up and "looked like a book," which became *Rose from Brier,* a book written not, as most books for the ill are written, by the well to the ill, but by the ill to the ill, "a rose plucked straight from a brier."

> The toad beneath the harrow knows
> Exactly where each tooth-point goes;
> The butterfly upon the road
> Preaches contentment to that toad.

Amy had often been that toad, and had found it hard to be grateful to the butterflies, even when they came "dressed like very good Christians." So she wrote the letters "before the sharpness of the prod of a single tooth" was forgotten. She had spent hundreds of days and nights under "the awful trampling power of pain" before she let that book go.

It seems inexplicable now, when patients are hounded out of bed and mercilessly exercised immediately after surgery, that an injury which seemed highly treatable should have resulted in her becoming a lifelong shut-in. It must be remembered that she had been a poor sleeper most of her life; physiotherapy was not available, the range of analgesic drugs was small. Perhaps she was overprotected. But she lived in a time when women were permitted to be invalids.

Amy was able to walk, though not without pain. Her "pain threshold" was very low. She could go to the bathroom, the verandah, occasionally the prayer room, and, whenever she wanted to during the first year or two, out for a drive in the Ford. "Such blissful drives. Godfrey used to bring his harp and two or three girls or Sitties came and we used to stop somewhere in view of the hills and they sang. It was heavenly. I often live in those evenings now," she wrote in 1943, "the dear love of all was like the blueness of the sea. Once we went to Caruniapuram and picnicked under the hills."

Neuritis took hold. Electrical treatment "played games with it," and her left hand was deformed for a while. Twice she was able to be carried up to the Forest, a long and rigorous journey even if you were riding. "One evening I all but raced down the Forest House verandah. It was the last time. Arthritis set in."

More than three times she prayed Paul's prayer that the

"thorn"[2] be removed. The answer was always the one that came to him: *My grace is sufficient.*

To one of the young Englishmen she wrote, "I wonder if the Lord is not saying not to me only but to you, my Own: See to it that you are in perfect accord with Me and then trust Me to withhold no good thing. If health be that good thing, O how joyful it will be, and every morning I waken with the hope, 'Perhaps today.' But I want first to want His will, be that will mine or not."

It was not Amy's will to be served. She who had come to India to be servant of all must learn to be served by all. "I had so fully expected to be like the old ox in *Mrs. Wiggs of the Cabbage Patch,* who 'kep' a'goin' an' a'goin' till he died a-standin' up, an' even then they had to push him over,' that I had been shedding my possessions, not accumulating them." Now she must accept luxury ("how I loathe it and fear it")—a proper bed instead of a mat on the tile floor, a room much larger and more beautiful than necessary, all manner of comforts and pleasures which flowed into the room from people who loved her. "My only trouble is that I have had so much too much. The Son of Man hath not where to lay His head."

---

2. 2 Corinthians 12:7.

Chapter 42
The Servant as Writer

Though the woman in the bed had no choice but to be served, "servant of all" was still her watchword. One kind of service still open to Amy, when pain did not make it impossible, was writing. As we have seen, she had been writing all her life, almost compulsively. An experience was not complete until she had given expression to it on paper. Sometime before the accident friends had asked her to write the story of the Dohnavur Fellowship and how it began—"just what is hardest to tell," she said, "because without foolish fuss it is impossible to escape the personal." Her publisher wanted "a religious document." She answered with a convenient Tamil word which means can't or won't, depending on the speaker's feeling. It would take a higher authority to persuade her. It came early one morning when "a quiet private word ended this ineffective unwillingness."

So it was that *Gold Cord* was begun, probably in 1931, and finished after she was confined to bed, though the reader could have no idea of that. The setting of the book she described as "a tragic page of history; not a date but is linked to great events in one or in many of the nations, or to those overwhelming distresses that the very names Armenia, Russia, China, Central Asia, suggest. And all that has happened in India is never out of mind. But the story holds to a single course. It looks across the open frontier to the Country whose forces move unseen among us; for they are the things that matter most, 'and the life of the spirit has no borders.' "

Like all Carmichael books, *Gold Cord* omits the personal whenever possible. There is no mention of the accident. It is nevertheless deeply personal, deeply revealing of the character and the vision of the author—dedicated to truthfulness, full of love, sensitive to beauty both inward and outward, large of heart and mind, seeing the visible always in the light that streams from the invisible. Though none of her books is "about" her, all are, like all books, the product of who the author is. "A man's heart determines his speech."[1]

Facing each chapter is a quotation from another's writing or one of her own poems or both. The end papers show a scale plan of the Dohnavur compound and a map of the southern corner of Tinnevelly (Tirunelveli) District. Sepia-tone photographs capture scenes in the compound: a moon-gate, a little girl polishing a brass vessel, close-ups of some of the more beautiful of the Dohnavur children, the House of Prayer, the Path of Quietness, to name a few; and outside: temple walls, plains, the Holy Washerman's Mountain. But pictures of Amy Carmichael? Not one, in this or any other book published during her lifetime. "There is nothing nice about me," was her view, "I am nothing and less than that." When someone persuaded her that she must allow a photograph for the sake of her children who loved her she gave in, "in a weak moment," thought it "horrid," and regretted it ever afterwards. "I never can understand how anyone can love such a thing. I often hope that those who have not seen me won't see me till I awake in His likeness."

The story is told of a noted American minister who had made up his very strong mind to take a picture of the by then famous Amy Carmichael of Dohnavur. He was Dr. Donald Grey Barnhouse of Philadelphia, a tall, powerfully imposing man with a booming voice. When I heard the story, I visualized the encounter with the small, gentle lady in the Room of Peace.

"Who won?" I asked.

"She did, of course," was the answer.

Gold Cord begins with a metaphor—the children's search for the source of "their" river in the forest. "A tree had crashed through the forest just where the banks were too steep to climb and the undergrowth was too entangled to penetrate. The trunk was covered

---

1. Matthew 12:34 (TLB).

with orchids, and was a beautiful thing, but it barred the way. Below it was a deep, clear pool." The children could not reach the source. Amy could not go back to the beginning of her story, so she began with the "pool," that day in Belfast when she and her brothers helped the old woman with the bundle, and a mighty phrase about gold, silver, and precious stones flashed through the fog. There would have been no Dohnavur story to tell if she had not made up her mind that day to build in materials indestructible.

When she had finished *Gold Cord,* she went on to write thirteen more books, making a total of between thirty-five and forty, depending on whether one counts those which appeared in different forms. Total sales of British editions exceed half a million, all this, of course, with nothing approaching high-powered advertising. By 1950 there were translations into fifteen languages. Twelve of the books had been put into Braille in England, eight in the United States. When a Christian magazine described them as popular she was distressed. "Popular? Lord, is that what these books written out of the heat of the battle are? Popular? O Lord, burn the paper to ashes if that be true."

She wrote very fast, by hand, on a table or, when in bed, on a writing stand. She seldom rewrote extensively. "Perfection I can never touch, but I do dislike loose threads lying about in a book, or weak lines and needless words."

She disliked pictures hanging crooked on the wall. She knew how to put her hand on any letter or paper she needed, and always looked "in corners and at the backs of things." She was in control.

Her style is graceful, often poetic, always lucid. Her descriptions have the power to give to the reader an experience. Her convictions about the handling of truth were sometimes in conflict. To a young biographer she said, "Generally speaking, I think the rule should be—the truth whatever people think. It is truth in a book that helps." Her test for every word, spoken or written: Is it true? Not always an easy question. Her loyalty to the truth did not bind her to tell the whole truth when there were other considerations, such as, Is it helpful? That depended on definition and other questions: helpful to whom? in what way? She had edited a good many things from the autobiography she wrote for the children because they did not strike her as helpful. "How can I be sure I am choosing those which will be of use to you?" she wrote. She could not be sure. There were three more questions: Is it kind? Is it necessary? Does it have the "seed of Eternity" in it? "Nothing is worthwhile if the seed of Eternity be not in it."

"There is a false suavity about most that is written from this land now," she wrote. "We are so afraid to offend, so afraid of stark truth, that we write delicately, not honestly." Her books give ample evidence of extreme delicacy where the reputations or the edification of others were at stake. Yet it was their edification she had in mind when she wrote at times far less delicately. Delicacy could be perilous. "Our smoothness glides over souls. It does not spur them to action, even though they be Christians to whom the thought of the glory of the Lord being given to another ought to be unendurable."[2]

Next to John 8:55[3] she wrote in the margin of her Bible, "To hide the truth is no less falsehood than to spread error." For reasons which her truth-loving soul thought sufficient, she carefully hid certain facts, and charged others to see that they remained hidden. Ambiguities, contradictions, errors, uncertainties, even certain mysteries she seemed peculiarly anxious to avoid mentioning.

She hated exclamation points on a printed page. When her publishers arbitrarily inserted them in *Things as They Are* she was incensed. "So fussy. They give an idea of overemphasis."

She must have written millions of words. Besides the books which were published she wrote privately for the Family. The long paper called *Roots* and the autobiography of her early years are examples of these. She wrote hundreds of songs and poems, thousands upon thousands of personal letters, in addition to those with multiple readership such as *Scraps, Life of Faith, Dohnavur Letter,* and *Dust of Gold.*

Most astonishing is the number of letters and notes she wrote daily to her own "beloveds" in Dohnavur. Many of these she re-

---

2. Frank Houghton, *Amy Carmichael of Dohnavur,* p. 330.
3. "If I should say, I know him not, I shall be a liar like unto you: but I know him, and keep his saying."

garded as her own long before she met them. Accepted candidates received loving, welcoming letters nearly weekly, sometimes for many months before they arrived. Especially notable is the intimate relationship developed with a young English girl, mentioned in an earlier chapter, who was engaged to a man already in Dohnavur. The girl was nineteen when she received Amma's first letter.

"Dear, perhaps Comrade-to-be," it began. There were expressions of warm welcome, followed by straight-from-the-shoulder words about the matter of marriage before language-learning. "We do not find we can lower our threshold, as Mildred Cable (missionary to Mongolia) puts it. . . . She has seen the weakness that follows making things easy and not soldierly . . . the battle to which we are committed is so terrific that only the tried and proven will stand, all others will give way and break at the moment of crisis. . . . Soldiers don't ask for ease or expect it."

Ill health delayed the girl's sailing. Amma fully sympathized with the anguish of separation from her husband-to-be. Occasionally she sent a snapshot of him, or wrote about him to Bee. "Bee darling, I love him more every month, and more desire him for you and you for him. He is one of the knightliest men I ever met. Every thought is knightly. He is one in whom a woman's love may safely rest, as a bird in its nest." She wrote of his progress in Tamil, his literary touch, and closed that letter with, "Now with you in my arms, Goodbye. Blessings on you, precious child. Your own Amma."

In another letter: "To His strength, to His tenderness, I commit you both. You are warriors, and when did warriors ask for an easy time? or no wounds? or no heart-breaks? But He healeth the broken in heart and bindeth up the wounds." There were other testings, "the beating out of the gold that makes us transparent, 'pure gold, like unto clear glass.' Goodbye, dear child, His trusted one, His tested one, His beloved one."

Bee's father was not happy with his daughter's traversing the globe and asked her to wait three years to be sure of her call, both to the man and to Dohnavur, suspending all correspondence with anyone there, including her fiancé and Amy Carmichael. She obeyed him. Here was her chance to prove the truth of Amma's words to her, "Home, with all its prohibitions and opportunities to die daily" offered training far greater than any Bible school curriculum. It was a long obedience, but the father decided not to insist on the full three years' silence and relented after two.

"If any least wisp of glamor is in your mind ask God to let His wind blow it away," Amma wrote after that hiatus. "There is none of that rainbow thing in the life here."

Week after week faithfully the letters went from India to England, letters filled with expressions of love, acceptance, oneness, sympathy and strong exhortations and encouragement. When Bee's fiancé came to Amy's room and kissed her, Amy saw it as an expression of a mystical union and wrote, "You are there—you and he and I." She told Bee that she did not speak to him of her "for I understand too well how much he loves you for that." Did she imagine that a man in love wants to avoid mention of the beloved? She wrote of the thought that had sustained her when she left her Dear Old Man—the thought of the Wounded Hands parting them, one laid on her, one on him. "He unites you closer than ever and binds you both together to Himself."

Amy had many terms of endearment for her children, *darling* being the most frequently used. For Bee, who was often "darling," she chose a special name, Child of my Bonds. In the pain and limitations of her illness she felt she had been given the gift of a very special child, a child who, she began to believe, might take a place which would soon be empty.

Chapter 43
Saint, Fishwife, Vegetable Marrow

I n the early evening, when the hills in the distance showed faint
and blue, in a patch of rough ground called the Field of the Dar-
ling-Pool a little girl stood alone. . . . She was wrapped in a sari,
bright like a blackberry leaf in September, or the breast of a forest
minivet, the one warm note of color there, and she waited, still as a
leaf, for something to happen, for someone to speak."

So goes chapter 1 of *Ploughed Under,* written two or three years
after the accident. It tells of the early life of Arulai, whom Amy
called Star, the girl on whom her hopes of the future leadership of
the work depended. As a child Arulai had thought, "If even for one
day I might be your daughter it would be as if the heavens touched
the earth."

Arulai was uniquely qualified. Spiritually she was fitted. She, like
Ponnammal, was the godly woman Amma had asked God to produce from the very beginning of her work in India. Intellectually
she was awake and alive, having at her disposal the English language, which gave access to Amma's collection of spiritually nour-
ishing books, and the Greek, in which she loved to read the New
Testament. "She was one who could go anywhere, do anything,"
Amy wrote.

Physically she was weak, due to smallpox and various other ill-
nesses. In 1935 she was ill again. Prayers went up, hopes for her
healing went up. Then they plummeted. For four years she was up
and down, but by 1939 she was confined to bed in a room within
sight of Amy's room.

She was so near me, not one minute's walk from this room, and yet I never saw her dear face after one day last October when she came to see me. I could have gone, but at first it was always that she was getting better, and it would have made a fuss to go. Then after March 10 it would have been too hard for her for it would have meant parting—and we never parted. I used to get up at night and look at the red roof of her room and *ache* to go over.

Amy began to put together a dialogue between "the son" (herself) and the Father, which was later published as *His Thoughts Said . . . His Father Said.* One of the fragments which may have come out of this separation from Arulai was this one:

"The son was in deep sorrow, and he said, Never, never did I think of not being with him who is my very heart, when he came to the brink of the river.

"His Father said, *Will he miss thy hand whom My hand holdeth?*"

Arulai was to Amy "perhaps the most precious thing I have on earth." On April 21, 1939, Amy read 2 Timothy 4, changing the pronouns in verses 6 to 8: "For now she is ready to be offered, and the time of her departure is at hand. She has fought a good fight, she has finished her course, she has kept the faith." Verse 9 was the one the D.O.M. had sent her, "Do thy utmost to come to me speedily." For years that verse had been like a knife thrust. "I could not go to him, and one reason was Arulai," she wrote in the margin of the passage. "Now I can read them without breaking down." She believed the same would be true some day of the verses which were then "so full of my Arulai."

Arulai died on May 24. Amy called it her Celestial Birthday. One of the Indian annachies, Arulai's nephew, Rajappan, who was very close to Amma ("my son-in-love"), came to the Room of Peace while the others went to God's Garden for the burial. They read together from *Pilgrim's Progress* about Christian's passing over, and passages from Revelation.

To the Child of her Bonds Amy wrote five days later of her "treasure child's" having seen the King in His beauty. "I am learning the lesson set to the weaned child. I am learning to do without. So are you, my very ownest. Let us learn the lesson together." She kept writing regularly to Bee, and began to call her by Arulai's name, "treasure child."

"You feel preciouser and preciouser with every letter, my *Sonthum* (own)," "Awoke with you in my arms—I have the *feel* of you."

People who worked closely with Amy Carmichael found it nearly impossible, after her death, to think of any faults. Perhaps memory did its beneficent work of erasure. One man, however, after weeks of thought, volunteered that Amma indeed had at least one weakness: Sometimes she misjudged folk. When asked in what way, he said, "She thought they were better than they were." If that, her single sin, qualifies for the name, it is rather more endearing than offensive.

The prayer-poem has been quoted which asks for

> the love that leads the way,
> the faith that nothing can dismay,
> the hope no disappointments tire,
> the passion that will burn like fire.

Her trust was firm that new recruits would give no cause for dismay or disappointment, would prove to be all they seemed to be in their letters. Amy was determined they would be. But would Amy herself measure up to expectations? That thought caused her to tremble. She begged them to expect nothing at all. "There are days when I hope I shall be gone before you come. I can't bear to be a horrid disappointment to you."

After listening to many unqualified eulogies I finally put a blunt question to some of the Old Girls: Was Amma a sinner?

"No," said one with a smile, "She was perfect."

"Yes," said another, "she must have been a sinner—the Bible says we all are—but I never saw it."

An Old Boy told me Amma never apologized. Others said they could not remember her ever apologizing, but that might be explained by the foggy memories of some and the fact that no apologies were due others. Perceptions differ. Some saw Amma weep. Not May Powell, who was as Irish as Amy. We may guess that

May was not one of those permitted to see Amy's tears. "We Irish don't cry," said May. "Tears don't come."

Some of the poems express an acute sense of the need of forgiveness and help. One confession from her collection of songs is this one:

The shadows of the underworld
Compassed about my guilty soul,
And thunderbolts were on me hurled,
And lightnings flashed; and on a scroll
Was written down, without, within,
The secret of my hidden sin.

Without, within, I saw it stand,
In clearest words accusing me;
Till, as it were, a wounded hand
Annulled its record, set me free;
With that the stormy wind did cease;
A voice commanded; there was peace.

O Savior, stricken for my sin,
O God, who gavest Him to grief,
O Spirit, who didst woo and win
My troubled soul to seek relief,
O Love revealed at Calvary,
Thy glory lights eternity.

One new arrival remembered her first glimpse of Amma—white haired, with a loving face, expressive hands; happy hearted, never gloomy, lively in worship, festive in rejoicing. "She wanted joy, triumph, tambourines, even after a burial."

When Bee arrived Amma enveloped her in her arms and in her love. Their first words were not to each other but to the Lord, thanking Him that at last she was there. Happily neither disappointed the other. A note shortly after her arrival assured Bee that she was still "treasure child." "Arulai knows it, I think, and is glad. You often remind me of what she was when she was your age."

The heart of the woman who could be so stern, so steeled to do the will of God, so intolerant of sham and shilly-shallying and shabbiness was an exceptionally fragile heart. The little notes to Bee are full of poignant hints of its fragility, of the indispensability of the smallest signs of another's love. "Arulai's last note has lain (for comfort) beside two or three special notes of yours. . . . I read your beloved little notes for comfort often."

When one young missionary was taken to meet Amma for the first time, she came out after only a few minutes. "I have seen the Lord Jesus," she said.

A very "down-and-out" widow was brought to see her. Amy talked about the Lord but nothing seemed to penetrate the poor, uneducated mind, further darkened by suffering. At last Amy pointed to a lily and said, "He made that." The woman gazed at it. Then, with the first glimmer of understanding, repeated, "He made that." For some time Amma had her come daily for teaching until she felt she could pass her on to someone else.

An Indian pastor who criticized the work of the Fellowship because children were brought up like "hot house plants," felt sincerely ashamed of his prejudice once he met Amma. "My doubts vanished. Instinctively I felt that here was a person just beside me who had realized God. I have never seen such a beautiful face."

A Canadian woman psychiatrist went to visit, expecting to garner an interesting case study of a neurotic old lady. Five minutes with Amma convinced the doctor she had picked the wrong lady.

Any display of the old Irish temper was rare, but it was still there. When someone described an emotional scene which had taken place, Amy said, "If I had been there I should have torn up a bush by the roots and laid on like a fishwife. But then I'm not a pacifist!" Something her dear friend Dr. Somervell wrote so horrified her she told him she wanted to throw a soup plate at him. A plaster saint? Hardly. She was much more interesting than that.

Today's mind, preoccupied with "self-image," would worry about Amy Carmichael's. She needed help. Her self-portrait: "I am a cross between a potato and a vegetable marrow."

Chapter 44
Broken by the Waves

By the middle of the 1930s it had become fairly evident that Amy Carmichael was not likely to be healed unless God gave a miracle. She was almost never out of pain, yet she maintained daily touch with the Family, seeing different ones every half hour all day, writing long letters to some, tiny scraps to others ("Welcome home, my child. Lovingest of welcomes. Your Amma"). Everybody got notes on special occasions: birthdays, holidays, return from a journey, Tamil exams. When Dr. Nancy Robbins was left for five days with the entire responsibility of the hospital, Amma wrote promising special prayer. To John Risk on his birthday in 1936 she wrote:

"My own David," using the name of the Bible character he reminded her of. "Did you think I had forgotten? Not a bit of it. Last night at midnight I longed to write (as I hadn't had time to do so all day) but if I had, there would have been protestations from my little nurse, so I didn't and then, alas, I woke too late for an early note.

"But He whom thy soul loveth, He has blessed thee already, my John, and His birthday morning blessings are like the dew and like His compassions, ever new, beautiful, heart-reviving.

"This has been a year of battle, but thank God, of victory, and we are nearer the Crowning Day this morning than ever we were before.

" 'And having done all to stand.' God keep us standing. 'When I said, "my foot slippeth, Thy Mercy, O Lord, held me up." ' "

It had indeed been a year of battle. There was never any other kind of year. The Family continued rapidly to increase. One member reported that there was a "crop of very naughty girls" about that time. Some of the older ones were a great disappointment to Amma. She sometimes had them come to her as nurses, which caused raised eyebrows—why should Amma choose such a one for her nurse? Someone who had thought at first that one of them was a poor choice, told herself that she must be "a nice, quiet girl who 'fit' Amma." Later she asked about her. "No," said Amy, "I saw the weakness in her from the first. I had her with me to strengthen her." Some responded. Some did not.

The same motive that inspired Amy to choose a girl who was not naturally appealing applied to her choice of a girl who was—she wanted always to encourage and strengthen. "Give all you've got to helping them." Eyebrows were raised in either case. "Never mind," she told one of the teachers. "Never be afraid of appearing to have favorites, provided you are truly seeking to help them for the Lord and not for yourself."

She sternly warned against "mushy" friendships. "They are pernicious anywhere, but on the mission field just deadly." She quoted 1 Samuel 20:42, "We have sworn both of us in the name of the Lord, saying, The Lord be between me and thee."

Kohila was a girl who had come to Dohnavur when she was four years old. She responded most eagerly to both the love and the discipline of the place, and was trained as a nurse. Vineetha, the accal in charge, needed Kohila's room for another nurse. Kohila "clung to her own small room as a cat clings to its home," Amy wrote in *Kohila: The Shaping of an Indian Nurse.*

In a case like this you who are responsible to God for such a soul stand for a moment at the parting of the ways. You may say, "I wish the thing to be done," and it will be done. There is no travail if you take that way; but it leads nowhere. It never leads to spiritual victory farther on. Or you may put the responsibility for decision upon the one concerned, and then you will travail indeed. But in the end, if your hands be steady until the going down of the sun, eternal gain will be the outcome of that prayer and that travail.

Vineetha said little and prayed much. When she felt the time was ripe she said, "Look, my child, give this room to the Lord Jesus and you will receive hundreds of rooms in heaven."

"Kohila went to her cherished little room for . . . one last precious minute. Then she went straight to the girl for whom the room was required, to whom she had spoken ungraciously, and she asked her pardon and 'willingly with joy I give you my room,' she said."

In September 1936, Kohila was in the forest. She wrote to her sittie, proposing that she share the new little room she had been given with a younger nurse who needed a helping hand. "It was the dearest thing she had to give—her privacy." Then one morning she climbed a steep rock to pick flowers for some of her friends. She slipped, fell, and was killed.

Three months before, Amy had reminded one of the DFs of the Scripture, "When I said, 'My foot slippeth, Thy mercy, O Lord, held me up.'" Amy did not put such items in juxtaposition. The mystery of the sovereign purpose of God she left with Him, never calling attention to seeming incongruities. She declared her certainties, not her questions. She shied away from any statement which might be taken as a complaint or a doubt, or anything which could make her Master look hard. When a little girl named Pungaja had her eye pecked out by a heron, Amma took her on her lap and said, "Darling, you must never ask God why." She comforted the child and urged her to trust His never-failing love."I was often tempted by that 'why,' but I have found power in the blood of Jesus," says Pungaja. One day she went to Amma with a burdened heart. "But when she hugged me all my sorrow went."

Amma asked about the work Pungaja was doing, caring for children. "Do you find your work hard?" she asked. Yes, said Pungaja. "These are soldiership years," Amma told her, and gave her a medal inscribed "Saved to serve." Pungaja responded to the soldier training, and later was placed in charge of the place of correction, a separate compound where the most difficult members of the Family live, some mentally ill, some merely intractable and rebellious. Once an outsider, who happened to be a doctor, remarked that it seemed strange to have such a place in Dohnavur. The only answer that could be offered was that if he knew the whole history, if he had come over the same road, he would understand. The conviction held that the light God had given for dealing with these problem people was sufficient. An outside opinion could not supersede that. It was still a family, but a very large and sometimes unwieldy family, and those whose behavior destroyed peace and unity had somehow to be sequestered. Pungaja, a gentle, quiet woman, is still in charge. "It is my joy to serve them," she says simply.

Amma's birthday letter to John had called 1936 "a year of battle." She went on to say, "Now as we look forward we see great stones and many of them. 'Who shall roll away the stone?' More and more I delight in that word that says, 'The angel of the Lord descended from heaven and came and rolled back the stone and sat upon it.' We shall see the angel of the Lord sitting upon many a stone during the coming year."

The next year brought "Adria." It was an experience Amy likened to the voyage of the apostle Paul to Rome in Acts 27, where they were "driven up and down in Adria," even to the point of desperation, "and falling into a place where two seas met, they ran the ship aground."

"Where the Will of God and the will of the flesh are in conflict there will be rough water, and if the flesh does not yield to the Spirit there must follow the painful breaking up of hopes and expectations, even as the timbers of that ship were broken up with the violence of the waves."[1]

"The flesh" in this case refers to two trusted workers who had to be dismissed for deception and disobedience continued over a long period of time. The peremptory manner in which they were dismissed was anything but delicate, and others objected. Some of them left or were asked to leave. There was misunderstanding in correspondence to other parts of the world, resulting in deep wounds to those who were disciplined and those (principally Godfrey Webb-Peploe) who administered the discipline. This was a "crashing sorrow" to Amy, for it "undid the work of years. Our white Dohnavur is being besmirched," she said, but declared she would rather be deceived a hundred times than distrust and misjudge once. She refused to publish abroad the truth of the matter. Vindication must rest in the hands of God.

1. Amy Carmichael, *Though the Mountains Shake*, p. 13.

One worker who did not know the details of what had happened wrote to Amy, "We are with you utterly . . . God grant it be *stainless steel* that comes out of this furnace."

When one matter "blew over" or was laid to rest, there was always another. At this same time the hospital was in full swing, which brought all kinds of people into contact with those who had been safely cloistered before. Rumors began to fly that Dohnavur children were bastards, which greatly upset the children, and some turned hostile. There were in fact some who had been born out of wedlock. If the mother was high caste, the child had to be got rid of. The children's genetic history was never divulged. All who asked questions about their origin received the same answer: You are where you are first because God brought you, and then because we loved you very much.

Amy found comfort in Samuel Rutherford's words, "O if my faith could ride out against the high and proud winds and waves when my sea seemeth all to be on fire!"

"There is no promise of calm waters for any mariner," Amy added. "But our Lord can give the faith that can ride out against any high and proud winds and waves. And He can come to our succor though our sea seemeth all to be on fire."[2]

---

2. Ibid, p. 17.

Chapter 45
I Hold Me Fast by Thee

A visitor with a serious heart condition told Amy that her doctor had said if she so much as bent over too suddenly she might die on the spot.

"However do you resist the temptation?" Amy wanted to know. Death had held no terrors for the child who swallowed the laburnum pods in Millisle. It looked like a lark then. It looked positively blissful now. When Amy's doctor suggested in 1934 that she might not have more than five years left, or even only three, before her Glory Day, Amy was elated.

"You would not have said such a blissful thing lightly," she wrote. "I know He might even now ask for longer than that five years, but that there is even a natural hope of that little while being enough, is purest golden joy. . . . Only pray that He will 'take from me all slothfulness that I may fill up the crevices of time' and truly finish all He wants me to do."

She felt like "a slug on a cabbage leaf." Her enemies, the various chronic ailments to which she gave biblical names like Sennacherib (who "came down like a wolf on the fold") and Goliath, did not leave her alone for long. Sometimes she was so hot with fever she got into the water tank in her bathroom. Between the accident in October 1931, and March 1939, she claimed to have had eight nights of "natural" (i.e. undrugged) sleep. Medicines, she believed, were gifts from God. When pills were administered she would take them into her hands, thank God, and ask Him to bless them. She was not fully convinced, however, of the need to use every means known to man to prolong life.

"You dear doctor people have something to answer for sometimes, I think, when you shut that shining door, or at least don't give it even the gentlest push open."

The mother of the Family was not the only shut-in in Dohnavur. Others began to feel increasingly shut in and isolated. Perhaps those on whom leadership responsibility had fallen were unconsciously protecting the place from outside contamination in order to preserve the status quo at least as long as Amma was with them. All decisions were referred to her, but full information on which to base her advice was not always made available to her, sometimes because people wanted to spare her such distress.

For many years no outside missionary or Indian Christian ever addressed the Family. One who spent ten years in Dohnavur remembers only three exceptions to this rule: a Chinese woman escaped from Singapore, and two members of the China Inland Mission, one of whom was Bishop Frank Houghton, author of the first Carmichael biography in English (Thyaharaj, one of the Family, had written one in Tamil).

Some of the younger members tired of breathing the rarified Christian atmosphere, unrelieved by any non-Christian breezes. When one of them mentioned this feeling to Amy, her imagination instantly latched on to a remedy. "Do you mean to tell me," said Amma, with mischief in her eyes, "that you'd really like to see one of the sitties *drunk?*"

Mrs. Webb-Peploe, mother of Murray and Godfrey, had a house in the hills to which Dohnavur people sometimes went for rest and refreshment, "but," says one, "you had to be insulated there from other missionary ideas and certainly from the rest of the European community. At the time of King George V's Jubilee we were invited to the Club to listen to the wireless description of the celebrations, but it was considered undesirable to go."

Both English and Tamil newspapers were available to the Dohnavur Family, as well as magazines such as *The Illustrated London News.* They listened to the broadcasts of the BBC, and Amy regularly read a newsletter called "The Essence of Politics." Because there were some German Sisters of Friedenshort in the Family, she was exceedingly circumspect in commenting on Hitler's activities in

Europe. She thought him a "mad dog" and a "devil incarnate," while one of the Sisters thought him "perfection." The rest of the Family had to be cautious and tactful in mealtime conversations touching on war news. While this could not but add to the feeling of isolation and stricture, it is a testimony to the power of love in the place that unity could be maintained at all with such a wide spectrum of nationalities (Indian, English, Scottish, Irish, Canadian, Australian, New Zealander, Dutch, German, Swiss—though not all of these were represented all the time), and ecclesiastical connections (Anglican, Presbyterian, Lutheran, Baptist, Plymouth Brethren).

Bee was Amy's confidante, a sort of safety valve to whom she could let off steam in private. Although she apparently wrote to everyone in the Family, and to some of them hundreds of times, it is difficult to see how anyone could have held a more important place in her thoughts, prayers, and correspondence than the beloved Bee. It was a mother-child relationship, very different from her relationship with her contemporaries in age or her near peers in experience. She allowed herself greater vulnerability with Bee.

"For some time I have been wanting you to have a room within reach; have been trying to get one for you. O Child of my Bonds, I love you very much. Your own Motherling." Often the time scheduled for Bee's visit had to be preempted for the sake of someone else. When this happened Amy trusted her to understand. "I wanted you tonight, but then Sittie proposed a 'new one.' You are not a new one now, but, my child, deep in, and so *ownest* that others can be put first." Again, "I have so many others I must see before I see you that I want you to have just a little love-note to bridge the gap."

In 1938 Amy speculated that Hitler, having got all he wanted in Europe by the "stand and deliver" method, might say, "Now for the colonies." "But I am breaking all my own rules in writing so. After all, no one yet knows much about anything." She was not sure it was right to pray for Hitler since God forbade His people to pray for one under His curse. The apostle Paul's injunction to pray for rulers applied when justice ruled, Amy noted, and John never said to pray for Nero or Domitian.

As we have seen, she was not a pacifist. She had gone to battle many a time for the sake of a child. Was not the same principle at stake in war? "What would you do if you saw a child tortured to death by a brute? Stand still and let him carry on? Swords may be required so much that coats must be sold to buy them," she wrote, with reference to Jesus' instructions to His disciples.[1] She did not find world peace in the Bible's list of signs of the last days.

When England went to war the DF again had reason to thank God for His leading them to settle in such an out-of-the-way place as Dohnavur. "This is a particularly safe part of India. We are just off the line of aeroplanes (I have never even heard, much less seen one!) and if there should be trouble in India this corner would be one of the last to feel it. This means we are left in peace to get on with the Great War." Airplanes, Amy Carmichael believed, trespassed in the territory of Satan, who is the Prince of the Power of the Air. "Birds only can be trusted in those regions."

They were not so isolated in Dohnavur as to make them oblivious of the world's suffering. Amy's letters during the war years make frequent mention of her heartbreak for the ravaged countries. In 1939 to John Risk, an officer of the British navy who was now a DF, she wrote of Poland, "A thousand killed in one city, many while at prayer, many ill and wounded, and little helpless children—and those beautiful Polish horses and dogs and pigeons." She felt sure that the Lord "has something" for the suffering animals.

Many of the letters include news of Amy's Scottish terrier, Scamp. He lived on her bed and made life dangerous for any who approached it. She tried to discipline him, but he was so adorable, so sinless, "poor dear little man." At last for the sake of Scamp's enemies, her nurses, she had to banish him. There was also a puppy named Tess. "Tess was delicious today," but posed another kind of threat, this time to Amy's own spiritual well-being. In her copy of Conybeare's New Testament, beside Colossians 3:2[2] she wrote, "not a puppy?" She longed for Bee, who loved dogs, to enjoy Tess, "but the War is the War," she wrote (no reference, of course, to the World War). "It doesn't leave much time for anything but it-

---

1. Luke 22:36.
2. "Set your heart on things above, not on things earthly."

self." Stick to business, the King's Business. That was the message.

One day Bee was called to go at once to Amma. She found her sobbing almost uncontrollably. It was the thought of London's maimed dogs that undid her. Who else could possibly understand her agony—for mere animals?

War stories she read eagerly and shared with the Family when she found in them something spiritually applicable. There was the "gallant lad," a young airman, who guided his burning plane to his death, refusing to use his parachute in order to prevent a crash into a town.

When a comrade in the Fellowship learned that her brother whom she had helped to bring up was missing, believed killed, Amy wrote, "What noble news. How little you knew you were training a young knight for the courts of heaven. You are honored, but—but—God comfort you tonight."

In 1942, with the imminent threat of Japanese invasion from Singapore, a plan was drawn up for evacuation of the accals and children between the ages of seven and thirty-five, of whom there were 316. They began quietly to send supplies up to the Forest but the plan never had to be implemented. Between 1939 and 1943 the price of flour increased nine-fold. When the work began in Dohnavur two hundred pounds per year supplied their needs. It was now costing between seven hundred pounds and eight hundred pounds per week.

It was a potentially frightening time for the Family. News of the war reached the children's ears, albeit in perhaps small doses, things for which their prayers were asked. Their Amma, whom some of them had hardly laid eyes on, but whom others still knew as mother, was apparently hopelessly ill. Prayer had not changed things in the Room of Peace, so far as the children could see. And prices—rising and rising, though rice and curry still filled their bowls. They joined in the prayers for God's supply.

There were many in the Family who were conscious, as Amy was, of being held by the One who controlled not only the price of rice, the health of each of His children, and incomprehensible matters like wars, but even the stupendous and mysterious celestial structures known as nebulae. She expressed her trust in that God:

A Chance to Die

Lover of all, I hold me fast by Thee,
Ruler of time, King of eternity.
There is no great with Thee, there is no small,
For Thou art all, and fillest all in all.

The new-born world swings forth at Thy command,
The falling dew-drop falls into Thy hand.
God of the firmament's mysterious powers,
I see Thee thread the minutes of my hours.

I see Thee guide the frail, the fading moon
That walks alone through empty skies at noon.
Was ever wayworn, lonely traveler
But had Thee by him, blessed Comforter?

Out of my vision swims the untracked star,
Thy counsels too are high and very far,
Only I know, God of the nebulae,
It is enough to hold me fast by Thee.

Chapter 46
The Voice From the Sanctum

To the burning spirit and the forceful spirit anywhere is easier than the rear. We always want to be in the van." The spirit Amy Carmichael thus described was her own—burning, forceful—from her enthusiastic guidance of her own little brothers and sisters and her earnest evangelism in the slums of Belfast and Manchester, to her ardent work with the Starry Cluster, leading to the Dohnavur Fellowship. She whose highest aim was to be a simple follower of her Master who made Himself nothing, who took the form of the lowest slave in an Eastern household—she had become, inevitably, it seems, a powerful matriarch of a very large and dependent family. She was no longer in a position to whisk everyone off suddenly to the Forest or the seashore when the fancy took her. Her control was of another kind. The accident, far from diminishing her matriarchal power, enhanced it to the level of a mystique. She was a *commanding* figure, as the figure of Beatrice seemed to Dante, "commanding as a mother."

The system—the Pattern Shewn in the Mount—was crystallized, not to say frozen, when she disappeared from view. She was not quite invisible. People saw her, of course. Many waited on her, children were brought to her room for Coming Days and other occasions, accals and sitties and annachies had access, but it was always controlled access, as in the case of any executive. For a given length of time, for a special reason, they entered the precincts. It could not have been otherwise.

The precepts given to Amy were the precepts perpetuated, not only by those who taught and exemplified them to the younger ones, but by constant reiteration and reinforcement in the reams of pages that poured out of the inner sanctum which was "Amma's Room." These included not only her many books and *Dust of Gold,* which was called a "private" letter for people all over the world, but daily messages she believed the Lord had given her for the Family. Many of these have been published as devotional collections under the titles *Edges of His Ways, Thou Givest . . . They Gather,* and *Whispers of His Power.* What God gave to her in the silence of her room she—always the mother, doing her God-given motherwork of nurturing—gave to her children on paper, to be read aloud the next day. So there was always a voice—still and small, gentle and loving, and a message—authoritatively prescriptive—issuing forth from that somewhat remote place.

In addition to these there were the personal letters, thousands of them, every one a perfect model of intimate concern for the individual, gracious encouragement in his particular need or task, and love—the warmest assurance, always, of *love.* There were papers: *Roots,* sixty-nine pages on what the DF was, what it did and why, written for insiders. There were instructive papers on subjects such as Fasting, Baptism, Prayer, and Guidance. She was able in this way to clarify what was to be done and why it was meet, right, and their bounden duty so to do, unless, of course, the Unseen Leader should lead them to do otherwise.

Could they do otherwise? It was often the conservative Indian establishment that stood most stoutly in the way of change.

"Amma never did it that way."

"Amma's vision has proved right down the years."

"Amma would not feel happy with the ideas you suggest." (This last was said sometimes even when one had access to her and she had said the opposite.)

"If only she were still about and could see the situation for herself," said one of the Europeans, "she would certainly change it all. She understands things clearly and would overthrow many of our traditions and contented routines." Some really believed this, at times at least.

Amy Carmichael's certainty that the lines on which the work had been established were divinely given was never shaken. Believing (in spite of numerous disappointments) that those who joined the work were divinely sent, she was willing to grant a hearing. "You could make suggestions without fear or inhibition," one of them assured me, "but you were not surprised if they were not accepted. She knew best." She was settled in her own mind, so anything which would shift the lines in any significant way she could not accept—until, as we shall see, certain radical changes were proposed in the last few years of her life.

In theory she wanted future leaders to be free from a sense of her hovering scrutiny. She wrote it down in 1946.

"There is one thing I have often said to you individually. I may have written it—I want to make sure you have it. It is this: when decisions have to be made, don't look back and wonder what I would have done. Look up, and light will come to show what our Lord and Master would have you do."

She wanted to be in the vanguard. She admitted it. But she saw that it was not her place. "Our place is always behind the scenes," she wrote, intending to emphasize the great importance of encouraging Indians for leadership. The effect of that effort was that she became the generator in the back room that ran the machine.

Amy tried to retire. Let it be understood that she really tried to turn over the reins to others. Annually she was reelected titular head, "kept on ice," as one DF put it. She wished that the next leader could be an Indian, but as she saw it there wasn't a man anywhere with the patience, the fixed purpose and grit, the courage, the vision, or the daring for the job. She had known two Indian women who, with more experience, more spiritual training, might have fulfilled the qualifications—Ponnammal and Arulai. She counted on other Indian women, up to a point, to do certain things. She delegated responsibility. Indian men were learning, she felt, but left something to be desired. Those in the Fellowship, after all, knew mainly what she had taught them, and that not always very thoroughly. She was still their mother. They were her sons and daughters. The time for cutting apron strings never seemed to arrive.

The danger of allowing herself to be the foundation of the work was very plain to Amy and she strove to prevent such a happening.

Hardly more than a year after the accident she had written one of her "Notes" to the DFs, citing Jesus' parable of the house building, and Hebrews 13:8, "Jesus Christ, the same yesterday and today and for ever."

"A work which is founded on anyone on earth is like the house that was built on the sand. When the rain descended, and the floods came and the winds blew and beat upon that house, it fell, and great was the fall of it. The only foundation that will stand through the floods is the eternal Rock. . . . Sooner or later every work is searched and tested and tried as by rain and the vehement beating of floods and winds. Then will appear its true character. If it falls it will be because it was built on sand; better then that it should fall. If it stands it will be because by the mercy of God it was built on the Eternal Rock, Christ Jesus our Lord." She went on to say that her heart's desire was that the thought of all might be forever fixed on the Eternal, not on the human—on Jesus Christ, the Rock, the same forever.

When she wrote that note she believed she would soon be either healed or dead. Fifteen years later, neither having occurred, she wrote another note, spelling out for May Powell, who was coleader with Godfrey, qualities to be looked for in a new leader: She must be just, a woman of character, able to make decisions, possessing the kind of love that is never tired out of loving, the power to ride the waves instead of being submerged by them, and a deep conviction about DF principles.

The fact that Amy addressed this note to May rather than to Godfrey or to Godfrey *and* May can hardly be ignored. She took it for granted that the leader must be a woman. A man could not be considered to make decisions which would bind the community.

Nowhere does David Carmichael, Amy's father, find more than passing mention in her writings. Her mother, in contrast to the vague figure of her father, is strongly portrayed. Amy was the oldest of the children and therefore the natural leader. Her brothers were cherished and adored, but they were her little brothers. Her relationship with the D.O.M. was certainly the most intimate she ever experienced with a man. Their mutual love and respect was of the deepest and tenderest, but there was little or nothing of male leadership and female response. She was probably by far the stronger of the two. Barclay Buxton was her "chief." She said so often. Thomas Walker, though not her superior in the same sense as Buxton, was a leader whom she gladly followed. They were gone. It was to her that the vision for this work had been vouchsafed. It was she who must bear the responsibility.

Amy had studied the New Testament passages on the ministry of women. To Conybeare's note on 1 Corinthians 14:34, "The women must not officiate publicly in the congregation," she added, "compare chapter 11:2 where they are told to be veiled if they pray or prophesy. Some muddle here?" and in the margin of 15:1–6 she puts, "Mary was the first messenger to men." She loved the Revised Version of Psalms 68:11, "The Lord gave the word: great was the company of the women that published it."

She believed that the apostle Paul's injunctions about the silence of women must have been meant for a certain group at a certain time. He was not articulating a doctrine of total silence, any more than he was commanding women, as Amy put it, "to go to church with their hair hanging down their backs," a horror of indecency for a lady of Amy's breeding.

Having explained the above convictions, she added, "Well, that's that. All the same I think men were as a rule meant for leadership and publicity and so on—not women, and the very day Godfrey knew enough Tamil for it—and even before—I pushed him into the pool and left him to swim. In other words asked him to take Prayers, the worship in the House of Prayer, and so on. And gladly, oh so gladly, I used to repeat John the Baptist's words to myself, 'He must increase and (I did not say *but* for I was very, very glad) I must decrease.' "

Chapter 47
The Razor Edge

The supreme gift of the soldier is the power to simplify amid confusion, to make a simple syllogism, which once it is made seems ... unquestionable, but which before it is made is in the power only of genius."

This, from John Buchan's *Cromwell,* is quoted in one of Amy's notes to the Fellowship.

"Instead of 'genius' read 'faith,' " she added, "and you will understand why anything like careless sureness was always far from the one on whom the final responsibility of decisions lay, and who would be, if the decision proved to be caused by a mistaken reading of the will of God, blameworthy."

She tells how, when a major purchase of land was to be made, she used to sign the checks kneeling by her desk, "so deeply did I fear." It was "the razor edge between faith and presumption, so exceedingly fine" that she had to walk. "I know we never moved forward without sureness, and yet there was always this prayer at the root of action. I won't attempt to explain the apparent contradiction except by this true saying, 'From the circumference even opposite lines run to the centre.' "

Sureness but not *careless* sureness. Fear and faith. Middle-of-the-night misgivings and dawn's renewed determination to take God at His word. The power to simplify amid confusion. Amy had all of the above. She was still a woman, a fallible creature like the psalmist: "When I said, 'my foot slippeth' "; like Paul: "the good that I would I do not"; like John: "yet if any man sin. . . ." Nothing exempted the Dohnavur crowd from being "miserable offenders," like the rest of the world. The whole lot was daily in need of that amazing grace which had brought them safe thus far, and would finally lead them home.

"All the conflicts were between what Amma thought God wanted and what others thought God wanted" was the diagnosis of one of the Family. "We all thought we had the mind of Christ."

Ronald Proctor, a practical man who confessed that he often saw mud where Amma saw stars, informed her that the old Ford needed to be replaced. It was a simple matter of what was going on in its insides. To Amy it was a spiritual matter, one for prayer and pondering. She told him she really did not "feel" it right to buy a new car. On the next trip the brakes gave out and the old Ford rolled straight for the water. "We were very nearly, feelings and all, at the bottom of the tank," Ronald reported. That was guidance. The car was replaced.

Then there was the shattering disagreement with one of Amy's most beloved, Murray Webb-Peploe, a man of loyalty and truth. Irresistible force met an immovable object. Murray's wife, Oda, had taken the twins to England for schooling. This meant a much longer separation for husband and wife than when the boys were at school in the hills. The time came when Oda could not go on without Murray. His loyalty to Amma and the work he had no doubt he had been called to was in conflict with his loyalty and love for his wife. There was a tug of war. His mother took Oda's side. "Years ago you sought my counsel," she wrote to Murray, ". . . but those days passed, and another woman (not Oda) took that place, though you may not have realized it."[1]

What was the man to do?

He understood and fully subscribed to the principles of guidance which Amy had spelled out for the Family:

The devil sometimes speaks and tries to deceive us into thinking it is the voice of God. He tries to get us, who long to walk in the light, to follow

---

1. Katherine Makower, *Follow My Leader,* p. 158.

instead a will-o-the-wisp into the marsh. In the matter of guidance there are three important points:

1. The Word of the Lord in the Bible.
2. The Word of the Spirit in our heart.
3. The circumstances of our lives, which have been arranged by God.

All three must point one way. It is never enough for any two of them to be taken as showing God's will. *If the voice is God's all three will agree.*

The thought of Murray's being drawn away "into the marsh," as she could not help thinking, was a major calamity for Amy. What could have been clearer than the guidance both she and he had had about his coming to Dohnavur? What could be more important than his place as director of the hospital? Why could Oda not have been content either to educate the boys in India or to send them, as most missionaries had always done, to boarding school? Furthermore, a commitment to the DF, in Amy's view, was a commitment for life.

This matter of how the Word of the Lord was received for guidance is illuminated in a letter Amy had written just after the Webb-Peploes had arrived in Dohnavur. They had had the temerity to take issue with Amma over a journey she proposed to make.

"The word came to me to go to Madura. . . . Nobody saw it possible, but it was clear to me and I knew it would soon be clear to them and so it was. Next morning dear Murray and Godfrey came to me, having got light, then the others most beautifully got light."

One of them had read that morning of the manger in Bethlehem, which, by what would appear some rather fancy mental footwork, gave meaning to the thought of the heat and the noise of Madura—if Jesus could come to a manger, she could go to Madura. "That settled it for him. Others got words of equal clearness and by noon all who understand this kind of leading were ready to pray through." So to Madura she went, confirmed in her guidance by the unity of her comrades.

The urging of Murray's wife, children, and mother were not by any means sufficient reason in Amma's mind for him to leave. Then he received "a jolly stiff letter" from none other than the home director of the China Inland Mission, who was also the chairman of the Keswick convention, W. H. Aldis, telling him to come to Oda. Under other circumstances such a man's counsel would have carried much weight with Amma. Not this time. She could not see this as anything but a grave mistake.

Early in 1947 Murray went. It was good-bye forever to Dohnavur.

"Pray that I may be directed in the writing of *Dust of Gold*" [about Murray's departure] Amy asked. "Unless it is clearly shown that it is NOT our DF way (though we stand by Murray in it for he has no choice) it will stumble many."

She could not bear disunity. Love, the Gold Cord which bound the Dohnavur Fellowship together, must bring about oneness of mind as well as heart. If God had shown her one thing, would He show the rest another thing? There is no instance on record of Amy's accepting another's guidance after she believed she had been given clear guidance in a matter.

Loyalty meant never questioning motives, always looking for an excuse for others' actions when they seemed out of line, never speaking about a person but always to him. To raise an objection to the Pattern was to skate perilously close to disloyalty.

One night, in great distress because there had been a disagreement between two people, Amy wrote a many-paged letter "To my children who are comrades in the war." There was truth on both sides. She reminded them of the need to go straight to the other. "O my children, if only you would make up your minds never to doubt the love of another sister or brother in Christ, but *always* to think the best and never admit an unkind thought in your heart, how happy, how heavenly, life would be . . . If this were the last time I could speak to you I should say just these words, Beloved, let us love, O let us love. We perish if we do not love. Let us love."

Chapter 48
Maintain a Constant Victory

On the stroke of midnight, August 14, 1947, Lord Louis Mountbatten took his pen and performed his last official action as the king's representative.

"Outside, at almost the same instant, his personal standard as the Viceroy of India, a Union Jack emblazoned with the Star of India, came down the flagstaff of Viceroy's House for the last time."[1] Britain in that moment relinquished the world's greatest empire.

"Never before had anything even remotely like it been attempted. Nowhere were there any guidelines, any precedents, any revealing insights from the past to order what was going to be the biggest, the most complex divorce action in history, the breakup of a family of four hundred million human beings along with the assets and household property they had acquired in centuries of living together on the same piece of earth."[2]

The effects of this stunning piece of history, so cataclysmic for the country, made little difference inside the red clay walls of the Dohnavur compound. Godfrey Webb-Peploe wrote,

"The great day passed off quietly. The village had a few fireworks and chorused shouting of 'Victory to India.' We had a very simple talk by Thyaharaj on the change of government, and then we put up the new flag of India and stood around it and prayed for the country. There was no visible difference on August 16th."[3]

---

1. Larry Collins and Dominique Lapierre, *Freedom at Midnight* (New York: Simon & Schuster, 1975), p. 288.
2. Ibid, p. 198.
3. Katherine Makower, *Follow My Leader*, p. 162.

One of the sitties felt liberated in a personal way. "We were sisters now," she said, "Indian and European. It was wonderful. I no longer resented everyone's knowing *everything* about me anymore. Before, I had held onto my British culture—I liked to be alone."

Amy did not think it was wonderful. A woman of her generation, she could not think that independence was a good thing, although she may not have shared Rudyard Kipling's view of Britain's divine appointment: "The responsibility for governing India has been placed by the inscrutable design of providence upon the shoulders of the British race." It is doubtful she felt pained for the same reason Churchill did: "The loss of India would be final and fatal to us. It could not fail to be part of a process that would reduce us to the scale of a minor power." Amy's thought was not for Britain's loss so much as for India's. She believed India was not ready for self-government and would suffer far more than she could benefit. Amy was tremendously loyal to her own people. She knew the worth of Britain's control, as did many Indians who looked with misgiving on the end of the raj and had fought hammer and tongs to prevent it. There were men in the civil service for whom she had great respect, men of honor who saw themselves not as conquerors but, like Amma, servants to the Indian people. The price of freedom was a terrible one—partition, war, murder, and pillage.

In the quiet gardens and lanes, in the lively cottages of the compound, things went on more or less as usual. Rice, by the ton, was pounded by hand, parboiled in the great pots, cooked daily, and eaten. Babies were fed and bathed and changed and rocked and sung to and carried out to play. Bottles were prepared, diapers washed, nurseries scrubbed, walks swept, tiles and brass vessels polished, gardens weeded. The children bathed under the pumps, ate their curries, learned their lessons. The bells of the Prayer Tower called the Family to prayer and rang out the evening hymn.

In the Room of Peace lay the mother, nearly eighty years old now, interviewing people for five hours a day, writing her love letters, working on a book—a simplified biography of Thomas Walker, *This One Thing*—writing always in longhand on the writing stand, giving the pages one by one to Neela her helper, who typed them and passed them on to a sittie for final draft.

It seemed to Amy that the Family had let up a bit on their prayers for healing.

"For years patiently the prayer meeting went on praying for me," she wrote in her private notebook. "It does not seem to do so now. I was feeling the need of prayer very much, but to ask for it would be selfish. So I had settled that I would not do so, when this word came: 'I have prayed for thee.' My dear, dear Lord."

Daily Amma called in one of her doctors, Nancy Robbins, to give her background in Hinduism, customs, histories of DF people. Nancy was writing a book, *Greater Is He,* for which Amma made suggestions and, to Nancy's surprise, humbly asked for suggestions on her own book. Dr. Robbins believed that the strongest psychological element of Amma's illness was her fear of the domination of pain over mind and spirit. This she managed to conceal from nearly everyone, but it was revealed again and again in *Rose From Brier* and her poetry, such as:

> Before the winds that blow do cease,
>   Teach me to dwell within Thy calm:
> Before the pain has passed in peace,
>   Give me, my God, to sing a psalm.
> Let me not lose the chance to prove
>   The fulness of enabling love.
> O Love of God, do this for me:
>   Maintain a constant victory.

"She never complained," Nancy said, "and was reluctant to discuss her symptoms with anyone, even her doctor."

At least one or two of the Indian women who cared for her saw a different side. Neela once said to Amma, "Your last word will be pain, pain, pain." Tired of hearing about Sennacherib and Goliath and Apollyon and the rest of her aches, she told Amma she ought to be thanking God instead that most of the ordinary functions were still functioning.

Nancy wondered at the large number of people who always seemed to be about, waiting on Amy. It made a strange impression at first, "but I realize that this attention was largely imposed on her by her anxious family, and that most of these 'attendants' were selected by Amma because no one else could cope with them and she felt they needed her help. So it was a complex situation."

The family thought of everything. Philip England, who built everything, designed a brick platform reaching from her verandah out to a place under the trees where she could sit without having to negotiate steps. Jeevanie brought powder for cooling and comforting, but when she put it on Amma's face, Amma said, "You must not think *you* can put powder on when you go to the House of Prayer." Powder for an invalid was one thing. Powder for vanity quite another.

Jeevanie was annoyed when Amma would have her open the bird cage so that the birds could fly through the room.

"She would be beckoning them—'Come, come, little birds!'—and I would be standing behind her shooing them away—'Go, go!' They landed in her hair, on her sheets—such a mess. I was very cross with her. But she loved them.

"Sometimes Amma imagined that I had bumped her bed. She chided me. I was angry with her. I threw the hot-water bottle at her and ran away."

Bee brought a bottle of cologne.

"Last night I used you to help toward sleep," Amma wrote in her thank-you note. "You are in a bottle with a red top, you know, close at hand. Nothing helps me more sometimes, and to have this extra means that I can use it without counting the drops."

Then someone thought of face cream. It was well timed—a gift from heaven.

"A few days ago I saw an advertisement for cream in the paper and thought, 'If I went in for buying such things I would try that stuff—it sounds cooling'—and here it comes! Did our angels (yours and mine) laugh?"

Besides the pain, heat and sleeplessness were constant torments. Before an electric fan was installed the seven- and eight-year-old girls would come in twos to "do punkah," pulling the rope that swung the fan for half an hour at a time. "If I got slow Amma would say, 'Oh darling child, are you asleep?' Then she would give me a sweet and give the other one a turn."

At night she asked her nurse to read to her. Jeevanie read John 14, 15, 16, Revelation 7:9–17, and chapters 21 and 22 so many times that she had them memorized, as well as the whole of Rutherford's hymn, "The Sands of Time Are Sinking." Then she would massage Amma's legs until she nearly fell asleep herself.

"Oh darling, what would I do without you?" Amma said. "You always make me sleep."

"She would make me take dictation in the middle of the night, and throw it all away next morning. 'What a waste!' I said. 'Never mind, darling, the Lord has given me something else,' she said."

Jeevanie was one of those who as a child had not believed Amma loved her as much as the others. She was very dark, not the coffee-with-cream color of Tara and Leela that Amma loved.

"But when she was sick I cared for her. I *had* to love her then, and I learned. I told her she had caned me often. 'Did I, darling?' she said. 'Yes, Amma.' 'Oh darling, I loved you dearly,' she said. All bitterness went. She was not at all a difficult patient. If Amma had not rescued me, where would I have been? She took me to a temple once so that I would know, but I saw the beautiful girls and their jewels and thought to myself, 'I would like that.' Now I understand. She saved me."

One of the tasks Amma had set herself very early in her illness was to write a letter to each member of the Family to be put into a box and kept until after her death. She did not keep a careful record of what was in the box, so some received several letters and probably there were some who got none. To Neela, who was both nurse and secretary, she wrote of the way the Lord had brought her to Dohnavur, through impossible barriers. "It was then our Father, yours and mine, said to me, 'No purpose of Mine can be hindered.'

"I don't want you to become so wrapped up in the work of this room," she went on, "that when it is empty you will feel your life is empty. So don't think of me, ever, in a way which would make it too hard if you had not me to help. Think of yourself as belonging first to your Lord and then to all, Servant of all. . . . Never, never let any human love come first."

To one of the sitties she wrote:

Margaret, for whom I thank my God, if ever you read this I shall be among the cloud of witnesses, looking with a deepened love and understanding upon you as you run your race.

I hardly know what to say to you. I think you know all I would wish to say, but you may not know how I count on you for the future—if there be a future—and how I thank God for the preparation of the years.

I remember your first letter coming and I remember your cable . . . and now you are deep in what seems to us a peculiarly selfless service. The spiritual training of children must be that. You work for the years you will not see. You work for the Invisible all the time, but you work for the Eternal. So it is all worth while.

Then follow words of encouragement for discouraging days, strong words for loneliness, and "Goodbye, my steadfast Margaret."

The letters I have been allowed to see follow a similar pattern—thanks to God, reminiscence of how they came, heartening words to help them toward faith, hope, and, beyond all, love.

This was her prayer for her children:

> Father, hear us, we are praying,
> Hear the words our hearts are saying,
> We are praying for our children.
>
> Keep them from the powers of evil,
> From the secret, hidden peril,
> From the whirlpool that would suck them,
> From the treacherous quicksand pluck them.
>
> From the worldling's hollow gladness,
> From the sting of faithless sadness,
> Holy Father, save our children.
>
> Through life's troubled waters steer them,
> Through life's bitter battle cheer them,
> Father, Father, be Thou near them.
> Read the language of our longing,
> Read the wordless pleadings thronging,
> Holy Father, for our children
>
> *And wherever they may bide,*
> *Lead them Home at eventide.*[4]

---

4. *Toward Jerusalem*, p. 106.

Chapter 49
The River Breaks Out

I t may be that decisions which seem to change the character of the work will now have to be made," Amy wrote in 1946. "But if the principles which have grounded us from the beginning are held fast there will be no real change. The river may flow in a new channel but it will be the same river."

Something told her that things could not go on forever exactly as they were, and it was as if she were bracing herself for the time when others would broach the subject they knew she dreaded. If the prediction came from her, their duty would not be quite so disagreeable. The education of the children had been often questioned in the past, and Amy had rejected suggested changes as an altogether different "river." When Arul Dasan, her faithful helper, arranged for his son David to attend the Walker Middle School nearby, the eight-year-old was excited. The first day of school arrived. All was in readiness. David had the books his father had bought for him and was about to leave the house when a message came. Amma wanted to see Arul Dasan at once. David was not told what Amma said to his father. He was simply told he was not going to the Walker School. In the early days Amma's children had attended the little mission school. Later she found that they did not learn to be truthful there, "rather the opposite," so began to educate them at home.

When Dr. MacDougall of the Women's Christian College of Madras had tried to persuade Amy to send her girls there, she consented at first but none went. For one thing, she was not sure the standards of the Indian teachers met hers. She had heard a conversation among missionaries from different parts of India, lamenting that the type of Christians turned out from their schools lacked certain qualities which make for character.

"I could not help wondering, as I listened to the talk of these seniors, how a new type could be expected to evolve from an old mould." Amy had set about changing the mould, and she meant to stick with that one.

Agnes Naish, to whom Amy had delegated responsibility for the children's schooling, took a hard line against college. After all, if the girls' primary calling was to be the care of children, was not a college education, leading perhaps to medicine and other ambitious professional fields, not only unnecessary but likely to eclipse the call? She reminded Amy of Amy's own words:

Our goal is service. It is not worth while to spend time, strength, money and energy on anything less. Settle it in your minds: our way of education is planned so as to prepare in spirit and in mind our boys and girls for the Service of the King of Kings. It must therefore from first to last be spiritual education. . . . And the result? No one need fear about that. I could give many proofs that an education such as our children have is indeed true education. The kind of letter a person writes is an index of mind. A letter written in a foreign language is a very searching test. Our children pass that test.

I was given some idea of the inflexibility of Agnes Naish ("three thousand years behind the times") when I asked why Amy Carmichael had stated adamantly that no American would be acceptable in the DF. The first answer: She did not believe Americans were prepared for the kind of sacrifice the DF asked. The second: There was no one known to Amy in America who might screen candidates. The third: "It was felt that a certain standard of the English language must be taught, and Agnes Naish dogmatized firmly on syntax and pronunciation (as she did on everything else). You said 'different from' and not 'different to,' kilometre was to be pronounced keelo-meeter."

It is to be wondered where the splendid Agnes Naish learned "American"—but then perhaps "different to" was used by some Americans in her day. It also needs to be said that when Dohnavur girls finally began going outside to school they found that they could speak neither Indian English (they spoke English English) nor Indian Tamil. Their Tamil was distinguished by a peculiar singsong such as often develops within a close-knit community. Possibly the accents of some of the foreigners lent their odd cadences, so that teachers in the outside schools had more difficulty understanding the Dohnavur girls' Tamil than the foreign DFs'.

One of Amy's most trusted older workers, Pappammal, who had come from a well-known Christian family and was in charge of the smaller boys, strongly disagreed with Amma about their education and finally left because of it. A close friendship of long standing came to an end and Pappammal was "erased." For the sake of example to the children, her name was not spoken again. Once more, "Dohnavur is a sign that is spoken against." So Amma, in spite of extreme sensitivity to any possible misrepresentation of her work, wrote, "like our Master we must hold our peace and answer them nothing."

India's independence began to impinge on the life of the compound far more powerfully than Amy had foreseen. New laws were passed, one of them bringing great joy to Amy and the rest—the *devadasi* (temple prostitute) system was outlawed. Its illegality did not stamp it out at once. It went underground for a few years and more recently has surfaced again.

Certain kinds of training which Dohnavur could not provide were now required by law for certain degrees. If they were to have government recognition for the teachers in Dohnavur they must have school-leaving certificates. Amy was able finally to see the necessity of a major change in educational policy. Thyaharaj was the first to break the boundary when he sat for the Senior Cambridge exams. Amy approved the boys' attending the Middle School in Dohnavur and the girls going to Tiruchchirappalli, though she wept when they left. She called the boys "Gideons," for a man who had courage and faith, and the girls "Timothys," for a man who learned to endure hardness. One of the sitties and an accal went with the girls to make a home, but the transition, not surprisingly, was less than smooth.

The relative freedom, so heady after the strictures of all their former years, was too much for some of the girls and, as Amma had feared, they rebelled. Furthermore it was discovered at first that Agnes Naish's system was not superior after all, and some of the girls did poorly in school. But the release into education in the public system was to lead into a new future for the work, with college graduates and other trained personnel moving into careers, often in Christian institutions in India and other countries. Some are now among the leaders of the present work in Dohnavur.

Studies in child psychology were brought to Amy's attention and she was able to accept the recommendation that children ought to be in mixed age groups in the cottages. They had always been divided into peer groups, ages two to six, six to eight, eight to ten, and so on. This meant that the children experienced several times, as they grew up and were moved from cottage to cottage, what amounted nearly to the death of their mother (their accal). Though the leaders had tried to make these moves gradual, having the children go first to play at the new house, the final transfer broke the children's hearts. It also broke the mothers' hearts. It took a long time before anyone recognized the reason for many of the difficulties that resulted.

Margaret Wilkinson, a university-educated woman from northern Ireland, felt strongly the need for some sort of a "break out" from the time-honored ways of Dohnavur. It was an out-of-the-way place. They were cut off not only by the war and by Amma's illness, but even, to a much greater degree than in Amma's early days, from other missions. They needed to establish links with the outside. There simply were not enough choices. Margaret's conviction was that the character of a young person is developed through learning to choose. She saw that they needed something other than spiritual training and proposed that Dohnavur girls be allowed to join the Girl Guides movement, of which she had been a leader in Ireland. She presented, for the consideration of Amy and the other leaders, her reasons:

1. It may not be possible to shelter future generations as we have sheltered past ones. I feel we must therefore try to prepare them to test things that differ and to weigh up other points of view, so that if

the day should come when they have conflicting ideals forced upon them from without they may be able to make a considered judgment.

2. Our senior accals had nearly all some experience of life outside the compound even if only as a child. The generation from whom the senior accals of the future must come have not that experience; yet not only may they have to fill the place held by the seniors of today but circumstances may arise in which they will have to shoulder responsibilities to carry which a knowledge of the world has been essential to sitties.

Then followed an explanation of the specific ways in which Girl Guides could provide just the help that was needed. The proposal was rejected, "but I did not feel I was not *listened* to," she said. Years later she broached the subject again. This time it received Amma's blessing and a Guide company was formed.

The interests of Amy Carmichael might understandably have been restricted by this time in her life to the Family. Weren't the burdens she bore for them quite an adequate load for an elderly shut-in who had a large share of pain to bear besides? In fact her attention and concern continued to range outside the compound walls where there were still huge numbers who did not know Christ. All new DFs were required to live for a time in a Hindu village with non-English-speaking companions in order to learn the language by the saturation method, and the religion and customs at first hand. She wanted news of them and their progress. When evangelistic teams of twos and threes returned from visits to the villages, Amma wanted to know exactly what questions they had been asked, how they had answered. What of the Tamil tracts and booklets produced and distributed in the DF book room—were they being read? Sometimes, until she became too ill, she asked to meet patients who had come to trust the Lord in the hospital.

Evangelistic efforts in Dohnavur suffered from too exclusive use of the Family's men as preachers. Yearly at Christmas a four-day convention called the Meetings of Vision brought together Hindus, Muslims, and others to hear again the Gospel which many had first heard through the personal witness of the hospital staff, or through visits to the villages by Dohnavur people. In 1948, at the suggestion of Dr. Kinnear, an outside Indian speaker (a "trusted" one) was invited to address these meetings. It was the thin edge of a most significant wedge, bringing to Dohnavur in due course many leaders of a new evangelical awakening in Tamil Nadu.

The Dohnavur "river" was certainly flowing in new "channels." It was a testimony to the vigor of Amy's mind that she was able to accept as many of the new proposals as she did. It was also greatly reassuring to those in charge. The question she had forbidden them to ask—*Would Amma have done it this way?*—was always there, spoken or unspoken. To have her blessing on the new channels obviated the question.

Chapter 50
Fettered and Yet Free

Three rules of prayer helped the Family to save time and energy in prayer meetings. It was Amma, of course, who wrote them.

1. We don't need to explain to our Father things that are known to Him.
2. We don't need to press Him, as if we had to deal with an unwilling God.
3. We don't need to suggest to Him what to do, for He Himself knows what to do.

Whether her children kept those rules as they prayed for her healing, we don't know. Surely they pressed the Lord often for the healing of their dear Amma. Surely they made many suggestions.

Amy Carmichael wrote a private note on June 12, 1948, "Not relief from pain, not relief from the weariness that follows, not anything of that sort at all, is my chief need. Thou, O Lord my God, art my need—Thy courage, Thy patience, Thy fortitude. And very much I need a quickened gratitude for the countless helps given every day."

Ten days later she was feeling pressed because of tiring interviews which came "before I had 'obtained access.' See 1 Kings 8:56: 'There hath not failed one word of all His good promise.' If we take time to let this soak in, there is rest in the midst of pressure."

The next day, June 23, was not different from other days, to begin with—the early morning cup of tea, the usual quiet time of reading and prayer, perhaps pills for the usual pain, and then the usual people to see. Someone brought word of another who was going through deep water. She wrote a note and made up a parcel to send to her. There was no one at hand to deliver them except the nurse. She sent her off, and then made her way to the bathroom. She slipped and fell. Neela was by her side almost at once. "Don't tell anyone," said Amma, "I shall be all right in the morning."

Neela promptly disobeyed, called the two doctors, Christian Rogan and Nancy Robbins, who came running. They found a broken right arm and a fractured femur. The shock to an over-eighty frame was nearly lethal, and without a blood transfusion and an injection she might quickly have passed through the Gates. She hovered very near for two days and then rallied. So, she noted wryly, those doctors had "slammed the Gates again."

Most of the responsibility for the men's side of the work had devolved on Godfrey Webb-Peploe since Murray's leaving. He had also the spiritual legacy left by Walker of work in the village of Dohnavur, not to mention "all that Shepherd-work means for the Family." Before Amma's accident in June he had been given doctor's orders to rest. A serious infection had set in after someone had kicked him in one of the boys' games, and the leg had not healed. Just before Christmas of 1948 he had a thrombosis.

Amy herself, though almost totally immobile since her fall, had snapped back sufficiently to be "deep in everything, and power to think has come again." She felt it was time for more " 'thinks,' together with one and another of this dear family"—about their allowing her to drop out altogether of the place of leadership, and implementing what had been decided seventeen years earlier: May and Godfrey were to be the leaders. Their appointment by Amma had been perfectly clear to the Family but they had stubbornly (or was it helplessly?) refused to acknowledge her abdication. "Up till now all I could say has been, as the Tamils put it, moonlight upon rock." What she wanted without further delay was validation by the formal election of May and Godfrey in the annual "Kingdom Business" meeting.

One evening seven weeks later Mary Mills came into the Room of Peace. Besides being the "Perfect Nurse" who had cared for Amy ever since her accident, she was one of the closest of her companions. Amy read in her face that something had happened.

"What is it?" she asked. "What is wrong?"

"There is nothing wrong," said Mary. "God has trusted us with a great trust. Godfrey is in heaven."

Godfrey, the beloved. Godfrey, her son. First it was Ponnammal, then Arulai, then Murray. One by one they had been given to her. One by one they had demonstrated the spiritual calibre she had asked God for, the character so desperately needed in a leader for her Family. And one by one they had been removed. Now Godfrey, the tower of strength she needed so much more in her old age, the one for whom she had so often thanked God. Godfrey. In heaven. We wonder what "her thoughts said" when she heard the stunning news. We wonder what "her Father said." What dialogue took place between those two during the rest of that night? It is not recorded. We guess that she said YES. We know that she wrote to the Family next day:

"Our God trusts us to trust Him. . . . Let us not disappoint God. Let us rise to this great trust."

She reminded them of the great promise of Romans 8:28, and of Jesus' having wept—proof that "tears are not sin. But to go on lamenting would be sin. It would be as though we doubted the love of our most tender Father. To wonder why this has been allowed to happen would be to dishonor Him. I found myself doing this very thing. 'Oh, why am I left—I who am useless to you all—and he, who could do so much for you, taken?' Suddenly I knew that even to think such a thought for a moment, was sin. Thank God for the cleansing Blood. But do not let us grieve His love by wondering why. Faith *never* wonders why."

Each of these deaths was a death far harder for Amy to bear than her own physical suffering. But she saw in each of them a chance to die, the opportunity to acknowledge once again the lordship of Christ in her life. He held all the rights. She had turned them over long ago to Him when she resolved to follow Him to the uttermost. The searing questions which crowded her mind she knew that she must refuse. It was one more way of saying no to herself and yes to God.

There was one question she could not possibly refuse. Who would pick up the reins? John Risk had the qualities of leadership she looked for, but was comparatively young and lacked Godfrey's experience. The Lord was aware of all that. John must be God's man. Who was to tell him so if not Amy? Who else was in a position to appoint him?

She wrote to him almost at once to say she expected him to take over. She was, willy-nilly, still the leader, still a prophet after the order of Judas and Silas who "exhorted the brethren with many words, and confirmed them."[1]

"As I was with Moses, so I will be with thee"[2] was the verse she gave to her "David."

Early in 1950 it was decided that it was time to invite Indians to join the leadership group which for twenty years had comprised only May Powell and the Webb-Peploes. There were two who had had all the training the DF could give—Mimosa's oldest son Rajappan and Ponnammal's daughter Purripu. They became associates, Rajappan working with John on the men's side, Purripu with May on the women's. Amy came to a settled peace that this now was the Pattern shewn.

Her phenomenal strength drained rapidly away after the fall in the bathroom. There was no more walking out under the trees or even across the room for Amma. She could not sit, let alone walk, stand, or kneel. She learned a new appreciation for each of these positions, which it had been her habit to use as helps to prayer. She was reduced to the one least conducive to prayer, the one she had never chosen—lying on her back. Throughout her life she had taken to her Lord every least thing, pleasant or unpleasant, in order to live the whole of life in Christ, discovering in each experience how He shared it with her. It was entirely natural that she should mention to Him this matter of being pinned flat. Could there possibly be a spiritual lesson there? Would it be something whereby to help somebody else? In answer, she "seemed to see Him, as He was for a few immeasurable minutes, not upright but laid flat on His Cross.

"I tell you this because some of you may find yourselves in hard ways. *Always your Lord has been before you.* Always He will come

---

1. Acts 15:32.
2. Joshua 1:5.

with a most heavenly understanding of what your heart most needs."

> Or doth another gird thee, carry thee
> Whither thou wouldest not, and doth a cord
> Bind hand and foot, and flying thought and word?
> An enemy hath done it, even so,
> (Though why that power was his thou dost not know)
> O happy captive, fettered and yet free,
> Believe, believe to see
> Jesus Himself draw near and walk with thee.[3]

If it was hard to pray while supine, it was at least as hard to write. But she kept at it, lying with the paper tilted against a blotter, conscientiously finishing *This One Thing* and courageously turning out her letters and tiny notes as long as her hand would do her bidding.

When severe neuralgia in the right shoulder and hand made her fingers almost immovable, her New Zealand nurse tried to encourage her to exercise to keep them from stiffening completely. One day she said, "Alison, I have been trying all day to join thumb and forefinger and I cannot. Do you think that I will be able to move them again?" Alison told her that probably she would not. She lay quietly for a time, then said, "I gave that hand to the Lord for Him to use"—she remembered the exact year—"and now He has taken it again." Further silence. Then she quoted the words of Jesus, "Is it not lawful for me to do what I will with mine own?"[4] She knew she would not write again. It was dictation after that.

Alison became ill and had to go back to New Zealand for further treatment. Before she left she was able to go and see Amma in her room. Each knew it would be the last time.

"Alison, we won't meet again in this world. When you hear I have gone, jump for joy!"

---

3. *Toward Jerusalem,* p. 86.
4. Matthew 20:15.

Chapter 51
One Thing Have I Desired

O n the wall of my study hangs a thin brass Celtic cross with the ancient inscription, IHS, for *In hoc signe vinces* ("In this sign conquer"). It used to lie on the table next to Amma's bed where she could finger it in the night and put her mind on those brave words. She would, by grace, by her Lord's cross and passion, keep on conquering, keep on climbing, keep on being God's "athlete" in her bed. She asked one of the men to cut a large cross out of black poster paper to be hung where she could see it in the dimmest light, to be for her a reminder "of pain far greater than mine."

Another comfort in the painful nights was the text which Nancy had given her to allay her fears about becomimg a burden. From Revelation 2:9, 10, the words I KNOW . . . FEAR NOT . . . were inscribed on a piece of teak and hung with a light over them.

Amy's friend Bishop Pakenham Walsh sent her the words of the hymn "In Heavenly Love Abiding," by A. L. Waring. She kept them also by her bed, especially comforted by the last stanza:

> Green pastures are before me
> Which yet I have not seen,
> Bright skies will soon be o'er me
> Where the dark clouds have been.
> My hope I cannot measure,
> My path to life is free,
> My Savior has my treasure,
> And He will walk with me.

In one of her last dictated letters she included these words, and added, "I am very happy and content. Green pastures are before me, and my Savior has my treasure—the DF."

Mary Mills reported in December 1950, "Our Amma is going through a very difficult bit of the way. She is definitely losing ground on this side, and the longing grows ever more for the day of Deliverance."

Poor Jeevanie, so often irritated with Amma in years gone by, but loving her now through the experience of ministering to her helplessness, had a new worry in the last two weeks. Amma had made her promise that she would see to it that no one put her in a coffin. No one had ever put anybody in a coffin in Dohnavur. It was always the simple pallet and the blanket of flowers. But Amma, not without reason, feared it might occur to somebody to do something special for her. She wanted none of it. So Jeevanie promised.

"But it rained for two weeks," she told me. "I could not help thinking. All that water—in God's garden—shouldn't we—?"

As the year 1950 gave way to 1951 the weather was stiflingly hot, a sore trial to Amy even in healthy times. Now it was almost more than the wracked body could bear. She stopped eating. The old cystitis recurred. Her circulation, in the doctor's words, "packed up." She whose eyes, both spiritual and physical, had been keen and quick and penetrating to see far more than most, lay without seeming to notice anything very much.

During the second week of January, 1951, Amy began to sleep a great deal. Then she fell into a coma, and it was then that some of her children saw her for the first time. She had been unable for a long time to have the large groups to her room as she used to, so there were people in the Family, which numbered nearly nine hundred, who had never seen her face. Now they could do so without disturbing her. They came quietly and were allowed to stand by her bed and look. The birds in the verandah cage, it is avowed, were silent then.

She loved Bunyan's story of the two pilgrims' welcome at the Gate of the City:

Now, while they were thus drawing towards the Gates, behold a company of the Heavenly Host came out to meet them; to whom it was said, by the other two Shining Ones. These are the men that have loved our Lord, when they were in the world, and that have forsaken all for his holy name; and he hath sent us to fetch them, and we have brought them thus far on their desired journey, that they may go in and look their Redeemer in the face with joy. Then the Heavenly Host gave a great shout, saying, 'Blessed are they that are called to the marriage-supper of the Lamb'. . . .

Now I saw in my dream that these two men went in at the Gate; and lo! as they entered, they were transfigured, and they had raiment put on that shone like gold. There were also that met them with harps and crowns and gave them to them; the harps to praise withal, and the crowns in token of honor. Then I heard in my dream that all the bells in the City rang again for joy; and that it was said unto them, ENTER YE INTO THE JOY OF YOUR LORD.

The children and their accals, the annachies and the sitties, the friends from the village who came to the Room of Peace could not help hoping for some last word, some glimpse of what the seemingly sightless eyes might be seeing. But Amy's prayer had been that there would be no rending good-byes. She believed the Lord had promised, in 1938, that He would take her while she slept.

She had written of those who died as having been "carried by angels."[1] "It is all we know of how they go."

So she went. By early morning of January 18, 1951 the appointed Shining Ones must have been dispatched to carry her on her so greatly desired journey. Others, we may believe, were waiting with the raiment, the harps, the crowns in their hands. Some were poised to begin the pealing of the bells.

From little Dohnavur she who had loved her Lord and very truly had forsaken all for His holy name was called, and the bells in the House of Prayer played the music she had asked for, that to which her own words had been set:

> One thing have I desired, my God, of Thee,
> That will I seek, Thine house be home to me.
>
> I would not breathe an alien, other air,
> I would be with Thee, O Thou fairest Fair.

---

1. *Toward Jerusalem,* p. 39.

For I would see the beauty of my Lord,
And hear Him speak, Who is my heart's Adored.

O Love of loves, and can such wonder dwell
In Thy great Name of names, Immanuel?

Thou with Thy child, Thy child at home with Thee,
O Lord my God, I love, I worship Thee.[2]

While she "went in and looked her Redeemer in the face with joy," those she had left behind, the people who loved her, came during the morning to see her face one more time. They covered her bed with flowers. At noon she was carried to the village church where, for an hour and a half, the boys of the Family sang while the people streamed by. One of Amma's oldest friends in India, Bishop G. T. Selwyn of Tinnevelly, led the service, with others taking part, including two Indian men who spoke of her and her work, giving glory to God. Between twelve and fifteen hundred cards were distributed, giving verses on eternal life and the way of salvation. Barbara Osman wrote:

As the chimes in the tower rang out the tune of "Ten Thousand Times Ten Thousand," Amma was carried to the House of Prayer and our own service was held there an hour later. The House of Prayer was filled with our men and women, school boys and girls, together with representatives from the servants and work-people, and friends from the village. The "Widow of the Jewels" was there, finding it hard not to sob aloud. Neela, who has been with Amma all through these long years, was standing erect as we joined in singing "Alleluia! The strife is o'er, the battle won."

John read some verses—Matthew 25:21, II Timothy 4:6–8, and Philippians 1:19–21—then, after thanksgiving and prayer, we moved slowly to God's Garden, singing all the time. It was a very long stream of people, mostly clad in white, with children among them, waving ferns instead of palms as a sign of victory.

By the graveside Devabakti read I Corinthians 15:50–58 in a gloriously clear and steady voice, though his eyes were full of tears. When Amma had been laid to rest, the boys led the way round the Garden, which we encircled, coming back to the huge old tamarind

---

2. Ibid, p. 116.

tree at the entrance, and pausing there for the end of the service.

It was Tara who led the unaccompanied singing, helped by a younger sister. Neither of them faltered. God's grace was seen in all those who are women now (some of them grey-haired)—Chellalu, Lola, and Leela, Preena, Suseela, Rukma, and too many more to mention.

At seven o'clock we gathered once more in the House of Prayer to sing of the Heavenly Country, where many of our Family are now, safe at Home forever.

None of the graves in God's Garden is marked by a headstone. Only one is marked at all. Under the old tamarind is a stone table for the pleasure of some of Amma's friends, the dear birds. On the pedestal is inscribed a single word, AMMAI. It is the polite form of her mother-name. Beneath it is the date when they laid her there under the tamarind.

Bird table marking Amy's grave.

Epilogue

So she finished her course—Amy Carmichael, one of the tens of thousands of lovers of the Lord who staked everything on His faithfulness. Her life is another case in point of how grace goes to work on the raw material of individual nature. Was she a fool? Yes, for the same reason the apostle Paul was: for Christ's sake. Were all her geese swans? Did she see stars where the rest of us see nothing but mud? Yes, they were and she did. Was she therefore deluded? Our answer must take into account that some are able to see the image of Christ in ordinary people and radiance in common things, while others cannot see either (His loved children or that pervasive radiance) as anything but common. Which are the more deluded?

"The unspiritual man simply cannot accept the matters which the Spirit deals with—they just don't make sense to him, for, after all, you must be spiritual to see spiritual things. The spiritual man, on the other hand, has an insight into the meaning of everything, though his insight may baffle the man of the world."[1]

Our enemy and God's is always busily at work distorting our vision, throwing confusion into our minds lest we see the glory that God is waiting to show us in everything that makes up our lives—the people we love, our homes, our work, our sufferings. Deep things he makes us believe are shallow, high things low, our deep hunger for the transcendent a will-o-the-wisp. Look for proofs, he whispers. Where are the proofs? Let's have statistics. Did it work?

---

1. 1 Corinthians 2:14, 15 (PHILLIPS).

Was she real? Is it true? The questions are valid ones. They cannot be ignored, nor can they be answered finally except in the realm where faith operates, the Unseen. We may and we must look at the visible, but let us remember that there is far more to be taken into account. We may not always insist on visible corroborations, for they don't tell the whole story. The gold, silver, and precious stones may be in safe deposit where we can't get at them.

Often as I sat at her writing table in the Room of Peace, studying the carved mottoes on the walls, fingering the tattered and stained logbooks, I wondered about these things. I heard the bells from the House of Prayer, the distant voices of children, the jingle of a bullock bandy. In front of me on the tiled floor were four marks where her bed had stood. Amy had been in the presence of the Lord for more than thirty years. The room was not a museum, the compound had not been turned into a memorial park. The place was alive. Work was being done.

Will "the work" last? In Dohnavur, no. The logbooks will crumble. The House of Prayer can't be everlasting. The children grow up and go. There will be an end to it. We may draw up a list of known results, but our criteria are restricted. What were the long-term effects in the lives of India and around the world? Some are visible. God knows the rest. None but He knows the steadiness of her obedience, the unseen struggle, the hidden offerings, the quality of faith.

If there should appear in the twentieth century one who was truly holy, a missionary who actually believed in the word of the Master and the worth of the assigned task, a Christian who never served Mammon, who, though human and failing, nevertheless kept a sense of the glory and dignity of having been redeemed and called by God—if such a person should appear, would we say "Away with him! Crucify him!"? Not out loud. There are other ways of banishing those who, because they live out the Truth, make us uncomfortable. We can deny the possibility of purity. We can refuse to tolerate superiority. If we are tempted to recognize them as true heroes, we can bolster our self-esteem by pulling them down to our level.

Was Amma "more human" when she sinned (or was sick or

lonely or Victorian) than when she prayed, wrote a poem, rescued a child? All are human, the latter perhaps *essentially* more so in that she therein fulfilled her God-given destiny.

> Make us Thy labourers,
> Let us not dream of ever looking back,
> Let not our knees be feeble, hands be slack,
> O make us strong to labour, strong to bear,
> From the rising of the morning till the stars appear.
>
> Make us Thy warriors,
> On whom Thou canst depend to stand the brunt
> Of any perilous charge on any front,
> Give to us skill to handle sword and spear
> From the rising of the morning till the stars appear.
>
> Not far from us, those stars,
> Unseen as angels and yet looking through
> The quiet air, the day's transparent blue.
> What shall we know, and feel, and see, and hear
> When the sunset colours kindle and the stars appear?[2]

---

2. *Toward Jerusalem*, p. 98.

The Dohnavur Fellowship

More than thirty-five years have passed since Amy Carmichael's death. The principles on which she founded the Fellowship remain the same, based on the pattern set in the Bible, but the Fellowship has moved with the times and is no longer the isolated, protected Christian community of Amy's day.

For some years boys, for whom there are other Christian Homes in the area, have not been admitted. The last boys left in 1984 after completing their education. Many of the Old Boys are active witnesses for Christ, and keep in touch and pay visits with their families.

Although the dedication of girls to the temples is now illegal, there are still many babies and young girls who, without protection, would fall into the hands of those wishing to exploit or abuse them. The Fellowship seeks out such children in order to give them a secure, happy Christian home. After completing their education and training, many marry or take jobs, and Amy's children can be found all over India serving the Lord, often in very respectable positions. They continue to regard Dohnavur as home, and some eventually return as fellow-workers.

The leadership of the work is now almost entirely Indian. For instance, the medical superintendent of the hospital grew up in Dohnavur from infancy. The hospital treats patients from the surrounding countryside, Hindus, Muslims, and Christians (who are in the minority), rich and poor, educated and illiterate. It aims to demonstrate the love of the Lord by the standard of its medical and personal care, and it works for spiritual as well as physical healing.

There are many different facets to the work and several outposts. Always the goal is the same: "We preach Jesus Christ as Lord, and ourselves as your servants for Jesus' sake."

For support the Fellowship depends on the faithfulness of the Lord, who leads His children to send what is needed and Himself balances the books. Most of all it depends on prayer.

The Dohnavur Fellowship   (In the United Kingdom)
Dohnavur, Tirunelveli Dist.   33 Church Road
Tamil Nadu 627 102   Wimbledon
INDIA   London SW19 5DQ
                                      ENGLAND

BOOKS BY AMY CARMICHAEL IN PRINT IN THE
UNITED STATES

Published by Christian Literature Crusade
   Candles in the Dark
   Edges of His Ways
   Figures of the True
   God's Missionary
   Gold by Moonlight
   Gold Cord
   His Thoughts Said . . . His Father Said
   If
   Mimosa
   Rose From Brier
   Thou Givest . . . They Gather
   Toward Jerusalem

Published by Fleming H. Revell Company
   Whispers of His Power

Published by Zondervan Publishing House
   If

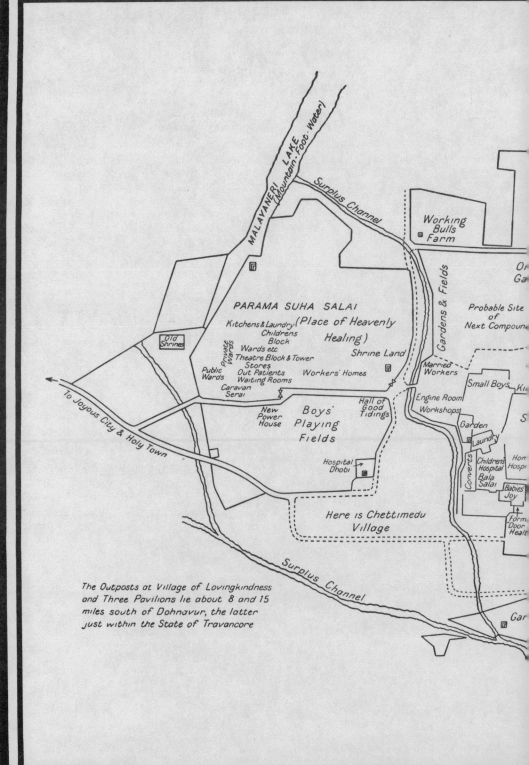

MALAYANERI LAKE (Mountain-Foot Water)

Surplus Channel

Working Bulls Farm

Or
Ga

Gardens & Fields

Probable Site of
Next Compound

PARAMA SUHA SALAI
(Place of Heavenly Healing)

Old
Shrines

Kitchens & Laundry
Childrens Block
Wards etc
Private Wards
Theatre Block & Tower
Stores
Public Wards
Out Patients
Waiting Rooms
Caravan Serai

Shrine Land

Workers' Homes

Married Workers

Small Boys

Ki

New Power House

Boys' Playing Fields

Hall of Good Tidings

Engine Room Workshops

Garden

S

To Joyous City & Holy Town

Convorts

Laundry

Childrens Hospital Bala Salai

Hom Hospi

Hospital Dhobi

Babies Joy

Here is Chettimedu Village

Form
Door
Heale

Surplus Channel

Gar

The Outposts at Village of Lovingkindness
and Three Pavilions lie about 8 and 15
miles south of Dohnavur, the latter
just within the State of Travancore